GROUNDED

GROUNDED

A Down to Earth Journey Around the World

Seth Stevenson

RIVERHEAD BOOKS
New York

RIVERHEAD BOOKS
Published by the Penguin Group
Penguin Group (USA) Inc.
375 Hudson Street, New York, New York 10014, USA
Penguin Group (Canada), 90 Eglinton Avenue East, Suite 700, Toronto, Ontario M4P 2Y3, Canada
(a division of Pearson Penguin Canada Inc.)
Penguin Books Ltd., 80 Strand, London WC2R 0RL, England
Penguin Group Ireland, 25 St. Stephen's Green, Dublin 2, Ireland (a division of Penguin Books Ltd.)
Penguin Group (Australia), 250 Camberwell Road, Camberwell, Victoria 3124, Australia
(a division of Pearson Australia Group Pty. Ltd.)
Penguin Books India Pvt. Ltd., 11 Community Centre, Panchsheel Park, New Delhi—110 017, India
Penguin Group (NZ), 67 Apollo Drive, Rosedale, North Shore 0632, New Zealand
(a division of Pearson New Zealand Ltd.)
Penguin Books (South Africa) (Pty.) Ltd., 24 Sturdee Avenue, Rosebank, Johannesburg 2196,
South Africa

Penguin Books Ltd., Registered Offices: 80 Strand, London WC2R 0RL, England

The publisher does not have any control over and does not assume any responsibility for author or
third-party websites or their content.

Copyright © 2010 Seth Stevenson
Cover design by Benjamin Gibson
Interior illustrations © 2010 Dan Halka and Mike LeGrand
Book design by Tiffany Estreicher

First Riverhead trade paperback edition: April 2010

Library of Congress Cataloging-in-Publication Data

Stevenson, Seth, date.
    Grounded : a down to Earth journey around the world / Seth Stevenson. — 1st Riverhead trade
pbk. ed.
        p.   cm.
    Includes bibliographical references and index.
    ISBN 978-1-59448-442-1 (alk. paper)
    1. Stevenson, Seth, 1974—Travel.   2. Voyages around the world.   I. Title.
    G440.S842A3 2010
    910.4'1—dc22   2009037877

PRINTED IN THE UNITED STATES OF AMERICA

10   9   8   7   6   5   4   3   2   1

For Rebecca

CONTENTS

GROUNDED

Introduction

Washington, D.C., to Philadelphia

W E'VE done this once before.

   Seven years ago, I was living in lower Manhattan with my girlfriend, Rebecca. She worked at a small start-up company. I was on staff at *Newsweek*. We both put in long hours, and our days bled one into the next. Week after week, we ordered takeout from the same set of restaurants, went to the same bars, hung out with the same friends. I spent inordinate amounts of time—sometimes lying awake, late at night—pondering how to get ahead in my career.

   We were comfortable, yet I couldn't shake this nagging sense that we were stagnating. We'd disappeared into our ambitions and our daily routines. As I ate another rushed lunch at the same Midtown deli, I wondered: Could a more transcendent existence be waiting somewhere out there, beyond the everyday grind?

Rebecca had the same thought. She and I started daring each other to make a drastic move. "Let's quit our jobs and just drive to Alaska," we'd joke.

These jokes became more frequent. Less jokey. And over time, we sort of forgot if we were joking at all.

One spring day, we did it. We quit our jobs—to the minor shock (and, I noted in a few cases, the self-loathing envy) of our friends and coworkers. We ditched all our possessions, hopped into a beat-up Honda, and drove.

We pulled off the road in dusty, nowhere towns. We got drunk on Tuesday afternoons in flyblown bars. We smoked a joint on a rickety veranda in Austin, laughing with an old friend. We camped on the Rio Grande, spotted a pod of whales off the California coast, and spent a full week in Salt Lake City for no clear reason. We never knew where we'd be sleeping the next night, and we loved it that way. From the concrete rote of Midtown, we'd escaped into a life that burst with color and immediacy.

After a few months, we woke up one morning, looked around, and discovered we were in Alaska. We'd taken our own dare, and our souls felt richer for it. We had zero regrets. Sadly, we were also out of money. Abject poverty (and the brutal Alaskan winter) loomed before us. We wistfully acknowledged that the time had arrived to reenter polite society. Time to turn the Honda around, hit the gas pedal, and plunge smack back into the drab bustle of the I-95 corridor.

We packed up the car for the long drive east and, as I slammed the trunk shut on our lovely idyll, I lingered a moment—gazing out at the cold gray swells of the Pacific. I could have sworn they were beckoning to me. Wouldn't it be wonderful, I thought, if instead of turning back we could just . . . keep forging on?

SEVEN years later, now in our thirties, we'd settled into a pleasant life in Washington, D.C. I was working from home and writing for various magazines. Rebecca had gone to law school and was now a litigator at a claw-your-eyes-out downtown firm. We ordered takeout from a new set of restaurants, drank in a new set of bars, and hung out with a new set of friends. Career ambitions and lifestyle routines had once again encrusted our lives.

We bought nice furniture and framed prints for our apartment. Ordered cable TV with all the trimmings. Set up wireless Internet and satellite radio in our living room.

By any reasonable measure, life was good. No suffering. No want. No ill health. Whenever the numbing trance of electronic entertainment failed me, various inebriants helped the days flip by. But again, I began to get a nagging feeling that life lacked a certain frisson. Spontaneity. Surprise. Above all: adventure.

The more I dwelt on this, the more restless I became. In the first paragraph of *Moby-Dick*, Herman Melville writes: "Whenever I find myself growing grim about the mouth; whenever it is a damp, drizzly November in my soul; whenever I find myself involuntarily pausing before coffin warehouses, and bringing up the rear of every funeral I meet; and especially whenever my hypos get such an upper hand of me, that it requires a strong moral principle to prevent me from deliberately stepping into the street, and methodically knocking people's hats off—then, I account it high time to get to sea as soon as I can." The hats are undoubtedly different in my day from those in Melville's, but I could sense myself eyeing them with the same bad intentions. Pushing my shopping cart through a too-crowded Whole Foods, or watching people in suits thumbing their BlackBerrys at a bar, I would feel a sharp, sudden, directionless rage. The itch to escape—from everything around me—flashed hot across my skin.

Meanwhile, Rebecca had hit the wall at work. She'd started at her firm straight out of law school and had toiled there for three years with nutty hours and little vacation. The life of a law firm associate logging seventy-hour weeks will, over time, take its toll on any thoughtful human being. (And yes, there are attorneys who qualify as such.)

Of course, society has a clear prescription for thirtysomething, water-treading couples like Rebecca and me. We're supposed to buy a house and start a family. And indeed, a wave of domesticity had lately crashed over our peer group. Conversations with friends always seemed to gravitate toward real estate and pregnancy. Prenatal vitamins. Good elementary schools.

These struck us as terrific notions to keep in mind for somewhere down the road. But our immediate impulses pushed the other way. We felt no urge to march forward within the socially sanctioned rut—its high walls guiding us smoothly toward parenthood, a mortgage, and on and on. We wanted to scramble out the top of the rut, dust ourselves off, look down from above with relieved smiles, and skip merrily away.

Around this time there appeared a familiar spark of mischief in Rebecca's eyes. And the dares began. "Let's quit our jobs and just hop on a cargo freighter," we'd joke to each other.

These jokes became more frequent. Less jokey. Soon enough, we realized we weren't joking at all.

AFTER some discussion, we concluded that it wasn't worth it to rip up our lives just to embark on some aimless, knock-around interlude—say, chilling on a beach in Central America until we got bored again. For one thing (while I admit this sort of plan did hold its appeals for me—hammock, spliff, sunset, etc.), Rebecca is not cut out for idle relaxation. She has a nonstop, hyperactive personality. "Like there are millions of tiny rabbits hopping around in my brain," she describes it.

This seems a decent place to mention that Rebecca is crazy. Only a wee bit crazy, mind you, but it's there. She will acknowledge this. Anyone who knows her will acknowledge this—as they close their eyes, nod, and chuckle. I love it about her. It's part of what drew me to her in the first place. But without some structure and a vaguely identified end point—for instance, Alaska—the blurry whir of possibility causes her brain to eat itself. You'll trust me when I tell you this must be avoided at all costs. Besides, what was missing from our lives was not the repose of a snoozy beach vacation. We had more ease and comfort than we could handle. What we craved was novelty. Challenge. Something to shake us from our trance and pop open our eyes.

I decided that the answer to our problems was to circumnavigate the earth.

*   *   *

THERE'S a certain romance inherent in circling the globe. It's the kind of mission that adventurers used to dream about—before globalization made the other side of the world feel like it was down the block and around the corner. Even now, though it's not nearly the challenge it once was, there's still a pleasing, physical absoluteness to making the full loop.

Granted, we wouldn't be the first to circumnavigate. That was Magellan—sort of. He left Spain in 1519, sailed west, made it all the way around to the Philippines, and then was killed there in 1521 while attempting to convert an indigenous chieftain to Christianity. (Any seasoned traveler knows you never argue religion with the locals. How dreadfully rude! You have no one to blame but yourself, Magellan.) In 1522, one of Magellan's original five ships limped its way back into a Spanish harbor, making its eighteen remaining crew members the first successful circumnavigators.

Since then, countless others have matched the feat. When an unadorned circumnavigation was no longer daring enough, people dreamed up ways to make the feat more challenging. Solo sailing endeavors. Nonstop, nonrefueled flights. Hot air balloons. Human-powered expeditions with Rollerblades and paddleboats.

Of course, the most famous circumnavigation of all never actually happened. First published as a newspaper serial in France in 1872, Jules Verne's *Around the World in 80 Days* recounts the madcap high jinks of the English gentleman Phileas Fogg. The ingenious plot has Fogg betting his friends twenty thousand pounds that he can circle the earth and get back to London within the titular time frame.

In the wake of the book's popularity, the journalist Nellie Bly tried to replicate Fogg's fictitious journey. Setting off from New York in 1889, she made it back home in a speedy seventy-two days. Which is a pretty decent lap time—though not as fast as some sailors on a catamaran did it in 2005 (fifty days). And not as quick as the Concorde's supersonic trip around the world in 1995 (thirty-one hours, including several stops). And it's a snail's pace compared to the time it took Yuri Gagarin, in 1961, to make the first manned orbit of the earth before falling back down to Soviet soil (about 108 minutes).

Rebecca and I are planning to circumnavigate slower than Gagarin (and without entering orbit) but quicker than Magellan (and, ideally, without getting murdered by a chieftain). We're not trying to set any world records here. We just want something we might look back on with pride. An accomplishment that's not about our careers, and not about raising a family. Something different, and all our own.

We've set these two initial rules for ourselves: 1) We need to cross every longitudinal line, plus the equator, for the circumnavigation to count. 2) We will not fly in airplanes. Ever. There's not a ton of challenge involved in buying an around-the-world airline ticket and, like, using it. Also, and more important: We despise airplanes and all they stand for.

Taking an airplane is like pressing the fast-forward button on your journey. It's a useful ability, to be sure. It lets us take a one-day business trip to Chicago or a one-week vacation to New Zealand. But with progress comes trade-offs. We've lost something along the way.

* * *

WHEN Jules Verne wrote *Around the World in 80 Days*, long before the airplane existed, it was an ode to the bracing new possibilities of travel. For the first time in history, Verne noted, you could circle the globe using almost exclusively commercial transport. Modernity had conquered the surface of the earth.

But if steamships and railroads made the world feel smaller, airplanes shrunk it beyond all recognition. In 1988, a little more than one hundred years after Fogg's romp, Michael Kinsley (later to become my boss at *Slate*) wrote a story for *Condé Nast Traveler* titled "Around the World in 80 Hours," which explored the possibilities of jumbo jet tourism. Mike flew to India, got off the plane for an hour, flew to Kathmandu, got off the plane for an hour, and so forth. The genre here was less travelogue than farce. For who could enjoy such a trip? It sounds like three days of pure torture. All the hassles of travel with almost none of the rewards.

"I dislike planes," wrote Paul Theroux, explaining why he'd hoped, in *The Old Patagonian Express*, to take only railroads from Massachusetts to the bottom of South America. (He was forced to fly on two separate occasions during the voyage, to his everlasting regret.) "And whenever I am in one—suffering the deafening drone and the chilly airlessness that is peculiar to planes—I always suspect that the land we are overflying is rich and wonderful and that I am missing it all."

I remember the sharp pangs I once felt flying over the Arctic on the way to Japan, when I looked down on a blinding-white ice sheet from thirty-five thousand feet above. I could imagine the howling wind down there, the fluttering snowflakes, and the crunch of the ice pack beneath my feet. And then I looked around at the faded floral fabric of the airplane cabin and listened to the white noise of the whooshing air filters.

There are countless good reasons to hate planes. Personally, I always walk off the jetway feeling buzzy and light-headed, as though the front of my brain has been dried to a brittle husk. There's jet lag, of course—your body has quite clearly decided it was not designed to go this far this fast. Also, when Theroux wrote his screed he could never have predicted all the hassles and humiliations of a post-9/11 security check. The pat-downs, the invasive questions, the bagging of liquids, the removal of shoes and belt. Businesspeople now stand in line with the sullen resignation of thugs at a county jail booking.

Once on board, there are further indignities. Tiny seats. Insipid in-flight movies. The airlines have begun to make you pay for every amenity, so you find yourself forking over cash for cheap headphones or a tasteless turkey sandwich.

As for the flying itself, there's very little romance to it anymore. Just claustrophobia, crying babies, and the ineluctable proximity of your seat-neighbors. The nosy retired lady. The loud drunk guy. The apologetic obese person whose haunches creep under your shared armrest.

For some among us flying is sheer terror. When Rebecca is in an airplane at altitude, she is a trembling wreck. We once took a plane together that left from Delhi and flew high up into the Himalayas. The mountain landing strip was surrounded by fog. Craggy rock ledges peeked out through the mists, seemingly inches from the tips of our wings. Rebecca gripped my hand with the approximate psi of a pneumatic vise while plowing through a pint of scotch and a triple dose of prescription sedatives. For the sake of her liver alone, I'd prefer we not try anything like that again.

And let's not ignore the environmental impact of planes. They burn lots of nonrenewable resources and emit kerosene soot and carbon dioxide directly into the atmosphere. Just taking a few flights a year can ruin any efforts you may be making to live green. Meanwhile, airports contribute to developmental sprawl, noise pollution, and possibly groundwater contamination.

All this aside, there's a more profound issue. Riding in a commercial jetliner simply isn't *traveling*, as far as I'm concerned. It's teleporting from point A to point B. You spend the entire time in the air just waiting to land, and afterward you speak of the flight only if it's to complain about the turbulence or the snoring of the dude who sat next to you. The trip itself is nothing. A blank. A means of skipping over instead of wading through. And it's precisely when we're wading through that we often stumble upon the joy, misery, serendipity, and disaster of a true adventure.

YEARS ago, Rebecca and I might have planned our journey by spreading open a big, dusty atlas on our coffee table. These days, we fire up Google Earth on a laptop. The computer application lets us spin a model globe around on the screen and zoom in on whichever country, or region, or street corner we please.

It's a fantastically fun and easy program to use. But it turns out there's a significant danger in this approach. On a twelve-inch laptop screen, things look mighty close together. Rebecca and I sat side by side on our couch one evening, tracing a hopscotch route across the pixels with our index fingers. "Okay, we can go here . . . then here . . . and then here." Voilà! Seemed so effortless—until we realized we were looking at a quarter of the earth's surface. And that the path we had blithely proposed went straight through the heart of the Gobi Desert.

It became clear that we'd first need to answer a few fundamental questions. Questions one rarely asks oneself in day-to-day life. Things like: How long would it take to sail from Singapore to Fiji? Or, scratch that—How fast can a camel traverse one hundred roadless miles, encumbered with two people, fifteen gallons of water, and a yurt?

Fortunately, Rebecca is a stone-cold genius when it comes to travel logistics. She knows all the angles and is lightning quick on her feet. When your flight gets canceled and everyone's stuck at a snowy airport with no rental cars, she's that fellow passenger you overhear murmuring calmly into her cell phone, arranging to hire a stage-coach and a team of Clydesdales. Her talents as a navigatrix made me so confident that we could face down any situation, I decided we could leave our plans vague for the time being. We knew we wanted to take a ship across the Atlantic and then trains across Russia. Our timing seemed to work, as it would get us in and out of Siberia before summer ended. (By all accounts, Siberia in winter is not a good place to be.) After that, everything—routes, destinations, schedules, accommodations—was left undecided. We'd build our journey piece by piece, on the fly.

Next step: packing. Rebecca and I had strong feelings on this matter. We share a severe disdain for travelers whose massive backpacks extend down below their knees and up over the crowns of their heads, dangling behind them bits of flotsam clipped on with carabiners. Walk through any backpacker district in Southeast Asia and you're sure to pass some sunburned schlub with a souvenir didgeridoo bumping along in his wake. We didn't want to be that guy. As a result, we risked going too far in the other direction, challenging each other to pack as little as possible. Rebecca at one point threatened to travel the earth carrying nothing but a lunchbox.

In the end, we settled on small backpacks—not significantly larger than the kind a book-laden college student might lug to the library. Into mine I tucked a minimal allotment of clothes, including just three pairs of underwear, which, if I hope to remain on friendly terms with Rebecca, will require frequent washing. For her part, Rebecca somehow managed to pack more digital gadgets than items of attire. (This is in her genes. Some people celebrate gold and diamond wedding anniversaries; Rebecca's parents celebrate the consumer electronics anniversary. Every year.) She included a small MP3 player loaded with songs, a shortwave radio for tuning in news broadcasts, an unlocked cell phone, and a handheld GPS to track our precise latitude and longitude at any given moment.

With the itinerary and provisions taken care of, we were left with only one more thing to do: systematically disentangle ourselves from every attachment in our lives. Rebecca gave notice at her office, and I told my editors I'd be off the grid for a good long while. Again, reactions to this news varied from total bewilderment to open envy.

We began scraping off the cushy trappings we'd built around ourselves. Our apartment building didn't allow sublets, so we ended our lease. We spent eons on hold with customer service hotlines— canceling the cable TV, the phone, the Internet, the gym membership. Automated telephone menu options rarely fit our situation. When the cable company's computerized voice asked me for the address we were moving to, I said, "A cabin on a transatlantic cargo ship." Replied the computer, "I'm sorry, I'm having trouble understanding your response." There were infinite odds and ends to take care of, and at times it seemed we'd never achieve full extraction. At frustrating moments, I pictured myself on the open ocean, a salty breeze in my face.

The final night in our apartment, we threw a bon voyage party. We tried to empty the place of all remaining objects, giving away as much as we could. By the end of the evening, Rebecca was pressing board games and toaster ovens into the arms of tipsy guests. The next morning, whatever we couldn't bear to give away or throw out we stuffed into a storage locker. Then I parked our car on a quiet street in a distant, leafy corner of D.C., dropping off my keys with some friends. They promised to watch the poor old thing rust until we came back for it.

That evening—our very last in D.C., until we closed the circle upon our triumphant return—we got drinks at our local dive bar, bidding a quieter good-bye to a few of our closest pals. When the gathering broke up, we crashed at our friend Ariane's apartment. We had nowhere else to sleep.

THE next morning, walking down the sidewalk, I instinctively check my pocket. There are no keys there, and it's a bit unsettling. I find I keep reflexively patting at the void. I feel a moment of panic each time. Until I remember there's nothing I need keys for anymore. No apartment, no mailbox, no car. I feel untethered. I'm carrying the whole of my existence in a backpack.

It's a bright August day. We're walking to the metro stop. Last week, my life lacked purpose, but today every step seems like a purposeful stride. Those people in front of us? They're going to their office. Us? We're going on an adventure.

We take the subway to Union Station, where we catch an Amtrak train up to Philadelphia. The very first leg of our trip is now behind us. At a Philly camera store we buy a pair of binoculars, figuring they might be of use out on the open sea.

In our hotel room that night, we watch TV as we drift off to sleep. There are promo ads for the new fall lineup of sitcoms and dramas. They wash over us. We'll be far, far away—in space and in mind—by the time they reach the airwaves. Tomorrow, we will board a cargo freighter and set off across the Atlantic.

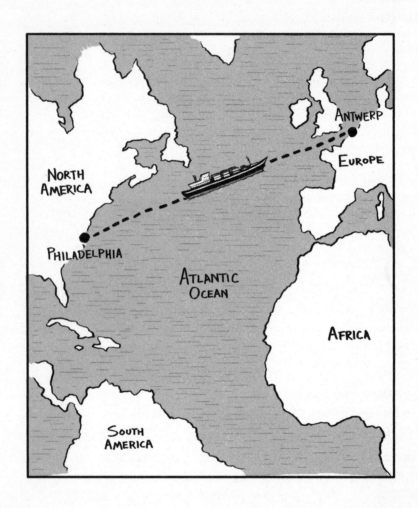

Chapter One

Philadelphia to Antwerp

O N a muggy Friday afternoon in early August, we catch a commuter train headed south out of downtown Philadelphia along the shore of the Delaware River. The train is crowded, filled with office workers clocking out early for the weekend. We lift our backpacks onto an overhead rack and find seats next to a napping, pant-suited woman. A half hour later, we hop off at an empty platform in a town called Eddystone.

It's a quiet, suburban neighborhood. On one side of the tracks are small, shingled houses and neat green lawns. American flags flap above front doors, and a warbling ice cream truck trawls the streets. On the other side of the tracks, a few hundred yards away, we can see ugly, rusty buildings lining the banks of the Delaware. That is where we need to be. We hoist on our packs and mosey down the weedy sidewalk.

Within a few blocks the landscape changes. We find ourselves in an industrial, waterfront wasteland. There are broken-window warehouses here and signs for a chemical company called Foamex. No other pedestrians in sight. The few vehicles rumbling by are eighteen-wheelers with faded paint. It's a species of place the average person will never have reason to set foot in and will recognize only from the climactic shoot-out scenes of low-budget action movies.

Before we reach the river, the street dead-ends at the gated entrance to a shipping terminal. As we approach, an elderly customs agent leans out of his lonely little booth and asks us for our passports. He has us unzip our backpacks and takes a cursory glance inside them before waving us through.

"How long will you be traveling for?" he asks out of polite curiosity as we walk away.

"Not exactly sure," I say over my shoulder, pondering the question. "As long as it takes to get around the world."

"No kidding!" He chuckles. "You've got less stuff than my wife takes with her for a long weekend."

This is the extent of our check-in. It's like the anti-airport: no departure lounge, no food court, no duty-free shopping. This terminal is designed for moving freight, not coddling passengers. As for security, the place is guarded by a chain-link fence and this solitary man—who seems neither equipped nor inclined to put up a great deal of resistance. There's no metal detector for us to pass through. We needn't take off our shoes and belts. Nobody confiscates our contact lens solution. It's a delightful contrast to the rampant civil liberties violations going on at your average air hub these days.

(Of course, there's a flip side to the lax protections. I'm pretty sure it would be easy to smuggle seventy pounds of ecstasy through this port. Or a few suitcase nukes.)

From the customs booth we walk toward the water, across an acre of crumbly asphalt littered with metal chains and shackles. We can see the jets taking off from Philadelphia's nearby international airport. A jumbo Lufthansa is currently screaming through the sky above our heads. It's no doubt headed across the ocean, just like us. But this plane and its passengers will get to Europe in less time than it will take our freighter to work its way out to the mouth of the Delaware River and into the open Atlantic. It occurs to me that, as a newly avowed surface traveler, I will need to dramatically rejigger my conceptions of speed and distance.

WE have no tickets for our freighter. Just a piece of paper I printed out at home so I'd remember the name of our ship—the *Independent Endeavor*—and the address of the terminal. The travel agency assured us our arrival would be expected.

A few decades ago, we wouldn't have needed a travel agency at all. Back then, you could walk out onto a shipping dock and talk (or buy) your way aboard a freighter. All you had to do was convince the captain to give you a bunk or a spot on the floor. Maybe you'd work for your passage by swabbing decks. Maybe you'd just slide the captain a wad of cash. Whatever the arrangement, it was not unusual for a cargo ship to accept last-minute passengers.

Those days are long gone. The golden era of freighter hitchhiking came to an end sometime around the mid-1970s. Nowadays, you can't get on a container ship without making reservations weeks in advance.

(Unless you secretly stow yourself inside one of the containers. Which I don't recommend. You could die that way. Even if you survived, you'd endure spooky darkness, brutal heat, and unbreathable air. A 1994 *New York Times* story about a group of stowaways from the Dominican Republic featured the evocative subhead "Three Days at Sea in Foul Box." The stowaways were discovered when a deckhand heard desperate shouting and banging coming from a container perched forty feet above the ship's deck.)

As with all great adventures, casual freighter travel stopped the moment the lawyers showed up. Shipping companies decided that, due to some pretty glaring liability and security issues, it would be insane for them to continue allowing their captains to take on random passengers. What if, for instance, one of those passengers experienced a health crisis while at sea, requiring immediate attention? If the captain diverted to the nearest hospital, he'd delay the cargo and lose money for the company. If he refused to divert, and the passenger croaked, hello, lawsuit. Either way, it was the sort of hassle the shipping lines could do without.

Enter the freighter travel agencies, which blossomed in the 1980s. The agencies' insight was that, because of increased automation, it took fewer crew members to operate a cargo ship. As a result, some officers' quarters were going unoccupied at sea. These cabins were private and spacious—just comfortable enough to be marketed as a cruise ship alternative. The agencies convinced the big shipping lines they could bring in added revenue by running a small, carefully regulated side business renting out the empty cabins to upscale passengers looking for a novel travel experience. And so freighter tourism was born.

To ride a freighter these days, you need to book your passage through a travel agency approved by the shipping company. You'll be required to sign a thick stack of release waivers. And you'll have to present a health certificate signed by your doctor, as well as evidence of an insurance policy that covers medical evacuations. If you're over eighty, even if you clear all these hurdles, you likely won't be allowed aboard a ship. There's too much risk involved when arthritic bone-bags wander around on slippery decks.

IN the corner of the shipping terminal, there's a shed that houses administrative offices. We knock on its door, and an oil-stained dock-worker answers. As promised, he's been expecting us. He tosses our backpacks in the bed of a pickup and drives us a few hundred yards to the ship's berth. It's not far at all, but walking this stretch isn't safe for civilians. The docks here are teeming with heavy equipment. One wrong turn and we could get impaled on the hook of a crane.

After slowing the pickup to a stop, the dockworker hops out, retrieves our bags from the back, and speeds off again. We find ourselves standing next to a wall of blue metal that blots out the sun. Closer inspection reveals this is the hull of our freighter.

The boarding process for your average cruise ship—one of those big, white Caribbean gluttony tubs—begins with thousands of passengers in a snaking velvet rope line on the pier. A squad of cruise ship workers, all fake smiles and elaborate epaulets, will load piles of luggage onto bellhop trolleys. They'll lug these bags to the passengers' cabins, make sure everyone's safely on board, and then point the way to the pasta buffet.

There's no such service as we board our freighter. Instead, a single Filipino deckhand, wearing a blue jumpsuit and orange hardhat, leads us in a scramble a hundred feet or so up a temporary metal ladder that's been lashed to the side of the ship. At the top of the ladder, we step over a yawning precipice and onto the freighter's deck. Here we're briefly introduced to the ship's first and second officers—one German, the other Romanian, both far too busy to pay us any mind. The deckhand leads us up a dimly lit interior staircase, then down a claustrophobic hallway lined with mysterious clamped hatches. He points to a door and nods. Apparently, we've arrived at our cabin.

I actually prefer this gruff efficiency to the icky sycophancy of a cruise ship's hospitality workers. In fact, Rebecca and I are sort of pleased that we're not—as we would be on a cruise ship—the central focus and purpose of this journey. We're just two ancillary pieces of cargo that the crew needs to deliver safely.

Despite this lowly status, our cabin turns out to be relatively posh. It's high up in the ship's superstructure, with windows looking out in three directions. We have a bedroom, an en suite bathroom, and a private sitting room with couches and a coffee table (all riveted to the floor, of course, so they won't tumble if the ship starts pitching). There's even a brass plate on the outside of our door that says "Owner's Cabin." Given that this shipping line is based out of Hamburg, I can't help but imagine a portly German burgher suddenly materializing to evict us and huffily reclaim his quarters.

Out our windows, we can watch the container-loading process. We've been told we'll be loading at least five hundred containers before we leave. Each box is forty feet long, eight feet wide, and eight and a half feet tall. The container stacks reach from the ship's deck far below us right up to our cabin windows' lower edges. They stretch the length of a football field from the superstructure toward the ship's bow.

We go outside to a railing for a better look at the action. What's happening down on the loading dock is like the wildest fantasy of a six-year-old boy. There's an entire fleet of large, deafeningly loud vehicles, each one with its own specialized job. They zip to and fro, hauling and lifting, beeping their safety signals when they chunk into reverse.

To suss out the routine, I follow a single container waiting on the dock: First, an oversized forklift picks up the container from the pavement and then places it on the back of a flatbed vehicle called a transporter. The transporter brings the container right alongside the ship, parking underneath one of the enormous dock-mounted cranes. These cranes tower over the ship. They roll on tracks that run along the pier, parallel to the freighter—so the crane can slide up toward the bow or back toward the stern to place the containers in different rows.

High above us, the crane operator—suspended in his little glass-walled cockpit—looks down at the transporter. He aims his four-cornered spreader bar (or, as I prefer to call it, "grabber") so that it lines up with and locks onto the four top corners of the container. Once the container gets lifted and maneuvered out over the ship, the operator carefully lowers it down onto the deck. Meanwhile, another transporter rolls into place. It has a new container ready for loading, impatiently awaiting the crane's attention.

An experienced crane operator can load twenty-five to thirty containers per hour—or about one every other minute. Today we have three cranes loading simultaneously. Along with the coordinated movements of the transporters and the forklifts, the whole scene makes for a synchronized ballet—a ballet in which the objects hoisted gracefully aloft are not ninety-five-pound women, but thirty-five-ton steel boxes.

This dock choreography repeats, over and over, for the next several hours. When we've seen our fill, we retire to our cabin to unpack, settle in, and eventually drift off to sleep. Around midnight, I'm stirred by the sound of the ship's engine firing up. I feel thrusters push us away from the dock. The propeller whirs to life and, gathering momentum, we start chugging down the Delaware.

WHEN we wake the next morning, we can see from our window that we've passed through the mouth of the river and into the open Atlantic. We're still close to shore, and the ship traffic is heavy. Other freighters pass us in both directions.

We tromp down the stairs to the officers' mess for breakfast. There we meet the only other passengers on board. They're a retired couple from Montreal, in their late seventies. Frank tells us he was an engineer (among other things) long ago, but he quit the rat race in his forties to become a painter. He's still a handsome man, with a long straight nose and high forehead. Daphne, his wife, was a university professor. She did genetics research, using mice as subjects. She's a bit mouselike herself—tiny, cute, and sharp featured. Her white hair is pulled back girlishly in barrettes.

Frank and Daphne are bound for a wedding in Europe. It will take them more than a week to get there, but they're in no rush. "We refuse to fly at all," says Daphne, "unless we absolutely must."

"Air travel actually used to be wonderful," says Frank, looking wistful. "But they ruined it. They take the planes designed for three hundred people and they fill them with five hundred. It's too crowded. And the air circulation systems can't handle it. Which is why you always get that kid's cold." Here he jerks his thumb over his shoulder at an imaginary, snot-snuffling tyke in seat 47G.

They'd considered taking the *Queen Mary 2* from New York to Europe (it still makes a regular transatlantic run—except in winter, when it putters around the Caribbean), but they decided it wasn't for them. "It's just a cruise ship," says Daphne. "We thought a cargo freighter would be immensely more interesting."

AFTER breakfast, the four passengers are led out to the main deck, where we receive a required safety lecture. It's delivered by the ship's third officer, a smiley Filipino guy named Gregorio. In halting English, Gregorio describes the procedures for various emergencies.

First, he demonstrates how to use the "immersion suits" the ship has provided us with. These suits are thick, one-piece, neoprene coveralls that zip over our clothing. They feature a built-in life jacket, a blinking distress light, and a whistle. They'll help us retain core body heat if, for some unfortunate reason, we are obliged to enter the frigid Atlantic Ocean without aid of a lifeboat. The suits look like a child's footie pajamas—puffy, to provide warmth, and bright orange so they can be easily spotted from the sky. Daphne is appraising them rather doubtfully. I picture her tiny frame bobbing gently in the swells, waiting for rescue.

The immersion suits explained, Gregorio moves on to the ship's alarm signals. Each different signal has a specific meaning. One pattern of horn blasts signals an emergency, "like if the ship sinks," as Gregorio delicately puts it. If we hear this signal, we're supposed to gather at a designated muster station. (This assumes the muster station is still peeking out above the waves.)

A second horn pattern signals a fire—in the event of which, again, we are to head for the muster station. (Assuming the muster station is not itself aflame.)

The third and by far most intriguing alarm is for a security alert. "Like if there are pirates," says Gregorio. I ask if, in the event of a pirate raid, we should gather at the muster station. "No!" says Gregario. "Stay in your cabins and wait for the captain to give instructions over the loudspeaker. Because the pirates might be at the muster station!"

With his lecture complete, Gregorio leads us on a tour of the ship to familiarize us with its layout. There's not much to it. The tall, multistory edifice at the back of the ship is called the superstructure, and it holds all the living quarters and the navigation bridge. In front of the superstructure are the endless piles of containers, stretching up to the bow.

What's in the containers? The crew has no idea. If a container holds refrigerated items or hazardous chemicals, the captain will be informed. (Refrigerated containers are tended by a crew member called "the reeferman," which is an enviably hip job title.) Otherwise, the contents of all those sealed boxes are a total mystery. They could be blue jeans. They could be antique cars. They could be scrap metal. Since the ship's previous stop was in Richmond, Virginia, it seems a decent bet there are tobacco products on board, but we can't know for sure. Freighter crews don't open the containers and don't ask questions. They just try to get the stuff there on time.

From the superstructure, Gregorio leads us on a walk to the bow. The ship is 550 feet long, so it takes us a while to get there. We walk down a narrow corridor between the ship's railing and the edge of the container stacks. The metal joints of the stacks groan as they shift with the rolling waves.

At last we reach a small open deck, about the size of a squash court, nestled at the front of the ship. It's called the "forecastle," and—for obscure nautical reasons—it's pronounced "folk-sul" and spelled "fo'c'sle." Here, at the pointy prow of the freighter, you have unobstructed ocean views to the front and the sides. You also have total privacy: No one in the superstructure can see you, because the tall container stacks looming behind you block the sight line. You're far enough from the engine that all you hear is the sound of the ship's hull slapping through the water.

"This is where I'm going to hang out," declares Rebecca. We expect to spend lots of time here, accompanied by suntan lotion, books, and binoculars.

AS we learn on our first day at sea, there's not much to do aboard a cargo freighter. No TV. No Internet. No restaurants, no bars, no fitness centers. No cliques of passengers to meet or planned activities to join.

There is, however, a lot of peace and silence. We'd grown used to the noisy bustle of our D.C. lives—cell phone calls, television blather, honking rush hour traffic on the streets outside our apartment. The quiet we experience lounging on the fo'c'sle is almost startling.

The isolation of the ship is also a very welcome data detox. I can't remember the last time, before today, that I went more than a few waking hours without checking my e-mail. Rebecca and I and everyone we know are all addicted to the constant flow of data and chatter. But after one afternoon out here on the freighter, I find I couldn't care less what's piling up in my in-box or streaming across my favorite websites and blogs. What does it matter? It suddenly seems so trifling set against the ancient silence of the ocean.

As for a social life, we have none. Our main human interaction comes at our thrice-daily meals with Frank and Daphne. (The crew eats at a separate table, and often on a different schedule.) Though they are delightful people, Frank and Daphne are not exactly in our peer group. We sometimes find ourselves struggling to converse across the generational divide.

During the day, when we're not at meals, Rebecca and I read in adjacent plastic deck chairs in the sun. When we want a break from our books, we stroll around the open-air parts of the ship—scouting with our binoculars for seabirds and maybe dolphins or whales. We've had no luck so far spotting ocean mammals, but hopes remain high.

At night, we put on sweaters and brave the salty evening chill. The stars twinkle against a pitch-black sky. No city lights here to turn the atmosphere milky.

We get our sea legs after the first day and become accustomed to the ship's slow, steady roll. It's wonderful to be rocked to sleep by it. It's so constant and powerful, it even seeps into our dreams. Rebecca keeps having this nightmare that she's back in her law firm's office tower and the building is undulating as though it's in an earthquake. File drawers rolling open. Casebooks spilling off shelves.

Then she wakes up and remembers that she left all those things behind.

OUR route across the Atlantic will begin at 40 degrees north latitude, near the southern tip of New Jersey. (Other places at this latitude: Portugal and Beijing.) We'll go pretty much on a straight diagonal northeast to 51 degrees north, where we'll pass through the English Channel. (Other places at this latitude: Calgary and Kazakhstan.)

The trip's first big visual waypoint comes fairly early into the passage, when the sea's color shifts from a dull gray-green to an indulgent purple. Bits of sargasso float past—a clear signal that we've crossed into the temperate currents of the Gulf Stream. The crew takes the opportunity to pump some warm ocean water into the little swimming pool on the ship's rear deck. Rebecca tosses on her bathing suit and hops in for a dip. The "pool" is more of a tub—just a bit larger than a Ping-Pong table—and watching Rebecca bounce off its walls reminds me of a neurotic otter I once saw at an underfunded zoo, frantically darting back and forth in his cramped aquatic habitat.

It's Sunday, which means it's the crew's day off. Several of the officers sunbathe. The chief electrician, an older Polish fellow named Witold, takes a shirtless constitutional around the aft deck in his

Birkenstock sandals and black socks. He has a pooching potbelly, scraggly gray chest hair, and a pair of mirrored, wraparound sunglasses. As he passes my deck chair, he pauses to chitchat about the weather. He predicts it will stay bright and clear for the entire trip. The Atlantic in summer is known for its calm, while the Atlantic in winter is famously nasty. "Een Septyember," Witold says with a guttural bark, "then mehbe storms start."

There are twenty-three crew members in all, representing six nationalities. The captain is German, stone-faced, and rarely seen. My understanding is that he doesn't have much to do on a daily basis—yet bears total responsibility if anything should go wrong.

The three navigational officers are a German, a Romanian, and a Filipino. These are the guys who actually pilot the ship. The Filipino is Gregorio, whom we've already met. The Romanian has made it clear, through an array of grunts and frowns, that he'd prefer not to meet us at all. The German guy, named Rikus, seems friendly, and I figure he's my best hope at becoming chummy with a crew member.

The four engine room workers are a Russian, a Ukrainian, and two Poles. They stick together—their own engineering-focused gang, separate from the navigational officers. Save for Witold, they appear to speak limited English.

Finally, there are the fifteen deckhands. These guys have titles like "oiler" and "wiper," and spend most of their time hidden belowdecks. They are without exception Filipino, as are the deckhands on most container ships at sea—regardless of the nationality of the captain or his officers. Like an Irish policeman or a Jewish gemologist, it seems the Filipino deckhand has become an ethnic occupational stereotype. No one I've asked can quite tell me why. Possible explanations: 1) Seafaring knowledge runs deep within the culture. 2) They work cheap.

MY self-assigned reading for this voyage is a book called *The Box*, which traces the history of container shipping. Its author, Marc Levinson, argues that the container hasn't gotten its due as a crucial element in globalization. I was intrigued by provocative blurbs on the book's back cover claiming that "the modern shipping container may be a close second to the Internet in the way it has changed our lives," and that, without containerization, "there would be no globalization, no Wal-Mart, maybe even no high-tech."

Before containerization, loading a cargo freighter was like piecing together a chaotic, 3-D jigsaw puzzle. Each item—a pile of lumber, a wheel of cheese, a batch of bicycles—had to be fit by hand into the ship's hold. This work was done by a team of longshoremen (think Marlon Brando in *On the Waterfront*), who used hooks, pallets, pulleys, forklifts, and elbow grease to lift the cargo on board. Loading a ship could take several days, and dockworkers were sometimes known to pilfer cargo as it waited on the pier.

In the 1950s, a trucking magnate named Malcolm McLean began to envision a new system. He wanted to drive his eighteen-wheelers into a port and then just load the trucks' cargo-filled trailers (minus their wheels and axles) directly onto a ship. He'd float this ship to a different city, thereby avoiding America's increasingly traffic-choked highways, and unload the trailers onto a bunch of eighteen-wheelers waiting at the other end.

On April 26, 1956—a date that may mark the Big Bang moment of globalization—McLean pulled off the exact maneuver he'd planned. Under his watchful eye, a retrofitted tanker called the *Ideal-X* was filled with cargo in the port of Newark. Instead of taking three days as it might have before, the loading process lasted just eight hours, with a crane lifting truck trailers onto the ship's deck. The *Ideal-X* departed the same day it loaded, and when it arrived in Houston its stacks of trailers were quickly and easily unloaded onto waiting semis.

By McLean's calculations, his new container system reduced costs to just 3 percent of what they'd have been on a similarly sized ship loaded with loose cargo. Much of the savings came from reduced labor requirements: All those longshoremen wrangling individual items could be replaced by a few crane operators lifting the containers. Containers cut down on pilfering, too, since the cargo was locked in boxes instead of sitting out on pallets. And the whole process was markedly faster, of course.

In the wake of *Ideal-X*'s successful maiden voyage, container shipping spread to ports around the world. The container's dimensions were eventually standardized for international use. These days, almost everything gets shipped in containers. Take a look around your house—chances are, more than 90 percent of what you see once spent some time inside a forty-foot-long corrugated metal box.

In Levinson's view, globalization simply could not have happened without containerization. Because containers dramatically reduced shipping costs—to the point that they almost ceased to be a factor at all—goods no longer had to be manufactured or assembled near the places they'd be sold. Factories and warehouses could be placed anywhere in the world. Preferably (and here we begin to glimpse the dark side of globalization) somewhere with very weak labor laws and easily exploited workers.

OUR fourth day at sea brings high excitement. In the morning, not far off the Grand Banks of Newfoundland, we spot a whale breaching a few hundred yards from the port bow. (The instant Rebecca finally relinquishes the binoculars and I lift them to my eyes, the whale disappears beneath the surface and never returns. Rebecca cackles.) Equally exciting: In the afternoon, we receive an invitation to tour the previously off-limits engine room and navigation bridge.

Witold the electrician leads our engine room tour. He is wearing a stained, threadbare jumpsuit that pretty clearly hasn't been laundered since the ship left port. He's zipped it open far down his sternum, allowing his chest hair to erupt forth. When he leans in close, to make himself heard above the noise-baffling headphones he's asked us to wear, his breath and body odor envelop me in a rank cloud that I fear I might never unsmell.

To get to the engine room, we follow Witold down stairways and ladders, lower and lower into the bowels of the ship. As we descend, we begin to feel the humming of the engine inside our skulls. At last, we reach the engine room door. "Welccchom to ccchyell!" Witold shouts gleefully, opening the hatch with a blast wave of heat and rumble.

"Thees ees engine!" he shouts, once we've entered the two-story chamber that holds the behemoth. The freighter's engine boasts seven cylinders and is roughly the size of a four-bedroom ranch house, but otherwise isn't fundamentally different from the engine in your car. Instead of turning wheels, its driveshaft turns the ship's single, enormous propeller. This simple operation burns 152,000 gallons of fuel per day.

The engine we're looking at, and the ship that it powers, were built in 1995. That's relatively old in container ship years. The German shipping company that owns this freighter will almost certainly sell it soon—likely to a Greek shipping line.

There seems to be universal, casual disdain for the Greek shipping industry among the crew members I've talked to. The term "rust buckets" has entered our conversations more than once. "A sheep like thees last fifteen years," says Witold. "And then the Greeks will use it for another fifteen!"

OUR tour through the ship's belly done, we climb about eight floors up. Here, at the top of the superstructure, is the navigation bridge. From its wraparound windows we can look down on the container stacks and see to the horizon in every direction.

The man currently on watch is the chief officer, Rikus. He's a tall, broad-shouldered, Teutonic cement block of a man. His smoothly shaven head is adorned with a pair of sleek, rimless eyeglasses.

Rikus begins his tour by pointing out the ship's steering wheel. I'd expected a wooden wagon wheel kind of thing—with thick, lathed spokes and shiny brass fasteners—but it turns out the wheel is actually smaller than the one on your average family sedan. It looks all out of proportion to the dimensions of the ship.

Also, it never gets used. There is a small dial, the size of a beverage coaster, embedded in a console in front of the wheel, and it is this little dial that does almost all the steering. On the dial are numbers from 0 to 359, corresponding to each different bearing on a compass. Turn the dial to 0, and the ship's autopilot steers a course due north. Spin the dial to 180, and the autopilot steers due south. In open ocean, with no ships or other obstacles to avoid, the crew generally sets the dial to a heading and forgets it.

Navigation, like steering, has become almost totally automated. The ship has three global positioning systems calculating its coordinates at all times, which nearly eliminates the need for the old-fashioned charts, rulers, and protractors. Of course, the computers aren't infallible. Rikus tells us that the U.S. government, which controls the GPS grid, can turn it off at any time and can also purposefully introduce errors—making you believe you're somewhere you're not. It's unlikely, barring some sort of global war or massive catastrophe, that the GPS grid would ever be disabled over the Atlantic Ocean. But just in case, the freighter's crew plots out their route every day in pencil, on paper charts. They even take daily sightings with a sextant, to confirm their location.

These cute, antiquated traditions aside, the life of the modern container ship officer is pretty bland. They work two lonely, four-hour watches on the bridge each day—Rikus does the 4:00 a.m.–8:00 a.m. and 4:00 p.m.–8:00 p.m. shifts—which are mostly spent monitoring the radar for other ships on possible collision courses. Were there any, the officer would have a solid half hour or more to make a minor heading adjustment and steer clear of an encounter. When not on duty, the officers read books, watch DVDs, smoke cigarettes, and work on their tans.

It's a classic hours of boredom/moments of terror kind of job. For the most part, the ship sails itself, but if things get hairy you'd better know what you're doing and do it quick. The real challenge seems to be maintaining a constant state of alertness. As he concludes our tour, Rikus wraps up his presentation with what is clearly a well-worn crowd-pleaser: "And finally, this is our most important piece of equipment," he says, pointing at the electric coffeemaker in the corner.

Life on a freighter wasn't always so rote and professional. Merchant seamen were once a breed of restless wildmen. As their ships sat tied up at docks in exotic ports of call for days on end—cargo slowly coming on and off—they would blow their earnings at local bars and bordellos. They'd wander back, drunk or worse, just in time to board the ship before it hoisted anchor.

Now, with containerization and automated loading, shore leave often lasts just a couple of hours, leaving enough time to eat a quick meal on land, and maybe buy some new DVDs, before heading back to the ship. There are also tougher rules and stricter enforcement with regard to drugs and alcohol. Today's sailors tend to be a staid, workmanlike bunch, less enthralled by the romance of the high seas than by the allure of a steady paycheck.

THE middle days of an ocean passage begin to blur together. There are no landmarks to break up the voyage and let you take stock of your progress. Hour after hour, day and night, the freighter chugs through the waves of an empty sea.

In open water, the ship maintains a constant speed of 17.5

knots—or roughly twenty miles per hour. Today's freighters are generally not expected to run at top speeds, as that would eat up expensive fuel. If a company needs cargo delivered very quickly instead of very cheaply, they'll use air freight.

Twenty miles per hour feels painfully slow, even by the standards of a surface traveler. For instance, picture yourself riding by bus from Seattle to Miami, without ever stopping for gas or food or lodging, keeping the speedometer locked in at 20 mph. That's essentially what we're doing as we cross the Atlantic—except that we're covering an additional thousand miles.

After twenty-four hours at sea, we were due south of Nova Scotia. After forty-eight hours, we were south of the island of Newfoundland. There's a small magnetic model of the ship stuck on a map that's attached to the metal wall of the mess room. At each mealtime, after politely greeting Daphne and Frank, Rebecca consults her GPS and moves the ship an eighth-inch hop—about 10 degrees of longitude. Our progress from meal to meal seems infinitesimal.

When it's as clear as the days have been so far, our visibility looking out from a railing is about twenty miles. So, at our 20 mph pace, we can look at the horizon's edge and know that's where we'll be precisely one hour from now. Of course, we know that when we get there it will look dismayingly similar to the place we'd been one hour before.

By my calculation, we can survey 1,250 square miles of ocean at any given time. And all of it is barren. We never see other ships out here. (When I ask Rikus why we're not seeing other freighters, his answer boils down to: It's a really big ocean.) There are no planes or contrails above, as we're not beneath any flight paths. Our view is of endless water and sky, punctuated by whitecaps and wispy clouds.

Until the fog rolls in.

A little more than halfway to Europe, almost dead center in the middle of the Atlantic, we wake up one morning to find the ship entirely shrouded. We can't see more than thirty feet beyond the railings. We can't make out the bow from the stern. It used to be our front yard was an infinite expanse of sea. Now it's an encroaching wall of mist.

The fog stays with us all day and night, and into the next day and night. It heightens the sense—absolutely true, as it happens—that the ship is an enclosed, self-sustaining world. The twenty-seven of us on board are the population of this lonely universe. And suddenly our little freighter is feeling very claustrophobic.

Rebecca's brain moves about forty-seven times faster than the brain of an average human. This is a great boon to her as a lawyer. But out here, with nothing to do, and naught to look at but an opaque curtain of gray, it's distinctly less advantageous. "I've been fantasizing about sneaking onto the bridge and slamming the throttle forward," she says. "If only I could somehow hydroplane the freighter at 200 mph all the way to Europe."

Instead she just paces antsily around the deck, carrying with her a small tote bag that holds her only diversions. First, she pulls out her shortwave radio and waggles the antenna around searching for BBC World Service. (No dice.) Then she consults her GPS. (Yup, still in the middle of the Atlantic Ocean.) Back to the radio. (Nothing but static.) In frustration, she resorts to teaching herself the Cyrillic alphabet from a book she brought along, preparing for our eventual arrival in Russia.

I stave off boredom by hanging out on the bridge as much as possible, peppering Rikus with questions. He's a sharp, thoughtful guy and seems eager for the company. He's also intrigued by our mission to circumnavigate the earth. Even the captains and officers on most round-the-world freighter routes have never actually circumnavigated in one go, as they usually swap out and fly home for a break before the ship completes the full circle.

With nothing to do in this fog but listen for radar blips that aren't blipping, Rikus helps me identify the whale Rebecca and I spotted a few days ago. We use a Greenpeace reference guide that's kept on the bridge in case the ship needs to report a collision with an animal. Based on silhouettes, I determine that what we saw was almost certainly a right whale—so named because early whalers deemed it the "right" whale to hunt, since it conveniently floated to the surface after being speared. (If this were 1730, the Grand Banks would have been swarming with whaling ships, and we'd have been sighting our mammal buddy down the shaft of a harpoon instead of through binoculars.)

Rikus also lets me leaf through the various operations manuals in the ship's library. I'm fascinated by the procedures recommended in the event of a lifeboat evacuation. The manual advises the captain to, early on, order everybody in the lifeboat to urinate over the side. Apparently, the stress and lack of privacy in the craft can build up and make some folks unable to go. Which, as you can imagine, becomes an awkward health issue. Though only slightly more awkward than having someone command you to pee before his eyes.

Our other friend on the crew, Witold the electrician, has also made efforts to alleviate our boredom. On a lazy afternoon, seeing that we're running out of ways to occupy ourselves, he invites Rebecca and me to his cabin to peruse his personal DVD collection. "Borrow as myenny as you like," he says, opening his door and ushering us in.

His cabin is tidy and compact, much smaller than ours, with a nice view of the fog. The cabin smells of Witold, which takes a moment to adjust to. But the most arresting aspect of the room is what's Scotch-taped to its walls. Upon them are arrayed at least nine or ten pinups of topless women, gazing out at us lustily from every angle.

I should note that these women are not just topless. They are top-heavy. To a comical degree. We're talking major bazooms. "I'm feeling a little inadequate," Rebecca whispers in my ear as Witold digs out his DVD collection.

None of us mentions the nudie shots aloud. Instead, having opened up his DVD album on his desk, Witold pauses to point at a different pinup photo on the wall, directly above his workspace. "Thees my daughter," he says with a proud smile. We follow his eyes to a snapshot of a plump, red-cheeked young woman. To our tremendous relief, she is clothed.

Aside from the odd fact that his daughter's photo is the only nonpornographic image in his cabin, and that her smiling face is flanked on either side by bulging bosoms, there's no denying Witold's affection for his kid. Beaming, he tells us that she's twenty-eight and is working in England right now. Later in the trip, when the ship docks in Liverpool for a couple of hours, she'll be meeting up with her dad for dinner. Witold, like many freighter workers, goes to sea for four months at a time, so he relishes even the briefest opportunity to see his family. On the wall next to the photo, just to the left of a set of boobs, he's taped up a calendar marking the days until he can return home to the town where he lives, an hour outside of Warsaw.

We flip through Witold's obviously pirated bootleg DVDs, looking for something that might entertain us as we wait for the fog to lift. Many of the movies are dubbed into Polish, which makes them of less use to us. Witold's written the names of the actors who star in each film in black marker on the DVDs, and as we sift through the collection two clear patterns emerge. First, the female stars are all extremely chesty. Not a surprise. And second, Witold appears to have difficulty distinguishing between different African American male actors. Specifically: Whenever a movie features a black actor in the lead role, Witold's marker scrawl will read "Denzel Washington." Even when the actor is not Denzel Washington. A movie starring Jamie Foxx? Witold writes, "Denzel Washington." Will Smith? "Denzel Washington." Wesley Snipes? Nope. "Denzel Washington."

WE borrow a couple of Witold's discs and watch them that evening on the TV in the ship's lounge. This offers a few hours of distraction. But when we wake the next morning—for the third day in a row—to a thick blanket of swirling fog, our ennui returns in force. It feels like we're not moving at all.

An exacerbating factor is the disappearance of our pet swallow.

Rebecca had been keeping tabs on him ever since Philadelphia, when she noticed him flying in and out of a crevice in the side of the superstructure. The little bird must have mistaken the ship for an apartment tower when we were docked in port. When we set sail, he came along for the ride.

Sadly, the poor guy just wasn't cut out for a life at sea. We sometimes see powerful, broad-winged seabirds swooping past the ship—skimming the swells and diving for fish. But when our tiny swallow makes his sorties out over the ocean, he quickly gets tired and flaps back to his nest. We began to grow concerned, as he couldn't be finding many bugs to eat out here. Now we haven't seen him at all for the last few days, and we fret for his well-being.

But mostly, it's the fog that's driving us nuts. It's so impassive, so oppressive, so monolithically dense and muffling. There's nothing we can do to shoo it away.

By evening three of fogfest, we're at our wits' end. There is but one surefire solution: copious amounts of alcohol. We purchase a bottle of whiskey from the freighter's slop chest—a little storeroom from which the crew can buy liquor and cigarettes—and polish off most of it in the course of an hour. Rebecca soon nods off. I, perhaps unwisely, stumble out into the foggy night with one last tumbler of good cheer.

I've brought the shortwave with me in hopes I might find a radio show to keep me company. But all I can manage to tune in on the world band are evangelical sermons. I pull out the earbuds and sit in silence, feeling the wet fog on my face and listening to the ocean slap against the hull.

As I continue to sip at the chest-warming liquor, entering ever-deeper states of inebriation, a maudlin thought begins to take shape in my whiskey-addled skull. My notion is this: We are each of us our own container ship, transporting our various cargoes through the ocean of life. At ports along the way, we may stop and pick up a new lover, a spouse, a child. At other ports we unload precious items—friends move away, relationships end, parents die. Even when we're lost in the deepest fog, we must try to keep our watch, not be the cause of any tragic collisions, and do what we can to keep our cargo safe.

In the end, of course, your ship rusts out and is no longer sea-worthy. So I suppose, in this analogy, the afterlife equates to being bought by a Greek shipping line.

WE wake up hung over, yet ecstatic: Outside our cabin windows is a bright blue sky. It's our next-to-last day at sea, the fog has lifted, and the sun on our faces is a warm bath of wonderful.

Rebecca and I run out to the fo'c'sle to enjoy it. There, we quickly spot our first sign of outside human life since before the fog descended. It's a fishing boat not far off our bow. A flock of yellow-headed gannets flies behind it, diving in for scraps.

An hour later, we spot something even better: land ho! To port, we can see the Isles of Scilly—an archipelago lying just off the south-western tip of England. There's more ship traffic now, and more birds. As we're about to head aft to the mess room for lunch, Rebecca hears some wet snorting sounds coming from the water below. She leans over the railing to look down. It's a pod of dolphins, surfing our bow wave. Fifteen or twenty of them—leaping out of the water, clearing their blowholes, swapping places at the spear tip of their formation. I basically explode the memory card on my camera trying to capture this.

BY evening, the crew are all standing out on deck with their cell phones. We're close enough to shore to get a signal now. It's their first chance in a week to make personal calls.

The next morning, on our ninth and final day at sea, we pass through the English Channel. We see the white cliffs of Dover to port, and Calais to starboard. The radio picks up both French and British pop stations. The water is thick with sailboats and ships.

In the late afternoon, we enter the Schelde River at its mouth in the North Sea, near the border between Belgium and the Netherlands. The harbor pilot's small boat comes alongside us, and we drop a rope ladder. The pilot climbs up on deck and—armed with his extensive local knowledge of tides, currents, and hazardous shoals—directs our freighter safely up the river, toward the port of Antwerp.

Just before sunset, we tie up to our dock in an Antwerp shipping terminal. The cranes immediately roll into place, ready to unload our containers. I'm ready to be unloaded, too. It's time to pack up our things, return Witold's DVDs, and say our good-byes to everybody on board.

I think of Christopher Columbus and his crew. They spent five weeks crossing this same ocean, not entirely sure whether anything awaited them on the other side. What relief must have melted over them as they collapsed to their knees on that Bahamian beach. I think I might be feeling a tiny morsel of that same resolution.

As we pull on our backpacks and get ready to disembark, an unfamiliar odor enters my nostrils. It's intoxicating. I can't quite place it. And then I realize: It's the freshly mown grass of a lawn on the opposite bank of the river. It's the smell of land.

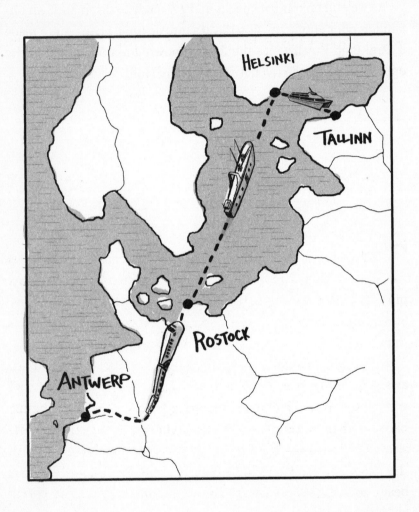

Chapter Two

Antwerp to Tallinn

THE swaying of a ship has a distinct flavor, as ultimately the hull is at the mercy of a liquid. We'd grown accustomed over the past nine days to the sensation of fluid dynamics asserting their whims. Stepping off the ship now, onto solid ground, we experience—as though for the first time—the eminent stillness of the earth.

Our freighter captain has kindly radioed ahead to shore, so a taxi awaits us on the pier. The taxi driver is a compact, muscular man with close-cropped hair and wraparound shades. He stands beside his cab with his arms crossed, his biceps flexing under a tight, short-sleeved shirt. As we approach him, Rebecca murmurs in my ear, "He looks just like Jean-Claude Van Damme." And indeed he does bear a striking resemblance to the world-famous Belgian thespian/kickboxer. It's extraordinary that the first person we meet on Belgian soil is an unmistakable doppelgänger for the nation's most glamorous

47

celebrity. (The five most famous Belgians, in my amateur estimation, are: Van Damme, René Magritte, Peter Paul Rubens, Tintin, and Papa Smurf. Possibly not in that order.)

It takes Jean-Claude forever to navigate out of Antwerp's enormous port, which is one of the busiest in the world. Having watched the loading operations at the dock in Pennsylvania, we're familiar with the rhythms of container shipping, so the bustle and noise of the forklifts and transporters here don't feel new to us. What *does* feel radically new is the taxi's velocity: When we hit 45 mph on a long back alley, between rows of container stacks, it's as though we've been strapped to a ballistic missile. This is more than twice the speed we've been moving at for the past nine days.

Our first stop is at the immigration center that gatekeeps the port, as we're required to check in and get stamped before we formally enter Europe. There's a long line at the passport window—mostly merchant sailors from other ships—so we wait outside for a bit. Jean-Claude, puffing on a menthol cigarette, decides to make small talk.

I had almost entirely positive expectations for our time in Belgium, with two exceptions. First, I predicted that at least one dude would direct an oily, sexual comment at Rebecca—because hey, this is Gallic Europe. Second, I predicted we'd see some mild xenophobia directed at Islamic immigrants—because hey, this is Gallic Europe.

What I didn't predict: that we'd encounter both these things within our first fifteen minutes in the country or that they'd both come courtesy of the first man we met.

When an adorable-looking South Asian family walks out of the immigration center, Jean-Claude complains angrily, under his breath, about "the fucking Mushlimsh." He explains that "they're lazhy" and "they all shell drugsh" and "they drive around in big carsh they can't afford." It's the litany of sins every culture attributes to its most underprivileged minority groups.

After customs stamps our passports without so much as glancing at our bags (damn it, I totally should have brought along that exotic monkey pet), we get back in the taxi for the drive into town. Along the way, Jean-Claude offers us an eccentric introduction to the modern Belgian economy. "There'sh a lot going on in Belzhum. We have a chemical indushtry. Alsho," he says, now grinning at Rebecca in the rearview mirror, "we make shilicone titsh."

ONCE we've checked into a hotel and dropped off our bags, we begin our explorations of downtown Antwerp. To my delight, it turns out the city brims with the sort of bizarre, medieval lore that I've come to expect from my continental hamlets.

For instance, near a pretty riverbank there's a statue of a mythical creature named Lange Wapper. Our English-language visitors' pamphlet describes him as a "water giant" who sleeps under the "meat hall." Mr. Wapper specializes in terrorizing drunkards and, perhaps less endearingly, little children. Another statue, near the town square, shows a man in the midst of hurling a large, severed hand. This pose somehow relates to Antwerp's name, which can be translated as "hand throw." The name is derived from a fairy-tale legend about a brave fellow who hacked off an evil monster's hand and then, for reasons not fully clear, threw it into the river.

Nowadays, Antwerp embraces severed-hand imagery as a kind of macabre municipal symbol. In the downtown shops, you can buy little souvenir chocolates shaped like hands. And in the sex district, a storefront window features lots of black, molded rubber hands—firmly clenched, as though preparing to enter a compact space. I'm not totally certain, but my guess is that these hands somehow get employed in a forceful salute to the city's proud history.

If Antwerp is known for one thing—besides civically oriented sex toys—it's the diamond trade. About 80 percent of the world's uncut diamonds (and half its cut diamonds) pass through this city each year. As we stroll through the diamond district, past its window displays of glittering necklaces, an armored truck suddenly prowls around the corner—flanked by four footmen wearing bulletproof vests and cradling submachine guns.

Have you ever been surprised by a man who is holding a submachine gun? If not, you should really try it sometime. Invigorating! I freeze in place, my eyes locked on the weapon, then step gingerly to the side, instinctively pulling my hands from my pockets and holding them out where the gunmen can see them. Meanwhile, a pair of orthodox Jews walks past nonchalantly, toting heavy suitcases chained to their waists. They don't even flinch. Visible automatic firearms are an everyday occurrence here and no cause for alarm.

BY the next afternoon, we're ready to resume circumnavigating the earth. We walk to the railway station and catch an intercity train. It's full of Belgian commuters, and everything about it—from its clean, shiny surfaces to its mobile phone–tapping passengers in business attire—screams efficiency. We get off in Brussels and connect to the high-speed Thalys line, which will zoom us onward to Cologne.

The Thalys locomotive used on this route is a French-made TGV model. TGV stands for *train à grande vitesse*, which roughly translates to "train of a lot of fastness." At one point, shortly after leaving Brussels, we reach a bracing 185 mph, according to the readout on Rebecca's GPS. If our taxi in Antwerp felt like a missile, this feels like a comet. When the train accelerates, the trees outside the window dissolve into a green-brown blur. Passengers sway gently in the aisle as we make the leap to warp speed.

Sadly, the Thalys sprinkles these high-speed bursts between much longer stretches spent slogging down older tracks, where the train tops out at a mere 60 or 70 mph. It's the same limitation you'll find on Acela, the U.S. northeast corridor's semisuccessful experiment in semi-high-speed rail. (Though that's about all that Thalys has in common with Amtrak. For instance, the Thalys café car is stocked with a wide, attractive selection of food and beverages, instead of three bags of chips and a rotting ham sandwich. European trains handle matters of sustenance far more skillfully.)

Our eventual destination is Rostock, a German city of 200,000 on the shore of the Baltic Sea. From there, our belief is that we'll be able to catch a ferry that goes to Finland. Quick surface-travel comparison: A flight from Belgium to Finland would take about two and a half hours. Our route—via rail and water—will take sixty-four hours. We'll be spending one night on a train, two on a ship, and none in a real bed. But we'll experience the charms of Rostock and the swells of the Baltic instead of the lifeless interior of a jet.

*   *   *

WHEN an airplane takes you to your destination three days quicker than a train or a ship, it's easy to see why people choose to fly, however boring flying may be. Planes are also cheaper than most forms of ground transport, which makes the decision even simpler. Ryanair, a budget carrier based in Ireland, has lately been offering flights between European cities for as little as twenty dollars. That's the price of two beers at an Antwerp nightclub.

Eye-popping fares like this have made Ryanair Europe's largest carrier. Also its most profitable. Despite handing out tickets like lollipops, Ryanair has maintained net margins higher than those of the traditional, long-haul airlines.

Most business analysts credit four strategic decisions: 1) Ryanair flies only one type of plane. 2) It only flies to secondary airports, where the cost of doing business is much cheaper. 3) It packs the plane with as many seats as possible. 4) It gives away those seats but charges passengers dearly for everything else.

The airline rakes in a fee if you bring too much luggage, and another if you check in at the airport desk instead of beforehand, online. The flight attendants sell snacks and scratch-card games once the trip is under way. Meanwhile, the interior surfaces of the plane are plastered with advertising, which brings in additional revenue streams.

In general, no budget-cutting opportunity is overlooked. Ryanair's CEO has, somewhat cheekily, threatened to charge passengers for using the onboard lavatory. One *BusinessWeek* story dubbed the airline "Wal-Mart with wings," noting several of the more miserly measures the airline has taken: "Seats don't recline, the better to cram in more passengers. Window shades have been removed, so flight attendants don't have to spend time resetting them between flights. Seat-back pockets have been ditched—one less place for clutter to accumulate."

Given Ryanair's success, at a time when air carriers everywhere are struggling, this sort of penury and squalor seems like the inevitable future of flight. To which I say: Leave me out of it. Having just crossed the Atlantic in a large, private stateroom, the thought of being herded into an airborne cattle car gives me itchy hives.

WHILE my personal objections to air travel mostly relate to comfort, aesthetics, and philosophic principle, there is the growing issue of air-travel politics to consider. Antiairplane activists in Europe have become vocal and aggressive of late. Recently, protesters set up a camp at London's Heathrow Airport, and a group calling itself Plane Stupid disrupted operations at an Airbus factory in Wales. Environmental concerns are the driving force behind this antiflying sentiment.

The fact is, jumbo jets burn up a lot of nonrenewable resources. Even taxiing them to and from the gate requires an absurd amount of fuel. (Virgin Atlantic has experimented with towing its planes out to the runway, to reduce this waste.)

Once aloft, airplanes belch kerosene soot into the sky at a rate of a million metric tons a month. Planes are major sources of carbon dioxide and nitrogen oxide emissions, which contribute to greenhouse warming. Eurostar, the railway line that zips back and forth between London and Paris through the Chunnel, has estimated that flying round-trip between those cities emits more than ten times the carbon dioxide the identical train journey does. What's more, the airplane deposits its CO_2 directly into the upper atmosphere, where it will do more damage.

Airports, too, have become focal points for environmentalist scorn. The chemicals used to deice planes in wintertime may contaminate nearby water sources. Also, airports often get built in isolated, exurban areas—necessitating new highways, new traffic jams, and new sprawl. By contrast, building a downtown train station can actually revitalize a city neighborhood.

Most travelers ignore the environmental impacts of flying, either out of obliviousness or indifference or because they refuse to live without the convenience. But awareness is slowly building. Some fliers attempt to offset their carbon emissions by donating money to organizations that plant trees or engage in other eco-do-gooder activities. Others limit their carbon footprint simply by vacationing closer to home.

A few brave souls, our spiritual comrades, have vowed to use only surface transport. One British newspaper recently ran a travel story addressing the fledgling "overland tourism" trend that's resulted. "In the 1960s people chose not to fly because air travel was too expensive," writes *The Independent*. "These days, a growing band of travellers are choosing not to fly because of the environmental cost of their journey."

Environmentalist or not, you may at some point be forced to confront a world without cheap, regular airline service. A couple of years back, a mechanical engineering professor at Stanford theorized that air travel as we know it is going extinct. Consider: While there are realistic alternatives for powering surface transport (cars and trains can already be run on electricity), no one has yet found an economically viable way to operate a large fleet of jets without using massive amounts of petroleum.

Experiments are afoot—again, Richard Branson and Virgin Atlantic seem to be in the forefront—but it's still not clear whether it will be possible to create a biofriendly, sustainable form of jet travel. Gravity is a tough customer, and it never gives up the fight. To beat it, you need to eat up a whole lot of energy. If the price of crude oil gets way out of hand—and no one figures out how to power jets with, say, vegetable grease—flying could eventually turn into a luxury affordable only for the rich, as it was in its early days. It's not inconceivable that middle-class travelers would literally be grounded. The clock would turn back to that relatively recent age when trains and ships still ruled the earth.

Which means Rebecca and I are both pioneers and historical reenactors. We're traveling as folks did in the past, and as they might again one day in the future. Ground-bound, while the rest of the world zips by thirty-five thousand feet overhead.

WHEN I was packing for this trip, a large segment of my effort centered on how best to erase all traces of my nationality. Not out of any distaste for America, but rather from a desire to blend in wherever I go. So: No shorts with white sneakers and tube socks—which, in addition to looking super dorky, is a dead giveaway that you're North American. Likewise, no baseball caps or recognizable brand logos.

Instead, my wardrobe consists entirely of drab, muted colors and conservative cuts. My clothes were all chosen based on their ability to deflect attention—much as a Stealth Bomber deflects radar pings.

The first test of my camouflage comes in Cologne. We get off the Thalys here and walk around a bit as we're waiting to connect with our next train. We're strolling across a large public square outside the station when a woman asks me, in German, for the time. I wordlessly angle my watch into her sightline. She thanks me—once again, in German.

To you, this may seem an inconsequential moment. To me, it is a hugely gratifying accomplishment. I've been mistaken for European! My disguise is a success. I've slipped off the shackles of national identity and now tread the road as the anonymous everytraveler.

Sadly, despite my best efforts, there's one element of my carriage that I fear I'll never be able to fully denature: my big, loose, floppy American walk. Americans, as a rule, walk large. We live in an enormous country, with room to spread out, and accordingly we let our limbs flail where they will. Not so with the Europeans, who favor a far more compressed bearing. They hold their knees closer together and their arms tighter to their flanks. The contrast is striking. With minimal practice, I've become able to distinguish New World gaits from Old World gaits at 150 yards.

We booked a four-bunk cabin for our overnight train to Rostock, but no one else is in the berths when we board. We claim the top two bunks for ourselves and have begun settling in when our cabinmate arrives and tosses his backpack on one of the lower beds. He introduces himself as Stefan, and tells us he's a policeman from Düsseldorf. He's a chubby blond guy in his midtwenties who's on his way to meet some friends for a vacation in a Baltic shore beach house. He takes off his shoes and makes himself comfortable on his bunk. Soon after the train starts rolling, he's asleep and lightly snoring.

Chatting quietly across the gap between the upper bunks, Rebecca and I calculate the ground we've covered so far. We went 140 miles from Antwerp to Cologne today, and we'll have gone another 330 miles by the time this train reaches the edge of the Baltic Sea tomorrow morning. Tack that onto the roughly 4,000 miles we racked up on our freighter crossing, and it's starting to feel like we've made some progress. Until we remember that the circumference of the earth is 25,000 miles.

Suddenly feeling smaller, I let the clacking of the rails lull me to sleep. When I wake after sunrise, Stefan is already gone, having disembarked in the wee hours of the morning to connect with another train. I drop drowsily from my bunk to the floor, rubbing my eyes. Soon after, we shuffle to the exit doors as our train pulls into Rostock at 8:00 a.m.

THERE are many ways to get overland from Belgium to Finland. Taking trains and/or buses is the obvious option. With both these, though, we'd have to make a big curve to get around the Baltic Sea. Looking at a map, the more elegant solution is to cut straight across the water on a ferry.

It's clearly the shortest path to Helsinki, mileagewise. We assume a ferry ride will also mean more time spent in the spacious, open-air expanses of a ship, instead of in the comparatively crowded compartments of buses and trains. Based on this reasoning, we've come here to Rostock to catch a ferry that boards later today.

Fifteen and a half hours later, to be precise. As we're beginning to learn—and will no doubt continue to learn, in painful detail—surface travel involves a lot of waiting around. It's no big deal to make a connection at an airport between a pair of four-hour flights. It's another matter entirely to make a connection between a ten-hour train ride (arriving at a downtown railway station) and a thirty-six-hour ferry voyage (originating at a pier in a far-off, neglected corner of the city).

Train and ship schedules rarely align, for one thing, since few people make this sort of transfer anymore. Even if the timetables miraculously coordinate, you'd be a fool to cut things close. If you miss a flight, there'll likely be another in an hour or two, and you can wait it out in a comfortable departures lounge. If you miss a long-haul ferry, the next ship might not leave for another three days, and you'll be stuck out at some remote, rusty dockyard, with no idea where you're sleeping that night.

Thus we've left ourselves some wiggle room. We'll consider it a chance to enjoy Rostock as we wait for our ferry to cast off. We pick up a tourist guide upon our arrival at the train station, and set off for a walk.

According to the guide, the focal point of Rostock's town square is something the locals have named the "porno fountain." We of course make a beeline for it. It turns out to be a standard fountain that's been ringed with sculptures of frolicking nudes—men, women, boys, and girls—arranged in embraces that, while intended to evoke an innocent joy, very easily lend themselves to darker interpretations. Perhaps you're familiar with an old joke about a family variety act that dubs itself "the Aristocrats"? If so, you'll understand what I'm getting at. Even the animal sculptures at the edges of the fountain seem sort of dirty. One of them appears to be an autofellating warthog.

After checking the porno fountain off our must-see list, we take a water taxi from Rostock to a nearby seaside resort called Warnemünde. It's a honky-tonk beach town, Baltic-coast style. Little rental sailboats zip around the harbor here, and T-shirt shops line the touristy streets. We lunch at a restaurant on the penthouse floor of a beach hotel. The panoramic windows offer a stunning view of the water, and a live, six-piece combo churns out easy-listening hits.

When the band launches into a jazzy version of "The Blue Danube," several elderly couples hobble eagerly onto the dance floor for a waltz. The men wear pastel blazers and white leather loafers. The women are built ... sturdily. Everyone smiles wide and nods in time. The scene feels familiar to me, but I can't quite place it. Until I realize: It looks like a troupe of actors re-creating, with careful attention to detail, a 1972 studio taping of *The Lawrence Welk Show*.

Which is interesting, given that this region was part of Soviet-controlled East Germany in 1972. I can't help but wonder if Lawrence Welk is, for this older generation, an embodiment of hip, off-limits capitalist culture. Either way, I can say with utter confidence that this is more interesting than an airport layover. I take a plate from the rolling dessert cart and nibble a bite of strudel as I tap my feet.

After lunch, we head back to Rostock to continue the long wait for our ferry. Once the stores close for the evening, and the crowds disappear, there's nothing to do but wander aimlessly through the dark streets, occasionally resting on park benches and stifling yawns. At 11:30 p.m. we at last catch the designated shuttle bus that will take us to the pier for our late-night embarkation.

OUR ship is named the *Superfast VIII* and is operated by an Estonian ferry line. Question: Why does an Estonian company operate ferries that travel between Germany and Finland? Answer: I don't know—but I'm sure looking forward to that legendary Eastern Bloc customer service.

The ferry boards everyone at night, but doesn't leave the dock until around sunrise the next morning. We're told that this lead time is necessary because so many people bring their cars onto the ferry, and it takes a long time to roll them all into the hold. Next question: Why must passengers like us, who are not bringing a vehicle, board the ship five or six hours before it departs? Answer: Again, I have no idea—but think I'm getting a taste of that legendary Eastern Bloc flexibility and attentiveness to individual needs.

A private cabin on this ferry costs $700, which seemed steep. Instead, Rebecca and I paid $125 each for what the ticket clerk described to us as "airplane-style seats." We'll be sleeping in these seats for the next two nights, so we envision they'll be like those wide, reclining thrones that you'd find in the first-class section of a plane.

Upon boarding, we discover that our seats are more like what you'd find in an airplane's economy section—if that airplane had no windows and was shaped like a small shoebox. The forty bolted-down chairs are crammed together in a dark, airless closet on a lower deck. When we arrive, the room is already filled with other people, and their piles of luggage, and their cranky children.

Having spent the previous night on a train, and all day today wandering the boulevards of Rostock, we're fairly exhausted by now. So we suck it up, find a spot against a wall to drop our bags, and settle into our assigned seats. We try to pretend they are fluffy beds instead of narrow, hard pews.

I can't fool myself. The chair's metal arms jab into my kidneys as I search for a sleeping position. My knees are jammed against the seat in front of me. From behind me emanates a sound I cannot for the life of me identify. Is it an armored personnel carrier grinding its gears? A high-powered blender liquefying coat hangers?

I crane my neck around. In the seat directly behind mine sits an elderly man swaddled in clumps of wool blankets. His eyes are closed. He isn't moving. Then suddenly the blankets rise up with great force. His mouth gapes open. And there's the sound! I'd never imagined it could be produced by a human being!

It is an atomic sort of snoring, with a relentless rhythm. One deafening blast is followed by another, over and over. I lie awake picturing the awful things I would like to do to this old man's trachea.

When a ferry employee making the rounds ducks his head into the room around 2:00 a.m., another sleepless passenger—having reached the limits of his patience with the snorer—unloads with a salvo of primal anger. "This man is snoring so loud!" he shouts, pointing his finger toward the heaving blankets. The ferry worker shrugs and makes it clear there is nothing he can do.

Frustrated, the angry man shouts, "It is also smelling!" Which is true. Many shoes are off. The air is thick with the odor of feet and there's no sign of a ventilation system down here. Again, the ship employee shrugs. When he turns and leaves, a sudden roll of the ferry slams the door behind him with a percussive force. It briefly stirs the snorer—but within a few seconds he's settled back into his groove, louder than before.

It's time to break out my secret weapon, which involves two ingredients. The first ingredient is a small bottle of scotch, bought from our cargo freighter's slop chest, that I have been saving for a special occasion. The second ingredient is a small bottle of Valium that I brought from home for just this sort of emergency.

Let me pause here to pay tribute to Valium and its many useful applications for the traveler. It's perfect when you can't fall asleep and need to tune out the bestial snorer in your midst. Also handy when you're nervous about missing your train or ferry connection. Or you can just use it to take the edge off the afternoon when you're lying out on a fo'c'sle.

Within minutes of downing the pills and chasing them with liquor, I am feeling no pain. The loud snores float off into the ether. I'm so relaxed, and so *not* fitting into this chair, that I slink down to the floor and melt into the space between our row of seats and the row in front of us. This position puts my face adjacent not only to the filthy carpet, but also to the snoring man's stockinged feet—which reek of a particularly fierce strain of toe jam.

No matter. I am in a haze of pills. Soon after, I am in a deep sleep.

* * *

WE'RE awakened at 9:00 a.m. by an announcement over the ferry's loudspeaker. It's the voice of an eastern European woman, I presume Estonian.

"Hi, keedz," she says, profoundly bored. "Now ees facepainting in cheeldren's area." Her tone straddles the line between droning indifference and mild hostility.

I rouse myself from my Valium stupor. Most of our cabinmates are already awake, and farting. It occurs to me that this is the worst room I have ever been in.

Leaving our packs behind (there's nowhere else to put them, so we just have to pray that nobody steals them), we climb several flights to the ship's main deck. The sunlight here is blinding, after all the time we've just spent holed up in a fluorescent-lit cave. We find a pair of seats in front of a window looking out across the water.

The ship left the dock four hours ago. We're now cruising along at a relatively speedy—for a ship—35 mph. But we've still got more than twenty hours to go before we get to Finland.

A small child scurries past. A few desultory streaks of facepaint wobble across his cheeks. Rebecca is inspired to do a quick impression. "Hokay, keed," she says, eyes half closed, one hand waving a pretend cigarette. She halfheartedly slaps at the nose of an imaginary toddler. "There ees paint. Now you leave."

Those of us booked in the cheap seats down below have been granted a one-hour time period during which we are permitted to take showers in the ship's "spa." When the designated time comes, and I make my way up there, I find that the men's side of the spa is a small tiled room with one plastic bench and one moldy shower stall. There are no lockers, no towels, and no attendant. (Were there an attendant, I imagine he'd just grunt and toss a wad of paper napkins at my face.) I leave my clothes out on the bench and take a quick, hot shower. It's my first since we left Antwerp two nights ago, and by far the best moment of the ferry trip thus far. I dry myself off with the T-shirt I slept in last night, on the dustballed floor of the world's worst room.

When lunchtime rolls around, we peruse the offerings at the snack bar. It has some unlabeled sandwiches wrapped in cellophane. The condensation droplets on the packaging make it impossible to see what's inside. All I can glimpse is a limp piece of lettuce, browning at its edges.

Unless you need to transport your car to Helsinki, and don't feel like driving it, it's difficult to see why *anyone* would take this ship instead of flying (or, for that matter, walking) to Helsinki. The ferry's not that cheap. And with its thirty-hour transit time, it's certainly not fast. It's also not luxurious in any way. The lounge areas are functional but boring, and from what we can see, the private cabins are pretty minimalist, too.

At the table next to us, two young, blonde backpacker women are playing cards. I noticed them last night in the windowless snore-chamber. They seem like nice, reasonable people. Which makes us wonder what on earth they're doing here. Rebecca's so curious, she leans over to introduce herself and ask their story.

After apologizing for their limited English (which turns out to be much better than your average American undergrad's), the two women tell us they've been traveling on Eurail passes through Germany and Poland. They're now heading back to Finland, where they live. "But why would you take the ferry instead of a plane?" Rebecca asks them, pointing out that a plane would have been not only much faster, but possibly much cheaper and also more comfortable.

"Because," says the taller one, "we thought we take ferry, big advwenture." She throws her hands high and wide on the last word, and the two women giggle. "But now we are here, no advwenture anywhere," she says, surveying the depressing vista of the ferry lounge. Their laughter fades. They return to their cards.

"What game are you playing?" Rebecca asks them.

After a quick discussion in Finnish, the shorter one answers, "English name is 'asshole.'"

CROSSING the Atlantic on our cargo freighter, I'd felt wonderfully protected. We had our safety lecture, and occasional drills where we all practiced boarding a lifeboat. In general the freighter crew seemed competent and careful. They also knew us by name. I got the sense that, in the event of an emergency, I'd be rescued even if I just sat in my cabin and listened to my iPod as cold, salty waves came crashing through the windows.

On the *Superfast VIII* ferry? Not so much. We've had zero safety instruction or drills. I've no idea where the life jackets are, and I haven't spotted any signs indicating where I might find them. Just looking around at all the elderly people puttering through the ferry's corridors, the children roaming the lounges unaccompanied, and the overall sloppiness and disrepair I've noticed as I've toured around the ship (muddy decks, rusty railings, etc.), I fear any crisis situation would quickly devolve into a colossal goatfuck. Loudspeaker announcement: "Hi, keedz. Boat ees seenking. You jump now."

Given all this, it is terrifying, and yet not surprising, when—flipping through a travel guide—I stumble across a reference to a ferry disaster that occurred on the Baltic Sea, on an Estonian-run ferry not unlike this one. The date was September 28, 1994. A ferry named the *Estonia* was headed west across the Baltic bound for Stockholm.

Just like our ferry, the *Estonia* was a "Ro-Ro"—meaning "roll on, roll off." Ro-Ro ferries have a drawbridgelike hatch in their hull that, when lowered down to a pier, allows cars and trucks to roll directly into a parking deck deep within the ship. On the *Estonia*, this drawbridge hatch was set into the bow, and the pointed prow of the ship swung out of the way to expose the door.

Passengers who'd traveled aboard the *Estonia* on previous journeys noted that this giant opening in the front of the ship was not exactly watertight. In fact, the mostly Estonian crew had sometimes been observed stuffing mattresses and rags into a big gap that seawater leaked through. This water would slosh around on the parking deck, and more and more of it would collect over the course of a voyage. Apparently, the crew had decided this was no big deal.

On that particular September night in 1994, the winds were gale-force and the Baltic swells were vicious. Though the ship pitched violently, the crew kept powering through the waves. Passengers became seasick and retired to their cabins. Some heartier souls stayed up to party in the lounges and bars—though at least one woman dancing to the live music was reported to have lost her balance and been thrown into the bandstand.

Sometime after midnight, a thunderous, metallic slam reverberated throughout the ship. The ship rocked erratically and began to list. Then it listed further.

The troubled car hatch—and the outer covering meant to protect it—had become dislodged as a result of the ferry's hard collisions with the waves. Because the car door was set into the bow, the ferry was scooping up water as it moved forward. The sea gushed straight into the ship's belly. When the weight of the flood became too much to fight, the ferry rolled on its side and began to sink.

Once the ship wallowed, its architecture was transformed into a cruel obstacle course. For instance, the ferry's strange new angle turned a hallway of open cabin doors into a series of treacherous pits. Those who fell into them found it difficult to climb back out. Stairways also inverted and became impassable.

Journalist William Langewiesche, in his book *The Outlaw Sea*, notes that those who made it out alive from the *Estonia* were overwhelmingly younger and physically stronger than those who died. The odds favored the quick-thinking and the athletic. Mothers were separated from sons, boyfriends from girlfriends. "Love only slowed people down," Langewiesche writes. "A pitiless clock was running." Life and death could hinge on a split-second decision between the right escape route and the wrong one.

Even those who got off the ship often died in the water. Lifeboats toppled in the wind and the tall waves. In some cases, it took hours for rescuers to arrive. When it was all over, authorities counted 852 dead and 137 still alive.

Some blamed the ferry's German shipbuilder for a faulty hatch design (though the ferry had been in service for more than a decade under other operators, with no prior problems). Others blamed the Soviet-trained, Eastern Bloc crew for lax safety standards (though the crew behaved courageously once the ship was in trouble, by most accounts). A few conspiracy theorists blamed a terrorist plot (though it's unclear what the imaginary terrorists' motives would have been). Whatever the cause, the sinking of the *Estonia* was among the worst nonwartime disasters in modern European history. Tonight, on our way to Helsinki, we'll pass almost directly over the wreck. It's at the bottom of the Baltic, some two hundred feet below us, and it's still full of bodies—people like us, just taking a ferry ride.

The *Superfast VIII* was built in 2001, so any flaws with the *Estonia*'s hatch design have presumably been remedied. Also, the weather tonight is quite clear and calm. Still, I can't help but picture the lounge we're sitting in filling with seawater and screams.

Would you rather find yourself aboard a sinking ship or a plummeting plane? For Rebecca, the answer is easy. "I can't stand the thought of a plane crash because I'd have no control over it. I'd have to sit there in my seat and hope the pilot knows what he's doing. I want more agency!"

I take the opposite view. A shipwreck is scarier, because my own decisions could determine my survival. I just imagine myself trapped shivering in some flooding chamber, awaiting my end, ruing my choice to take a left down that corridor instead of a right.

IT'S getting toward midnight, and the ship is due to arrive in Helsinki at 6:00 tomorrow morning. Going to sleep now would mean a return to our seats in the "room of despair," as Rebecca has dubbed it. We just can't bring ourselves to ever go down there again.

Instead, we find a table at one of the onboard nightclubs, check out the drinks menu, and order shots of an obscure Estonian liqueur made from tree bark. Surprisingly tasty. The first pleasant surprise on the ship. Over the course of the next two hours, we swallow several more shots. There's a band here playing cheesy Europop, and an older Finnish couple is dancing to the electro-beat. We're digging the vibe, as well as the tingle of the bark booze.

Around 2:00 a.m., when we can hold our eyes open no longer, we curl up on a pair of benches in a far corner of the lounge. The music has stopped now, and only a few stragglers still sit at the tables. Within moments, we start drifting off to sleep. If only we'd had this brilliant idea last night. Sleeping in a public lounge is way better than suffering through the dense, foul air of that jail cell a few decks below.

At 5:30 a.m., a thin morning light comes trickling through the windows of the lounge. Rebecca blinks open her eyes and finds there is a strange man sitting about eight feet away, staring intently at her face. He's a little bald fellow, maybe sixty years old, wearing sandals with black socks. He's angled his chair so it points straight at Rebecca. He must have been watching her while she slept.

Rebecca nudges me awake. I rub my eyes and soon become aware of her creepy admirer. Without a word, Rebecca and I stand and walk quickly toward the other end of the ship.

THE ferry arrives at the dock in Helsinki a little after 6:00 a.m. Having spent the last three nights attempting to sleep in a wide variety of subpar conditions, all we desire at this point is to check into a hotel, shower away the last seventy-two hours, and crash into a deep, fully horizontal slumber. Tragically, no hotels will make a room available for us until after noon. So we trudge the streets like zombies, bent forward under the weight of our packs.

When the Helsinki City Museum opens for the day, we are the very first visitors through its doors. We make a beeline for a bench in a distant, quiet exhibit hall, far from the entrance. Here we sink into sleep, leaning our shoulders against one another, running the risk of being mistaken for vagrants. We manage a forty-five-minute nap, during which not a single soul enters the room.

When we wake, feeling vaguely refreshed, we glance around at the dusty display cases all around us. I'm pleased to find them chock-full of more wacky medieval Euro-lore. Helsinki's civic history is rife with tales of fire-breathing dragons and shape-shifting goblins. Also, there's mention of something termed a "dung fork." I have no idea what this is and am afraid to Google it for fear that the search results will include some searingly traumatic images.

After further hours spent dawdling in bookstores and coffee shops, we eventually manage to check in to a hotel, wash up, and feel human again. That night for dinner we meet up with our friend Andrew, who's been vacationing in Europe and e-mailed us with a plan to rendezvous here in Helsinki. Together we spend the next couple of days strolling around the city.

My first impression of Helsinki is that it looks like a TV commercial for a high-end optician. Everyone here seems to favor complex, rhomboid, asymmetrical eyewear. Also, everybody's very tall and sleek—often flaxen-haired, with piercing blue eyes. Andrew, Rebecca, and I are of average height in America, but walking around Helsinki we feel like stunted hobbits. Our faces are like a foot below the typical eye level of the locals. Have you ever been at a party where you swore you were invisible? That's how our entire stay in Helsinki feels. "I swear," Andrew muses over dinner, "I could walk into a bank here, rob money out of the vault, and walk out, and still the Finns wouldn't notice I exist."

Our resulting inferiority complex has prodded us to look for faults with the city. But we just can't find many. It's cute and walkable. It has a terrific public transportation system that has been zipping us around with great efficiency. There are windswept, grassy islands in the middle of the harbor where you can hike and have a picnic.

I guess if I were to name a flaw, it would be Finnish cuisine. While there's lots of delicious, fresh fish, the food as a whole here is a bit too mushy for my taste. Foreign dishes attempted in the restaurants often go awry—as with the "bruschetta" we were served, which turned out to be cold, floppy pita bread. Perhaps I'd feel differently if I'd worked up the courage to sample the pressed, canned bear and reindeer meat for sale in the gourmet markets.

AT almost exactly 60 degrees north latitude, Helsinki is as far north as we plan to get in the course of our circumnavigation. We do feel some temptation to make a run for the Arctic Circle, at 66 degrees. But making a detour of some nine hundred miles just to cross an imaginary line probably isn't worth the trouble.

Instead we decide we'll brave another ferry, due south to Estonia. It will drop us off in Tallinn, the capital city. From there we can hop on an overnight train to Moscow.

Most single-hulled ships can't exceed 41 mph, as at high speeds a wall of water builds up at their bow and becomes tough to fight through. A catamaran—like the ferry we catch in Helsinki—distributes the load onto two hulls, allowing the ship to go a bit faster. Our catamaran ferry cranks up to a top velocity of 47 mph, cutting across a narrow corner of the Baltic Sea at the mouth of the Gulf of Finland. The ride is silky smooth and comfortable. In contrast with our previous ferry, it's almost elegant. People are reading magazines and ordering cocktails from the bar. Most of the passengers on board are Finns, who often make the ninety-minute journey to Estonia because they can get a better price on beer there. (Many have brought along folding carts, all the better to lug back bulk quantities of brew.)

When the catamaran arrives in Tallinn, we disembark and start walking into town to look for a hotel. As we stop at a corner to wait for a traffic light to change, we notice a wild dog—and not a small one—loping casually down the middle of the street. A few other nappy, feral dogs join up with the leader, forming a confident pack.

Toto, I've a feeling we're not in western Europe anymore.

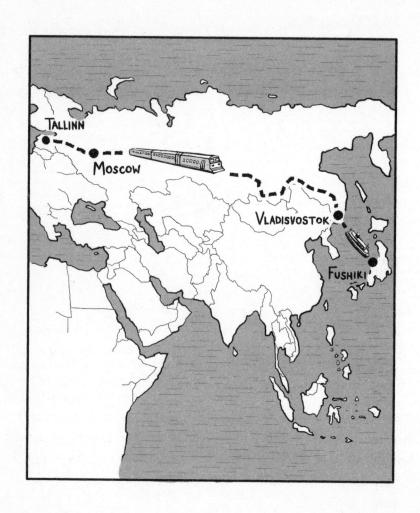

Chapter Three

Tallinn to Fushiki

THOUGH only a short ferry ride from Helsinki, Tallinn feels galaxies apart both in its architecture and its mood. The old part of town is a cluster of medieval buildings set into a hillside—all pointy spires, rust-red roofs, and jutting stone turrets. It's so theme-park cute, I half expect a troupe of merry jesters to come juggling and cartwheeling down the cobblestone lanes.

And yet *merry* is not a word I would use to describe most of the Estonians we encounter. More like *slouchy*. Or *shruggy*. Perhaps because we've now crossed behind the old Iron Curtain, I detect something different in the air. Less sunny optimism. More public urination. Also, fashionwise, it appears all the natural fibers got confiscated at the border.

We've happened to arrive in Tallinn on Estonian Independence Day. Or rather, one of multiple Estonian independence days. There are at least two. (Opportunities for newfound independence are frequent, if short-lived, when your country gets routinely invaded and occupied.) This particular independence day celebrates Estonia's most recent liberation, in 1991, from several decades of Soviet rule.

Hundreds of people have gathered in Tallinn's town square, before a festooned stage. Six little blonde girls wearing green tunics sing a traditional Estonian folk song. A portly singer belts out an emotional, no doubt fiercely nationalistic ballad, punctuating the high notes by extending his arms and throwing back his head.

There's a strong current of Estonian pride running through the audience—so much so that when some teens standing near us start to chatter over a politician's speech they're immediately shushed by older folks in the crowd. The main vibe I'm picking up on, though, is not collective excitement about Estonia's bright future. It's more a collective relief that the miseries of living under Russia's thumb seem to be mercifully over.

IN *Around the World in 80 Days*, our hero Phileas Fogg leaves London and makes his way southeast through the Mediterranean and the Suez Canal. He cuts across India, then up to Yokohama and on to San Francisco. We'd thought about retracing Fogg's route. But in the end something drew us north, to Russia, with equal parts fascination and fear. We can't resist a visit. Russia is an incomparable place: its vast expanses, its epic themes, its rich cultural history, its shoddy consumer products.

There's also the lure of the Trans-Siberian. I'm attracted by the sheer enormity of the world's longest railway, stretching a nearly unfathomable six thousand miles from Moscow to the Pacific. I want to gaze out a rolling picture window as I watch Europe slowly dissolve into Asia.

With dusk falling in Tallinn, we leave behind the independence festivities and head to the railway station for a Moscow-bound train. The frowning, polyester-tracksuited woman at the window sells us tickets for an overnight sleeper that leaves within the hour. Upon boarding, we discover our four-berth cabin is already inhabited by our two new roommates.

INTRODUCTIONS inside a train cabin are always a chaotic, claustrophobic affair. There is much shifting of backpacks, ducking of heads, and careful shuffling of feet. When this tempest subsides, hands are shaken. We learn that our cabinmates are named Vladimir and Alexandr, and that they are Russian.

In fact, they're almost too Russian to be believed. It's like they're animatronic robots programmed to embody various Russian stereotypes. After the train starts rolling, Vladimir (the older, balder one) produces a giant bottle of vodka from a duffel bag. Meanwhile, Alexandr (the younger, pudgier one) digs out crumpled plastic bags of cheese, dark brown bread, and cucumber slices. The two each take a healthy slug of liquor and then hungrily chase it with a chunk of food. After a brief exchange between them in Russian, Vladimir pushes the bottle at me with a dun-toothed smile and a vigorous nod of his head.

I take a swig. It tastes like recycled paint stripper. I immediately cough and tears rise to my eyes. Our Russian friends find this supremely hilarious. I pass the bottle to Rebecca, who of course knocks her shot back cleanly, with a satisfied exhale at the finish. More uproarious laughter from the Russians—while pointing at me. They offer us bread and cheese chasers, which we gratefully accept.

Though these two men speak little English, and we speak no Russian, by some miracle—possibly the miracle of inebriation, as those vodka shots keep flowing—we are able to carry on a conversation. For instance, we manage to establish that Vladimir and Alexandr are airplane engineers. Communicating this fact involves them holding out their arms and making airplane noises.

We also determine that they both live in a town called Vyazma. Rebecca hands Alexandr her GPS and, after some fiddling with the buttons, he finds Vyazma on a map and holds out the screen for us to see. It's a town of fifty thousand people, about 130 miles west of Moscow. It turns out to have suffered occupation by both Napoleon's and Hitler's armies, with battles decimating it first in 1812 and then again during World War II. I would like to tell Vladimir and Alexandr that, as an American, it's hard for me to relate to all the tragic history that's been overlaid on the cities of eastern Europe. But I'm not quite sure how to convey this notion using only funny noises, hand gestures, and facial expressions.

Eventually, the vodka overtakes us and it's time for sleep. These have been the best trainmates we could have hoped for. (With two minor drawbacks. Vladimir is snoring a little. And when Alexandr changed into his nightclothes, he inadvertently stuck his crotch directly in my face.) When morning comes, they disembark in Vyazma, and we continue on to Moscow.

IT'S about 9:00 a.m. when we arrive at Moscow's musty Leningrad Station. After disembarking from the train, my first encounter with Russia involves the vilest public restroom I have ever seen. The squat toilets here (wait, squat toilets? We're still in Europe, yes?) are spattered with all manner of foul matter. Half the sinks are broken, and several have screwdrivers and wrenches lying dormant in their basins—as though the repairman recognized the futility of maintaining any order here and just walked away with his hands in the air.

While Rebecca searches for a ruble-friendly ATM, I wait with our backpacks in the station's lobby and people-watch. I spot two little Russian boys, maybe ten years old, standing with an older woman I assume is their mother. The three of them look pretty hard up— grubby clothes, beaten-down faces, plastic bags to hold their belongings. Suddenly, the boys' heads swivel. I follow their eyes to a family of French-speaking tourists walking through the lobby.

One of the little French kids is wearing a pair of those roller sneakers that have pop-out wheels. The two Russian boys are spellbound as the kid glides by on the smooth station floor. They've never seen roller sneakers before. Their jaws literally drop. It's like the French kid has superpowers.

Once the kid has rolled out of sight, the boys start pretending to skate around the station—sliding the worn soles of their shoes across the floor, leaning their shoulders left and right, making whooshing noises with their mouths. They even stomp their feet on the ground once or twice, to see if some wheels might magically pop out from their heels. Perhaps this feature was always there, in every pair of shoes, and they simply hadn't been informed?

After a minute or two, one of the boys gets frustrated and pushes the other. They start fighting. I think mostly they're just trying to forget what they can't have.

OUTSIDE, it's ninety-degree August heat, with stifling humidity. (Not how I'd imagined Moscow.) Having no hotel reservation, we death-march through the city in search of lodging. Eventually we stumble on a little guesthouse tucked in an alley. The young woman at the desk says she has one room left and guides us upstairs for a tour.

It's a tiny, hovelish chamber, with no air-conditioning. A rabbit-eared TV gets three grainy stations. The wall-to-wall carpet doesn't actually reach the walls, and instead peters out a few feet short, unraveling into a fuzzy, ragged fringe. We take the room.

Back outside, blissfully unleashed from our packs, we explore the city. After walking through a few construction zones, we almost accidentally arrive in the middle of Red Square. It's a shock to stumble upon the kaleidoscopic, Technicolor onion domes of St. Basil's Cathedral. The church's familiar visage is recognizable from every on-location-in-Moscow TV news shot you've ever seen.

Sadly, most of the tourist destinations we'd like to see here are closed—and for no clear reason, as it's the middle of the week and not a holiday. Lenin's tomb? Nope. Kremlin? Nope. There is one his-

80

GROUNDED

torical museum open, though, and we're pleased to discover it includes an exhibit about the history of the Trans-Siberian Railway.
One of the displays is a detailed drawing of a disastrous and bloody
train derailment.

This is sobering, as we'll shortly be riding on a lot of Russian
trains. Further reason for concern: Just as we arrived in Europe,
someone detonated a bomb that derailed a train traveling between
Moscow and St. Petersburg, injuring about sixty people. We saw footage of the wreckage on TV when we were in Antwerp. News cameras
focused on a pair of trench-coated Russian investigators casually
lounging in front of the twisted metal. One detective was smoking a
cigarette. The other was eating a floppy sandwich wrapped in wax
paper. They seemed in no hurry, though they hadn't yet identified the
perpetrator (and still haven't, as best we can tell). The whole scene
did not inspire a ton of confidence.

The next morning, we attempt to take a midmorning stroll through
Gorky Park. But a wrong turn gets us lost in some kind of dilapidated
Moscow hospital complex—all peeling paint, cracked asphalt, and
wilting chain-link. A bandaged man wheeling his own IV drip stops
in a third-floor window to silently observe us. When at last we emerge
from the maze of crumbling buildings, we find ourselves directly
across from the New Tretyakov Gallery—a museum of twentieth-
century Russian art.

Outside, in the museum's sculpture garden, there's a collection of
Lenin and Stalin statues. They were ripped down in the days after
Communism fell. The statues look naked and vulnerable without
their pedestals beneath them.

Inside the museum's lobby, there is a line of at least twenty-five

81

people waiting to buy admission tickets. This line is not moving. Like, at all. We wait fifteen minutes without advancing an inch.

The situation offers a study in glacial Russian bureaucracy, and also in comparative patience as a factor of nationality. Consider: The laid-back German guys standing in front of us in line are cheerfully patient. The granite-faced Poles in front of the Germans seem gloomily, fatalistically patient. And the Koreans in front of the Poles are yelling and waving money in the air.

My own instincts are probably closest to the Poles', but Rebecca's fall squarely in the Korean camp. Accordingly, she makes an antsy reconnaissance mission to the head of the line to figure out what's going on. The deal is, she informs me upon her return, the museum's ticket-printing machine has broken down. It's unclear why the museum workers can't simply improvise by giving us, say, handwritten notes granting entrance. But they don't.

Instead, we continue standing in place for another fifteen minutes, during which time not a single person succeeds in buying a ticket. We would leave, but at this point we're less interested in the museum than in the resolution of this dadaist one-act play. In a new plot twist, one of the Koreans—speaking English, as it's the closest thing anyone here has to a shared language—has loudly declared his group a "special guided tour," in the vain hope that they might thereby circumvent all ticketing procedures.

"I'm doing a thought experiment," says Rebecca, hands on hips. "I'm trying to imagine what this would look like if it happened at MoMA."

"And?" I ask.

"It's not working. I can't picture it at all. By now, the ticket lady would have been fired. And someone in line would be taking witness depositions for a class-action lawsuit."

Eventually, the impasse is broken. A batch of uncut, unprinted tickets is produced from a back office, and the ticket lady begins to tear them out individually—using a ruler as a guide, and maddeningly licking her fingertip before each careful rip.

After all this drama, the museum's collection is of course anticlimactic. Though it does feature some fabulous Communist Party–approved art. It's all broad-shouldered Russian peasants together forging steel and harvesting grain in beautiful harmony.

Rebecca—never a huge fan of abstraction—discovers she has a soft spot for social realism. "First of all, the spirit of group endeavor here is sort of inspiring, if you ignore what actually happened," she notes. "And second of all, these guys are really hot!" She points to a sculpture of a beefy, chisel-faced worker wearing overalls and wielding a sledgehammer. "Look at those biceps!"

IN the late afternoon, we take the Moscow metro to the official government railway ticket office. It's like stepping back in technological time: the scraping noises of the dot-matrix printers, the amber glow of the monochrome computer screens. We ask at the information desk if there's anyone here who speaks English. Our question is met with indifferent shrugging and frowning. We'll have to wing it.

We check the timetables, write down specific numbers for the trains we want, unfold a map so we can point to our desired destinations, and approach one of the ticket windows. As we'd pretty much anticipated, things do not go smoothly. The clerk speaks zero English

SETH STEVENSON

(which is fine—I don't expect people in other countries to speak my language) and seems disinclined to make any effort to understand our map-pointing or our elaborate pantomimes (I'm less forgiving about her unwillingness to meet us halfway). When she eventually prints out tickets for us, we examine them and determine they're for a train that leaves a month from now, instead of for the one we want that leaves tomorrow. It takes several minutes, with much arm waving on both sides of the window, to explain this.

After the clerk rips up those tickets and prints new ones, we once again pore over the details, deciphering the Cyrillic. This time we discover that the tickets are round-trip instead of one-way. It takes several more minutes, and lots more arm waving, to make her understand that we don't want to return to Moscow (possibly ever, I'm beginning to think). She cancels this set of tickets and tries again. Third time's the charm.

By now we're hungry for dinner. But at this point we can't face the wearying thought that ordering our food will necessitate further charades and require us to endure the inevitable frowns and shrugs of the waiter. When we pass a McDonald's on the way back to our hotel, we break down and enter—mostly just to remember what it's like to have an effortless transaction with a service worker.

I cannot tell you how cathartic it is to pronounce "McNuggets" in a confident tone and, an instant later, receive exactly what I've asked for.

THE next afternoon, we go to Yaroslavl Station to catch a train out of town. The station's enormous waiting room is filled with battered-looking luggage and even-more-battered-looking people. Scowling faces. Sullen children. And, oh, the clothes. There are men in sleeveless mesh muscle shirts. There are *women* in sleeveless mesh muscle shirts. Beer bellies strain at threadbare polyester. Enormous bosoms erupt from spandex tube tops.

The female fashions in particular are . . . provocative. As Rebecca delicately observes, "The women here all look like eight-dollar hookers."

"That's an unfair stereotype," I tell her. "Some of them look like at least fifteen-dollar hookers."

We find a small space to situate ourselves amid the waiting-room masses, and Rebecca goes off hunting for provisions for the trip. There's no air-conditioning in the station and the air is fetid and still. By the time Rebecca returns with some snacks, she finds me sprawled across our backpacks, my shirt unbuttoned far down my sweaty chest, a look of utterly resigned doom on my face. In other words: I blend right in. "Dude," says Rebecca, "you've gone Russian." She says this with equal parts apprehension and respect.

When we board the train, we can see other passengers through the half-open doors of their private cabins. They are in various states of undress, wilting in the heat of the motionless train. Clothes are strewn about the cabins. Large, shirtless men wallow on their bunks like postcoital sea lions.

When we get to our own cabin, Rebecca closes the door behind us and gives in. "I'm going Russian," she declares, wiping sweat from her forehead. She unhooks her bra and slips it out from under her shirt. She flops supine on her bunk with a guttural sigh. "Going Russian is awesome," she says to the ceiling.

* * *

THE train itself actually has an elegant shabbiness to it. Our carpeted first-class cabin is paneled with dark, worn wood. There's a stately picture window and a small wooden table with a little white tablecloth. The two narrow bunks are made up with crisp sheets and firm pillows. This genteel mood is dampened by the bad Russian pop that plays through a speaker bolted into the ceiling. (There's a knob on the speaker that reduces the volume but—in a rather Orwellian detail—there is no way to turn the music all the way off.)

We'll be riding in this cabin for three days and two nights. The nine-hundred-mile trip east from Moscow to the city of Yekaterinburg is at least three times longer than either of our previous rail journeys, from Antwerp to Rostock and from Tallinn to Moscow. We're giving ourselves a sudden, full-on immersion in the culture of the Trans-Siberian.

There are three classes of tickets on Russian trains. First class (called *spalny vagon*), which we're riding in now, has private cabins with two bunks each. Second class (called *kupé*) has four-bed cabins, much like the one that we shared with Vladimir and Alexandr on the train from Tallinn. Third class (called *platskartny*) stuffs fifty-four bunks into a single, open carriage.

We're intimidated by *platskartny*. It's a lot of humanity in not a lot of space. When our train makes its first station stop, we watch the *platskartny* passengers piling out like escapees from a P.O.W. camp and at that moment basically rule out the idea of ever casting our lot with them. A pair of incidents at subsequent stops reinforces our feelings on this matter: 1) We watch a *platskartny* rider buy a whole fish—eyes intact, slimy gleam reflecting off its scales—from an old woman on a station platform, which he then brings back onto the train. (You could smell this thing from thirty yards away. I have no idea how he planned to cook or eat the fish, and I wept for the other people in his carriage.) 2) At another stop, we see a drunk, vomit-flecked man hauled out of a *platskartny* carriage by a pair of angry policemen. (If there's one thing that smells worse than a whole fish, it's a whole pool of vomit.)

There's also the issue that the fifty-odd *platskartny* passengers share a couple of painfully oversubscribed toilets at the end of the car. We're much better off in *spalny vagon*, sharing a toilet with only fifteen or so people. Though even in first class, the bathroom is bare-bones. It's all hard metal surfaces and constantly reeks of bleach, which I suppose is better than reeking of dead fish. There is no shower, so people take sponge baths using the sink.

On the floor next to the toilet is a flush pedal—which I'd assumed would trigger a rush of antiseptic blue liquid, ushering the toilet bowl's contents into a chemical tank. Instead, pressing the pedal just opens a flap at the bottom of the bowl. When this flap opens, it sends a shock of sunlight up into the bathroom, revealing the blur of the train tracks beneath the car and carpet-bombing the ground with human waste. We're not permitted to use the toilet while the train is stopped at a station, for obvious reasons.

No matter which class we ride in, we will be forced to deal with a *provodnitsa*. Perhaps the most iconic figure in Russian rail, the *provodnitsa* is the person (usually a woman—if he's a man he's called a *provodnik*) who is in charge of each car. She rules her fiefdom with an iron fist. You can find her vacuuming the hallways, restocking the bathroom with unnecessarily coarse toilet paper, and generally clucking at her subjects as they disappoint her with their behavior.

Our car has two *provodnitsas*. They work in shifts and are constantly bickering. Both sport dyed hair the color of maraschino cherries. At station stops, whichever one is off duty will stand on the platform in a tattered robe and slippers, puffing on a cigarette and scowling at all who pass. If you step outside to get some air, and are the least bit slow reboarding the train before it sets off again—perhaps because you are fascinated by a transaction involving a fish—she will wag her finger at you and bark angrily in Russian.

A couple of hours and several stops outside Moscow, we move beyond the crowded city sprawl and into the countryside. We begin to pass a series of mournful-looking towns. People walk aimlessly along the train tracks, and feral animals roam about. The view out the window is sometimes patchy forest, sometimes clusters of small wooden houses, and sometimes crumbling, cement-block factories surrounded by barbed-wire fences and stagnant puddles of mud.

At each station stop, locals wait on the platform with baskets of food for sale. Sausages, cucumbers, blocks of cheese, potato chips. Many of the merchants are wrinkly babushkas, with thick ankles and deep-set, suspicious eyes. Often they wheel their goods around in baby strollers. Given the state of things in these towns, it would not surprise me if some of these women were selling actual babies.

That evening, as our train rolls through a moonlit Russian forest, Rebecca fiddles with her GPS to see where we are. She sits up straight in her bunk with a start. "Hey!" she says, still looking at the screen, wiggling her hand to get my attention. "We're about to be in Asia!"

The Ural mountain range marks the divide between the continents, with the official boundary falling at just about 60 degrees east longitude. We turn off the lights in our cabin and press our faces to the window, keeping our eyes peeled for some sort of marker. Rebecca glances down at her GPS to track our progress. "Should be any second now. . . ."

And there it is. A small white obelisk by the side of the tracks. The train rumbles by it at 50 mph, but I manage to make out Cyrillic letters spelling "Europe" and "Asia" etched into the stone, with corresponding arrows pointing in opposite directions. There's nothing else here but a quiet glade of birch trees.

Unexpectedly, a wave of accomplishment passes over me. We've conquered the Atlantic Ocean, and now Europe. An entire continent in our rearview mirror. To celebrate, Rebecca goes to the dining car and brings back a bottle of vodka. We drink it all, chasing it with a tube of Pringles we'd bought from a babushka on a station platform earlier in the day.

WE disembark at Yekaterinburg, taking a break from the Trans-Siberian's interminable march, and buy a locally published "English-language" tourist pamphlet from a vendor at the station. The pamphlet opens with a welcome from Mayor Arkadiy Chernetsky. "Dear readers! The cities got their own biographies and family trees like we people are," he enthusiastically and semigrammatically begins. "Yekaterinburg takes very special and significant place in time and space of the whole Russian State. Dear friends! Let Yekaterinburg bring much novel and enchanted into your life!"

A city of about 1.5 million people, Yekaterinburg is infamous for being the site of the Romanov massacre. In 1918, at the height of the revolution, Czar Nicholas and his family were brought east by train here, much like we've come. (Though they were in the custody of armed Bolshevik guards, and their train's arrival was greeted by a bloodthirsty mob.)

After two months of imprisonment in Yekaterinburg, during which the Romanovs endured constant torment from their jailers, the royal family was herded into the basement of the house they'd been confined in. Twelve soldiers opened fire on Nicholas; his wife, Alexandra; and their five children. After the first volley of shots, some of the children—who ranged in age from thirteen to twenty-two—remained alive. The guards waded in to bayonet the survivors. The bodies were hauled to a forest, dismembered, burned, and unceremoniously dumped in a mine.

The house where the Romanovs were killed was eventually turned into an "antireligion museum," seemingly in an effort to change the subject. In 1976, it was torn down. This order was given by Boris Yeltsin, then the regional head of the Communist Party, who claimed there was an urgent need to fix the stretch of street that ran beside it.

On our first afternoon in Yekaterinburg, we take a stroll around the grassy hill where the house once stood. It is now the site of the evocatively named Church of the Blood, constructed in 2000 to honor the Romanovs. That same year, the czar and his family were literally sainted—canonized as martyrs by the resurgent Russian Orthodox Church.

As we approach the cathedral, we see a man high up in its belfry, ringing the hourly bells. He's a frenzy of motion, all four limbs pushing and pulling different bell ropes. This guy is like the Yngwie Malmsteen of bell ringing. He slams out a furious minor-key riff, with flurries of notes piling up on each other. I had no idea the pealing of church bells could sound so angsty.

I'm fascinated by the Romanov murders—mostly because I have the reductionist instincts of a simpleton when it comes to history. I find it hard to wrap my brain around the rise and fall of Russian Communism. But I find it easy to imagine the Romanov family, ripped from their lives of opulence, huddling frightened in a dank basement. I can also imagine the Bolsheviks convincing themselves that, in the name of crushing monarchy once and for all, it was imperative for them to murder the innocent Romanov children. In this one moment, you see not just the passionate certitude of the Communist revolutionaries, but also the miseries that certitude would continue to inflict upon anyone who dared get in the way.

There's a tabloid dimension to the Romanovs' story, as well, with a lively cult having formed around the memory of the czar's daughter Anastasia. Several women have claimed to be the grand duchess herself, miraculously escaped from the Yekaterinburg slaughter. Among the more successful impersonators was a woman named Anna Anderson, who stuck by her Anastasia story right up until her death in 1984 and managed to fool all of New York society for a time in the late 1920s. (DNA research has recently confirmed the identification of all the Romanov corpses, thus putting an end to any speculation.)

With the tremendous interest that the story of the Romanovs inspires all over the world, I felt sure the good people of Yekaterinburg would try to monetize the tragedy—eking a living out of the city's major claim to fame. Perhaps a slick Romanov museum with an expensive entrance fee and a well-stocked gift shop? Or at least a row of pushcarts selling Anastasia T-shirts and coffee mugs? But there's none of this. Even downtown, on the main Yekaterinburg shopping drag, I can't find a single Romanov-themed souvenir.

I still remember, very clearly, the first time I saw a 9/11 T-shirt for sale in lower Manhattan. It was no more than six months after the planes hit the towers. Initially, I was shocked that anyone could want to profit from something so awful. But after a moment's reflection, I found it oddly comforting: Tacky capitalism marches on, terrorists be damned.

It's been a solid ninety years now since the Romanovs died. Still, it appears the Russian people harbor no interest in making a ruble off that family's misfortune. And my response this time is the reverse of what it was that day in lower Manhattan.

At first, I'm dumbfounded that there's no exploitation going on in Yekaterinburg. Here's an obvious tourist draw, and yet no one is milking it. Is it a lack of Russian entrepreneurial instinct? Did decades of Communist rule permanently deaden the profit motive?

On reflection, though, I begin to see a certain nobility in the Russians' restraint. Perhaps it speaks to the fundamental seriousness of the Russian soul. They've accepted capitalism, yes, but they refuse to give in to its basest elements. They won't engage in a race to the bottom that culminates in selling nine-dollar T-shirts commemorating violent deaths.

I feel sudden shame about the fact that I would have quite happily bought an Anastasia refrigerator magnet.

LATE that evening, we board the train again. Soon after it chugs out of the station, we do a couple of vodka shots—it's become our routine as we work toward going fully native—and settle in for the night. The next day, as we stare out the window, the passing scenery begins to shift. The forests get thicker. The towns get bleaker.

Rebecca starts joking about abandoning me the next time we make a stop in a particularly grim-looking village. "I'll push you off the train right when it's pulling away," she explains. "You won't have your passport or any money. You'll just have to make a new life for yourself." I look at her sideways. "Oh, don't worry," she reassures me, "you'll be very happy in Magnetogorsk. You can work at the blast furnace. You'll marry a babushka. Plenty of cozy quiet time with her when the snows come."

If we were to ride on the Trans-Siberian from Moscow to Vladivostok without ever getting off, it would take about six and a half days. We're planning to make stops to break up the journey and to spend time in some of the cities and towns along the way. Still, we'll be enduring a few fifty-hour segments on the rails.

For entertainment on these long stretches, I'm plowing through a collection of Chekhov short stories. Meanwhile, Rebecca's having a brave go at *War and Peace*. (It was she who first taught me the joys of contextually appropriate reading material, and we've made it a habit ever since.) There's only so much reading you can do on a multiday train ride, though, before you're forced to set your book down on your lap, rub your eyes, and wonder: For fuck's sake, are we ever going to get there?

Around the World in 80 Days portrays Fogg's journey as a frantic, nonstop sprint. Admittedly, Fogg was racing against the clock. (And the frenetic pace also suited Jules Verne's prose. As a contemporary put it: "Jules Verne! What a style! Nothing but nouns!") But consider Fogg's nine-day passage across the Atlantic, which Verne describes in a few breathless, breakneck pages. Having now been on an actual nine-day trip across the Atlantic, I can assure you there is nothing breakneck about it. The ship inches along through the endless ocean, and meanwhile you eat twenty-seven-odd meals, do laundry once or twice, and generally pass those 216 hours reading books or looking for whales or whatever. I imagine that for Fogg, this downtime might have involved playing a lot of whist, his favorite card game. Perhaps he'd also bugger his manservant Passepartout for kicks. (Who knows—the book never fully addresses their relationship.) The point is: Life continues, even in transit. You will get bored sometimes, guaranteed.

Luckily, there is a powerful weapon at our disposal in the war against boredom. It's called vodka. After we finish off a bottle over the course of a lazy afternoon—and become fearful that we might lose our pleasant buzz—Rebecca runs out to buy another liter from the dining car.

She returns moments later, mission successful. "Wow," she slurs, a little giggly, "my Russian when I talk to male bartenders is *great*. They totally *love* me!"

The fact is, *not* to drink vodka on the train would be to reject the cultural norms of the Trans-Siberian. Even at our prodigious pace, we can't keep up with the gallons being consumed by all the Russian dudes on board. The dining car actually runs out of liquor sometimes, in the face of constant demand.

Once, at a station stop, we watched a group of eight shirtless men leap off the train before it stopped rolling. They sprinted off the platform and down a short slope to the village below. We knew exactly where they were going. Only one thing on earth could compel a fat Russian man to move that fast. Sure enough, the men were soon running back up the hill with their arms loaded full of booze. One fellow was balancing so many bottles that I was obliged to hold open the carriage door for him, as he couldn't spare a free finger to open it himself.

We've noticed that a lot of these shirtless dudes sport fat lips and swollen, black eyes. Rebecca's reasonable theory: "Drunk people get in fights and hit each other a lot."

THE towns roll past, one after another. We are officially in Siberia now—though it's harder to recognize the place in summer, there being no snow, and no Dr. Zhivago zooming by on a sled.

In the middle of the night, our train reaches 103 degrees east—a spot exactly halfway around the world from Washington, D.C., longitude-wise. Coincidentally, at almost this same moment the train slows to a stop. I wake up, drowsy and disoriented. (I always wake up when the train stops in the night. It's the sudden absence of that steady rocking motion, and that relaxing clackalack of wheels on tracks.) Loudspeakers on the station platform suddenly blare to life. A stern male voice bellows something in Russian, and the words echo out through the brisk night air. I squint, trying to look through the window. All I can see is thick fog, diffusing the bright light from the lamp poles on the platform.

We're in a four-berth *kupé* cabin, and we have one roommate, who is presently sleeping on an upper bunk. When this middle-aged man first boarded the train and entered the cabin, he said something to us in Russian. Upon realizing we couldn't speak his language, he said not another word to us for the following eighteen hours. Now I keep hoping he'll stir, and somehow—through his body language—convey that there is nothing for me to be alarmed about. But he doesn't budge.

I am riding on a Russian train headed east, into deep Siberia. I am cold. I am confused. And I swear I'm experiencing an embedded cultural memory handed down from my mother's eastern European ancestors. When I hear a cluster of loud bangs coming from somewhere down the platform, I figure it's about fifty-fifty: They might be linking up a new locomotive, or they might be shooting Jews and wealthy landowners. I decide that either way it's out of my hands, and drift back to sleep.

THE next morning, we arrive in the city of Irkutsk. You may remember this name as one of the territories on the Risk game board. I half expected to see ten-foot-tall, plastic Roman numerals wandering the streets.

The main attraction in Irkutsk, as far as Rebecca's concerned, is a small aquarium that features a pair of nerpas. Nerpas are the earth's only freshwater seals, and they are adorable. They have eyes as dark and deep as nearby Lake Baikal, where they live. (Lake Baikal is in fact the deepest lake in the world. It's more than a mile from its surface to its bottom—which at least one Russian minisubmarine has reached.)

The nerpas' "aquarium," when we find it, turns out to be three rooms in the basement of a strip mall, located beneath a retail store called Fashion House. The seals' aquatic habitat is essentially an oversized bathtub. The two nerpas—one male, one female—do a show here every half hour, ten shows a day.

The audience for the show we attend consists of me, Rebecca, and two small children accompanied by their grandmother. It kicks off with a trainer leading the nerpas through a set of tricks. These tricks include "singing" (making fart noises through their nostrils); "breakdancing" (turning around in a slow circle); "painting" (having a brush shoved in their mouths, which they then whack intermittently against a piece of paper); and "the lambada" (a sort of awkward flipper shimmy).

The promotional brochure at the aquarium claims that nerpas have the power to "hypnotize" people with their huge, black eyes, and that sometimes the trainer, under the spell of this hypnosis, will begin feeding the nerpas and then forget to stop. I have no doubt that this is true, as the male nerpa here is so grotesquely fat he can barely perform any of the tricks. He struggles just to haul his blubbery mass up onto his designated, floating platform. Mostly, he bobs upright in the water like an overinflated buoy. He has about eight chins, and his facial expression conveys at all times a childlike anticipation that he might be thrown a fish.

"Except for you," Rebecca says to me when the show has ended, "that is the most ridiculous animal I have ever seen. In its defense, it's much cuter than you."

FROM the aquarium, we go to the Irkutsk regional museum. The exhibit text is all in Russian, but there seems to be a display about the creation of the "BAM"—the "Baikal-Amur Mainline" branch of the Trans-Siberian Railway. The BAM breaks off from the main Trans-Sib route and shoots farther north, into the largely uninhabited wilds of Siberia and the Russian Far East.

Construction on the original Trans-Siberian route (the one we're taking) began in 1891. Czar Alexander III decided the railway was crucial to both economic growth and military might, as it would connect Moscow and St. Petersburg with the Russian hinterlands bordering China and the Pacific. In 1916, it became possible for the first time to traverse the width of Russia by rail, from Moscow to Vladivostok.

The idea behind the BAM branch extension was to provide better access to the rich natural resources in the remoter, northern parts of eastern Russia. Construction on the BAM began in the 1930s but quickly got bogged down. One major challenge was the region's permafrost, which required dynamiting before tracks could be laid. For a long time, prisoners (plucked from the Siberian gulags) were the central source of labor on the railway. Later, idealistic students were encouraged to pack off to Siberia and work on the BAM as part of a gung-ho national service initiative.

As recently as 1991, large sections of the BAM were still not complete, though with various detours it was possible to reach the terminus. The whole project has turned out to be costly, dangerous, and—many would argue—completely idiotic. Still, at least one Russian transportation official wants to double down, proposing a $50 billion BAM extension that would include an undersea tunnel across the Bering Strait to Alaska. Were this to happen, you might eventually be able to ride a train from London to New York, the long way around.

We're currently skirting along the northern edges of Mongolia and China. The freight trains rolling by in the opposite direction are loaded with hundred-foot pieces of timber and gigantic oil drums. This part of Siberia is a mix of forested hills, prairies dotted with hay bales, and the occasional wide, gray river. It's pretty—in large part thanks to its emptiness. At times it looks a bit like the Catskills, minus the billboards, the gas stations, and the Jewish summer camps.

There's a fundamental difference in the quality of the light here, though. For some reason, everything in Russia looks much drabber than in other countries. The sunshine is thin. The colors are drained. Even the faces are sallow. It's the opposite of a vibrant place like India, where everywhere you look is the orange shock of a marigold or the wild purple of a woman's sari.

Granted, there's a pleasing rusticity to the wooden houses here, with their herringboned slats, their corrugated roofs, and their tiny square gardens. But these villages somehow look wintry even now, in August, on a sunny afternoon. I imagine they'd be positively funereal under a thick blanket of snow.

Rebecca's taking a breather from *War and Peace* and has moved on to *Gulag: A History*—journalist Anne Applebaum's definitive take on the Soviet prison camp system. The facts, figures, and anecdotes Applebaum collects are just as depressing as you'd imagine. One of the strange, heartbreaking revelations in the book is how truly arbitrary the whole gulag system was.

People were sent to the Siberian camps for no clear reason, often at the whim of a powerful official. Once there, a surreal randomness reigned. Prisoners could become guards, and guards could become prisoners. Convicts could be set free with no notice and without knowing why. Life felt haphazard. Many tragic deaths were the result of pure laziness. For instance, some guards on the trains headed to the camps would refuse to give their prisoners any water—because the guards didn't want to deal with bathroom breaks. Soon enough, as the prisoners dehydrated, the guards were dealing with corpses.

From what I've witnessed, this indifferent half-assedness continues to be the overriding Russian mood. We see it in the way people treat us in stores and restaurants and in the crumbling infrastructure all over the country. The sidewalks are pocked with rubble, the wall-to-wall carpets never reach the walls, everything's broken and nothing ever gets fixed. It's as though the whole country just grew bored with its collective existence. No one ever seems happy, and yet no one is moved to do a thing about it.

Having traveled pretty widely, I've become a student of comparative body language. I enjoy identifying the nonverbal cues that prevail in different regions. In parts of India, for instance, people will frequently perform a head waggle—a bobble-headed bouncing of one's cranium from side to side, indicating general assent. In Japan, the bow is a highly ritualized indicator. Here in Russia, I've discovered that the signature gesture is a shrug. Note that it is not like American shrugs, which can convey indifference or even, sometimes, mild agreement. The Russian shrug says: "Go fuck yourself, retard." It's a hateful, aggressive popping of the shoulders—often accompanied by a frown, an eye roll, a loud exhale, and/or upturned palms. Every time we encounter it (and we've encountered it quite a bit), the shrug cements my notion that this is the land of the can't-be-bothered.

Yet there's a contradiction here. Any look at Russian history reveals a country with almost *too much* passion. Its great writers—Tolstoy, Dostoyevsky—grapple with grand themes and bold choices. Its brilliant dancers and composers radiate romanticism. And of course, if Russia were truly a nation of shruggers, it would never have shed so much blood in the wild-eyed pursuit of abstract ideals. I realize the country may be suffering an extended hangover after the fall of Communism, but still—it's hard to reconcile Russia's fiery past with its seemingly listless present.

To better understand this dichotomy in the Russian character (and also to pass time on the train), I've been reading Chekhov short stories from the late 1880s. They're off-the-charts bleak. Chekhov once described his ambitions thusly: "All I wanted was to say honestly to people: 'Have a look at yourselves and see how bad and dreary your lives are!' The important thing is that people should realize that, for when they do, they will most certainly create another and better life for themselves."

Chekhov died in 1904. Not long after, Russians did indeed attempt to create a different way of living. The emptiness gnawing at Chekhov's characters seems to predict the cultural dissatisfaction that led to the Russian revolution. People were searching for a more profound and harmonious existence. It was a beautiful dream, though it ended in tatters.

To be sure, I've met some smiley, friendly people in Russia. And I've seen evidence of forward-looking optimism. The little girls crushing forehands on the public tennis courts in Irkutsk looked determined to be Wimbledon stars. The far eastern town of Khabarovsk built a lovely park along the Amur River—as pretty and peaceful as a stroll along an Amsterdam canal.

Still, if I were to identify a defining attribute in the people I've interacted with here, it would be this: Most Russians seem viscerally aware of the fact that day-to-day life is an absurd endeavor. This explains their mad desire to create a different and better way of being (a response Chekhov foretold, and Lenin channeled into revolution). It also explains why, once that utopian vision faded, Russians grew bored, gloomy, and resentful of quotidian tasks.

Toppling a government, creating a new political system, and defeating Hitler? These were soul-stirring missions that Russians could get excited about. Fixing sidewalks, laying carpet competently, and being polite to American tourists?

Shrug.

THE clackalack of the train rolling over tracks is sometimes a perfect 3/4 shuffle. Other times it morphs into an exotic polyrhythm. Occasionally, in the steeper turns, it's a scary cacophony of groaning, popping metal. When it's smoothly clackalacking along, though, it mostly reminds me of all the ground we're covering, day and night, as we roll onward toward the next line of longitude.

GROUNDED

We're less than thirty miles from the Chinese border now. The facial features of the villagers we see as we rumble by have, on balance, shifted several ticks toward the Asian end of the racial continuum. This region actually belonged to China until 1858, when a Russian military buildup strong-armed the Chinese government into ceding territory.

This is our very last leg on the Trans-Siberian, and it's a relatively short twelve-hour, overnight ride. For this final segment, we've booked ourselves into a shared, four-berth cabin, betting on the hope that we'll get interesting roommates and not the shirtless, fish-toting kind. The gamble pays off, as our cabinmates turn out to be friendly and easygoing and even speak a bit of English.

Natalia is twenty-seven and a petite, pretty blonde. Much excitement ensues when we learn that she, like Rebecca, is a lawyer. She tells us she's on her way to a legal conference in Vladivostok, and that there are several other attorneys on the train, all headed to the same gathering.

I'm trying to picture a bunch of D.C. lawyers traveling together to a conference in Indianapolis (an approximately equivalent distance). Would they opt to take an overnight Amtrak instead of the two-hour flight? Admittedly, Rebecca—given her crippling fear of airplanes—might actually do this, but she's the exception. I assume Natalia's reasons for taking the train have to do with the economics of Russian law firms and Russian airlines, but my polite attempts to ask her crash up against the language barrier.

Albert, our other cabinmate, is thirty-eight and tells us he has four children. He lives in Yakutsk, which is a city in northeastern Russia, not far from the Arctic Circle. (Yes, you are correct; it's also another important territory in Risk. If I had a set of dice, I'd challenge Albert to roll for ownership of his house.)

Albert is an ethnic Sakha. His skin is bronze, his hair black. The Sakha are a Russian indigenous group, and Albert says he shares genealogical roots with the Eskimos. Things get a bit hazy here, with a lot of frustrated searching for simple words to convey complex ideas. But it's my understanding, based on Albert's scribbled drawings and notations, that temperatures in Yakutsk can drop as low as minus ninety degrees Fahrenheit and routinely hover around minus fifty. Albert's family actually lives in a house built on stilts, elevated thirty feet above the ground, to escape the permafrost of the soil below. At least I think that's what he's drawing. It's either that or his family lives inside a giant spider.

After an hour or so of pleasant semiconversation, during which at least two-thirds of the sentiments get lost in translation despite the goodwill and enthusiasm of the participants, it's time to go to bed. Natalia just falls back on her bunk in her blouse and jeans. Within moments, she's fast asleep. We know this because she snores with a ferocity that belies her ninety-five-pound frame. Curses—just when we least expect it, the dreaded snoring stranger strikes again.

THE first dawn light finds us pulling into Vladivostok. We've reached the end of the Trans-Siberian. After more than six thousand winding miles, Russian trains will take us no farther. It's a bit shocking to see those endless, parallel rails suddenly come to a halt at the Vladivostok station.

As a major base for the Soviet navy, less than one hundred miles from the North Korean border, Vladivostok was completely closed to foreigners (and even most Russians) up until the fall of the Communist regime in the 1990s. Recently, it's seen a jump in tourism and trade. I arrive with high hopes that it might be a sort of Pacific Rim melting pot—the cosmopolitan center of the increasingly wealthy Russian Far East, and the region's main touchpoint for businesspeople and travelers from nearby China, South Korea, and Japan.

The physical setting of the city is spectacular—a hilly, misty peninsula surrounded by ocean. It looks a little like San Francisco might look. If San Francisco had been attacked by marauding zombies.

With its rubbled sidewalks, muddy streets, and rampant litter, Vladivostok suffers from the all too common Russian affliction of municipal deterioration. There is an additional problem here, though: a building boom gone horribly bust. Next to our hotel, we can see a high-rise under construction. The first two floors are finished; the next twenty-eight are just roughed-in concrete. The project appears to be ongoing, but every time we look it's just one guy with a jackhammer, taking long breaks every half hour or so. At this rate, he should be finished single-handedly constructing this tower by, oh . . . never. And that's not all: There are three other half-finished towers on this same block. All have wide-open, unenclosed upper floors with wind and rain rushing through and loose Tyvek sheets flapping wildly.

It's our understanding that there's a ferry from Vladivostok to the west coast of Japan, so our first order of business is to confirm its existence and get ourselves tickets. We manage to locate the ferry company's offices in a marine terminal next to the harbor. But the woman at the front desk has disastrous news. The ferry leaves only once a week, and the next departure is not for four days.

Four days! Phileas Fogg would never stand for this stagnation. He'd be bribing a freighter captain or somehow commandeering a naval destroyer from the Russian Pacific fleet. But we are not Fogg. Concluding we have no workable alternatives, we buy two ferry tickets and resign ourselves to an undesired interlude in Vladivostok. As we leave the terminal, a thick rain begins to fall. It will continue to fall, without cease, for the next four days.

UNLESS you can wrangle a tour of the Russian navy ships in the harbor, the two main tourist attractions here (aside from the natural outdoor beauty, which is hard to enjoy in this constant drizzle) seem to be the regional museum and the aquarium. The regional museum is like every other regional museum in Russia: Creepy taxidermy. Old oil portraits. Dusty maps.

As for the aquarium, we got excited when we read that it hosts a pair of beluga whales. But this excitement turns to dismay when we see the whales' home. They're kept in a small, netted pen at the end of a pier that juts into the harbor. Bored Russian children gather on the pier so they can throw garbage into the pen. (With their parents' encouragement. The parents think it's a riot.) The beautiful, pale white whales surface into the rain with plastic bags and orange rinds stuck to their fins. They open their mouths and let out long, bending squeaks that sound like sad moans. The whole scene is unbearable. If we weren't deathly afraid of spending time in a Russian prison, we'd dive into the frigid water right now and cut the nets with our pocketknives.

On what we hope will be our final night in Russia, we get celebratory drinks at the bar in our hotel. I order a beer. Rebecca experiments with a mysterious local liqueur. We toast and take big gulps. Rebecca gasps for air.

"What does it taste like?" I inquire.

"You know how sometimes a bad batch of moonshine can make you go blind?" she asks me.

"Yes," I answer.

"This tastes like blind."

WHEN at last it comes time to board our ferry, we arrive at the dock a few hours early. We're taking every precaution. There is simply no way we can endure another week in Vladivostok.

The main customers for this ferry turn out to be automobile arbitrageurs. They ride over to Japan to buy used Hondas and Toyotas and then bring the cars back with them on the ship to sell at a profit in Russia. (This explains why so many cars in Siberia have their steering wheels on the wrong side. In Japan, you drive on the left half of the road, while in Russia you drive on the right.) The car traders are burly, tough-looking guys, clad in flashy leather jackets. They all seem to know each other. I assume they make this trip back and forth together every week. Once on board the ship, they immediately head for the bar on the top deck and start pounding alcohol. It's a two-day passage to Japan, and I've a feeling they'll be spending the whole time drunk. I've a feeling I might, too.

Besides the Russian car salesmen, the other people on the ship all seem to be travelers like us, making similarly absurd overland journeys. Frankly, there just aren't a lot of other reasons to be on a forty-hour ferry leaving from the Pacific coast of Russia. While there are only a handful of us nutty adventurers on board, we instantly gravitate toward each other. We end up gathered around a table in the bar, swapping stories from the road.

A cheerful Japanese guy tells us he drove to Vladivostok all the way from Paris—by himself, in a three-wheeled, one-seat delivery cart. He leads us down to the vehicle deck to show us. The cart looks like something a Dutch florist might use to putter around Amsterdam, with tulip bouquets spilling out the back. Why this guy decided to drive it across the whole of the Eurasian land mass . . . is not clear.

The two Serbian guys sitting at the table rode here on motorcycles, all the way from Belgrade. They conquered the featureless deserts of Mongolia on their bikes. At one point, they ran out of water and went a full day without a sip—praying they'd reach the next village of yurts before keeling over with a last dying gasp. The two Serbs are huge, strapping dudes. They're covered in a hard-earned layer of dust that looks like it doesn't wash away even when they shower.

We're all enjoying each other's company, getting steadily drunker. Eventually, a few Russian guys come over and join our table. They're visibly hammered. Rebecca appears to be the only woman left at the bar, and these Russian men are very big fans of her. They keep nudging their chairs closer to hers, while subtly edging my chair farther away. They buy round after round for the table and direct all their toasts to Rebecca.

At this point, Rebecca is deeply in her cups. She's enjoying the attention, though she deftly deflects it. Which makes the Russians try that much harder. "Rehb-yehk-ah," slurs a guy named Sergey, his eyes glazed and his forehead sweaty. "Vweel you danz vwith me?"

I am becoming terrified. I sense an imminent fistfight. I can vividly picture myself dangling over a ferry railing, one of these drunken brutes gripping my ankles and cackling. Meanwhile, Rebecca will be out on the dance floor, obliviously grooving to bad Russian techno.

Thank God for the Serbs. I'm pretty certain they have my back if the going gets weird. Nobody's gonna mess with the badass Serbs.

Around 4:00 a.m., I manage to at last shepherd Rebecca away from her new friends, out of the bar, and back to our cabin. She passes out instantly. I watch the moonlit Sea of Japan through our porthole for a minute, and then follow suit.

THE next morning, Rebecca wakes up horribly hung over. "I'm just seasick," she insists. Last night remains a bit of a blur for her. When she steps outside for fresh air, thirty Russian dudes excitedly yell "Rehb-yehk-ah!" across the open deck. This both confuses her and troubles her greatly.

With the sunlight streaming in, I now realize that our cabin is a squalid shithole. The floor is buckling. The shower has no water pressure and yet somehow still floods the bathroom. There is a dented, nonfunctional rotary phone bolted into the wall. This ship was constructed in Poland in 1986, and I can't say—having been made aware of the disaster of the *Estonia*—that I'm hugely psyched to be riding in a twenty-year-old car ferry, built by eastern Europeans, operated by a Russian crew.

We order dinner in the ship's café, but our waitress shoos us out before we can eat the last few bites on our plates. "Feeneesh time," she barks, clearing the table. I look at her in amazement. In return, I get a classic shrug.

We thought we'd left Russia when this ship cast off from the dock in Vladivostok. But it turns out the ship is a floating microcosm of the country—complete with hateful shrugs, beefy drunkards, and failing infrastructure. I am counting down the hours until we set foot on Japanese soil.

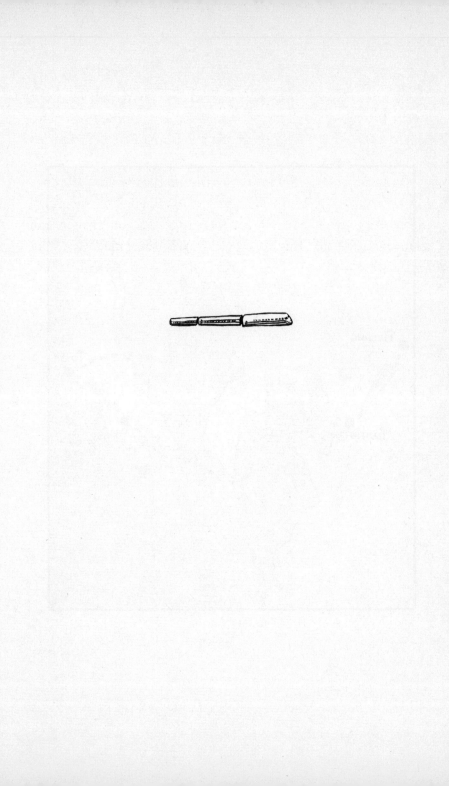

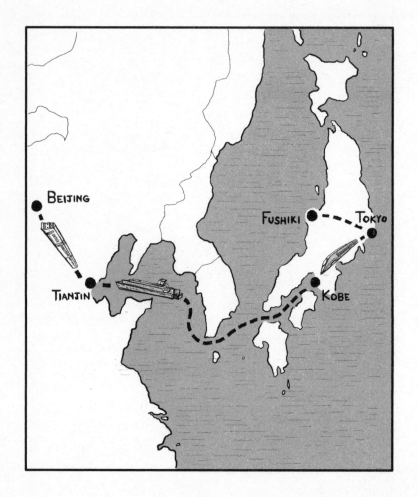

Chapter Four

Fushiki to Beijing

O UR Russian ferry arrives midmorning in the port of Fushiki, a small town on Japan's west coast. As I step down off the gangway, the heavy gloom of Russia lifts away at once—like a Cossack cloak. I feel newly at ease. Freshly bathed in first-world stability.

While on board the ferry, we'd struck up a friendship with a fellow passenger named Satoshi. He's a Japanese university student coming home after a semester of study in Moscow. Satoshi's headed for Tokyo, as are we, so we agree to make the trip together.

The Fushiki railway station is so tiny and adorable that it looks like an accessory for a child's model train set. There are no English-speaking clerks and the ticket window does not accept credit cards. Coincidentally, Rebecca and I don't speak Japanese and, fresh off the boat and with no ATMs in sight, we have no yen in our pockets. Our new friend Satoshi volunteers to do the talking for us, booking us all on a commuter line that connects to a Tokyo-bound bullet train. Satoshi also fronts the three hundred dollars for our tickets, which he happily lends us without even knowing our last names.

I love this about Japan: the extreme goodwill toward strangers. (Superficially, at least. Foreigners attempting to assimilate into Japanese society encounter some entrenched and impermeable barriers.) A few years ago, on the platform of a Tokyo subway station, I felt a tug at my elbow. I looked down to see a little boy holding out a five-yen coin. I must have dropped it about a hundred yards back. The kid had sprinted the length of the platform to catch up with me and hand me, essentially, a nickel. Later that same day, I asked directions from a stranger on a street corner, and the guy—instead of pointing and grunting, which would have maybe been a best-case scenario in Russia—walked a half mile out of his way with me just to ensure I wouldn't get lost.

Chatting with us across the aisle as the train rolls out of Fushiki, Satoshi tells us he took the Trans-Siberian straight from Moscow to Vladivostok without once getting off. That's a continuous week on a train that doesn't have showers. And he did it all in third-class *platskartny*, surrounded by the Russian masses. By way of explanation, he proclaims himself a Russophile, and says he can't wait to get back to Moscow when he finishes university.

"It's interesting that you like Russia so much," I say. "Japan and Russia seem so . . . different."

"I like the chaos," Satoshi says, grinning mischievously. "Everything in Japan is so ordered. It's too predictable!"

There may in fact be no more jarring cultural contrast than to travel directly from Russia to Japan. Russia was blustery, slovenly, and rough around the edges. Japan is reserved, neat, and carefully squared off. Out the window of our Trans-Siberian trains, the view was all emptiness and vastness, dotted with occasional, dilapidated outposts of human existence. Looking out the window of our train in Japan, it's all compartmentalized neighborhoods. Well-tended, fenced gardens. Paved streets with brightly painted lane markers.

During the layover between our train connections, Rebecca finds an ATM so we can pay back Satoshi. We treat him to a *tonkatsu* lunch for good measure, at a restaurant around the corner from the station—because nothing says "thank you" like deep-fried breaded pork. Soon after, the three of us board the bullet train, which quickly accelerates to a buttery-smooth 140 mph. I fall fast asleep and don't wake up until Tokyo, where we bid Satoshi a fond farewell.

Traversing Russia by train from west to east took us a couple of weeks and a bottomless vat of perseverance. Riding the rails from Japan's western shore to its eastern shore takes a few hours—mostly spent napping in plush reclining chairs.

AFTER checking in to our sparkling clean Tokyo hotel room, we drop our packs, flop onto the crisp white sheets of the bed, and flip on the flat-screen TV. Again, we're reminded that we've arrived in a very different country. Back in Russia, where they're still getting acclimated to the whole capitalism thing, most TV advertising took a straightforward approach to persuasion. Thus, even though I don't speak Russian, I had no trouble understanding Russian ads. They were all along the lines of: "Oh, no, there's a stain on the tablecloth! What will Mom do? Thank goodness for this effective detergent!"

Not so in Japan, where sophisticated consumers have grown bored with simple persuasion, forcing advertisers to get wildly inventive. Japanese TV ads have at this point evolved into an abstract mishmash of symbols and sounds. Your average thirty-second Japanese commercial is something like: Here's a man holding a giraffe. Now the giraffe morphs into a rainbow. The rainbow is friends with a talking pencil, and they live together on a spaceship. A few seconds of laughter! A snippet of loud reggae music! Fade out. At least half the time, I have no idea what the product being advertised is or what it does. And yet I very much enjoy the ads. They're like short-acting hallucinogens.

Amid this psychosis-inducing television content, we manage to learn that there's a major sumo wrestling tournament going on this week. I've always wanted to experience sumo live. We figure out where the stadium is and take the subway there the next morning.

Like New York, Tokyo has a plate-of-spaghetti subway map. But Tokyo's straphangers are a far quieter bunch, and its subway cars have floors so clean you could lick the spaghetti sauce *off* them. It's contrasts like this that make Tokyo a bizarro-world Manhattan. It has at least as much bustle, glamour, and skyscraping density, but it has very little of New York's foul odors, rampant litter, and casually rude behavior. Even the cabdrivers here are loath to honk their horns in anger.

After a short subway jaunt in a crowded but silent car, Rebecca and I arrive at Kokugikan arena. At the gate, we buy a pair of cheap tickets up in the nosebleed seats. Rebecca rents a tiny handheld radio from a kiosk out front so she can listen to the English-language simulcast from the commentators' booth.

Reflecting Japan's near-religious reverence for sumo, Kokugikan is more a temple than a sports facility. A decorative, peaked wooden roof dangles thirty feet above the ring, where the JumboTron might hang if this were a basketball court. It's as though the wrestlers are competing within a sacred shrine. There's also no advertising anywhere inside the main hall—unlike the rest of ad-plastered Tokyo—and there's no music blaring over the sound system in between bouts. The seats are a plush, velvety burgundy. There are pantalooned servants who float through the aisles with tea and snacks. The crowd is enthused, but always attentive and respectful. In general, it's pretty much the opposite of the atmosphere at your average NFL game (which is often like a cross between a death metal concert, a bikini contest, and a public hanging).

Sumo's rules are simple. You must either knock your opponent down or force him out of the fifteen-foot-diameter ring. There are eighty-two officially recognized winning techniques. Among them are the "twisting backward trip," the "thigh-grabbing pushdown," the "frontal crush-out," and—I imagine this one being lovingly administered—the "hug and shove." Rebecca's listening to the announcers on her radio and happily calling out the takedowns as they happen ("Yes! Frontal crush-out!"), while also munching on the bag of fried octopus balls she bought from one of the food vendors.

Sumo matches typically last less than a minute and can sometimes be over in the blink of an eye. Elaborate ceremony pads out the time between bouts. Before any wrestling begins, all the combatants march out together and form a circle around the ring. They wear handmade, jewel-encrusted, million-dollar aprons that cover their stomachs, thighs, and knees, but leave their buttocks and nipples exposed to the world. Whoever decided that these blubbery fellows should wrestle in what is essentially thong underwear had an excellent sense of humor. Or, possibly, a bizarre fetish for the dimpled fat of an outsized butt cheek.

SITTING here observing this quintessentially Japanese tableau— eating teriyaki with chopsticks from a bento box balanced on my lap—it suddenly dawns on me, with a jolt: We have made it to the other side of the world.

In my mind, I trace our route as a fast-forward flip book. I visualize our path as one smooth glide over the gray waves of the Atlantic, the crowded cobblestones of Europe, the empty forests of Russia, and the gentle swells atop the Sea of Japan. It's taken mere weeks to go from sitting on our couch in D.C. to sitting in this arena in central Tokyo.

True, with the aid of a 757 we could have made this same trip in roughly fourteen hours. But by the same token, imagine if we'd tried this a few hundred years ago, before modern advances in surface transport. It took the Pilgrims sixty-six days to cross the Atlantic, for instance. Our freighter did it in nine. Likewise, before the Trans-Siberian, it took months to hack through the wilds of Russia from one end to the other. Now, trains cross that same ground in less than a week.

Back when we began this journey, I'd imagined that the surface of the earth would feel enormous. Certainly, we've earned every mile we've traveled—sitting on the floors of train stations, waiting on windy piers, muddling through border checks. And by no means do

I wish to make our voyage sound effortless, because that's far from the case.

Still, the most surprising revelation of the trip so far is that the world seems relatively conquered. Even without a plane, you can get between any two populated regions with comparative ease and quickness. We could have gone westward overland from D.C. to Tokyo in about thirteen days, maybe less, if we'd committed to a flat-out sprint. Japan is in actuality a lot *closer* than I'd thought it was. As of this moment, the world seems *smaller*—and, as a result, more connected and fragile—than it did before we left home.

Yet this sense of smallness is misleading, too. In truth, we haven't gone halfway around the world. We haven't really covered much of the globe at all. We've been zooming along in the middle latitudes of the Northern Hemisphere, where the sphere is narrower. We haven't dipped far enough south to feel the earth's true bulk.

We could hop on a freighter out of Yokohama Harbor tomorrow, continue our wussy Northern Hemisphere jaunt, and arrive in Los Angeles ten days from now. But that would be cheating. To fully understand the size of this planet, we need to halt our eastward momentum. The time has come for us to hang a sharp right turn and start crossing some latitudes instead of just longitudes.

FOR a 100 percent no-messing-around, officially recognized circumnavigation of the earth, you must accomplish three things: 1) Start and end in the same place. 2) Cross every line of longitude moving in the same direction. 3) Touch two antipodal points.

Antipodal points are two points that are diametrically opposite each other on the earth's surface. The most obvious example of a pair of antipodal points is the North and South Poles. Hitting antipodal points eliminates opportunities for circumnavigational funny business, because it forces you to make a "great circle." A great circle divides the surface of a sphere into halves. (The most obvious example here is the equator.) Without the antipodal requirement, you could cross every line of longitude without covering a significant distance. For instance, imagine two adventurers racing to complete a circumnavigation: One guy makes an arduous trek that follows the equator for its entire length, while the other guy skips in a little circle around the North Pole. Both have crossed all the longitudinal meridians, but I think you'll agree that the feats are not quite comparable.

Rebecca and I haven't exactly been doing a jig around the North Pole, but we also haven't been making a great circle. For amateur overland adventurers like us, unfortunately, touching our toes to two antipodal points presents extreme difficulties. The bulk of the world's land is in the Northern Hemisphere, and it's tough to find reciprocal points on land below the equator. There's one antipodal pair with points in Indonesia and Ecuador, another touches down in a town in Chile and a village in China, and a third nuzzles Spain and New Zealand. It's hard to see a realistic scenario for us in which we hit any of these pairs without going far off course. (Some of the places involved are distressingly remote, to boot. I can only imagine the surface transport we'd have to take to reach both Valdivia, Chile, and Wuhai, China—the latter awaiting us somewhere out there in the Inner Mongolia Autonomous Region.)

As for antipodal points located in the middle of oceans: To hit them, we're at the mercy of extant freighter routes and passenger lines. And as best we can tell, these won't do the trick. Unless we can buy, borrow, or steal a seaworthy vessel, and then navigate it into isolated corners of the South Pacific, it seems we're out of luck.

But we're not giving up. After much careful research and debate, Rebecca and I have decided we can legitimately claim to have circumnavigated the earth if we meet the following four conditions: 1) Start and finish at the same place. 2) Cross all longitudinal meridians going in the same direction. 3) Cross the equator. 4) Cover at least twenty-five thousand miles—the length of a great circle around the earth. There's some precedent in the annals of amateur adventuredom for allowing this alternate set of criteria, so we don't even feel like we're cheating.

What does this mission directive mean for our route? It means we need to move much farther south, toward the equator—so we can cross it. Since we're currently on an island, this action will necessitate a ship of some sort. On the Web, we've found a ferry line that goes from Tokyo to Shanghai. We figure once we reach the Asian mainland, we can head south by train, bus, or car toward Singapore, which is very near the equator.

Unfortunately for our ferry hopes, the weather is not cooperating. "I'm checking the maritime forecast," says Rebecca, clicking around the Web, "and it's looking grim. There appears to be a major typhoon headed straight for Japan." The next forty-eight hours could be a dicey time to be at sea. We'd prefer not to spend two days vomiting over a ferry railing into thirty-foot waves.

Impulsively, we decide we'll hop on the next train going south out of Tokyo. At least we'll be headed vaguely in the right direction. And there appears to be another China-bound ferry that leaves from Kobe a few days hence. We're betting the typhoon will have petered out by then.

Going south to Kobe also provides another excuse to ride on a bullet train. These things are without doubt the coolest form of practical, everyday surface transport in the world. (Yes, to answer your inevitable question: that includes the Quebec funicular.) The bullet trains are sleek, quiet, and stylish, and their on-time rate is simply astounding.

Watch the digital clock above the station platform as the bullet trains pull in: Invariably, the wheels will shoosh to a stop, and the doors snap open, within a few seconds of the scheduled arrival time. One train after another, after another, after another. Anyone who's dealt with Amtrak on a regular basis will, upon witnessing a parade of on-time bullet trains, experience shock, followed closely by anger, settling into resigned sorrow.

Our own train pulls in precisely as scheduled, of course, and we find our assigned seats next to a big picture window. Cabin attendants roll carts of tasty Japanese food down the aisles. By the time I take off my sweater and settle in for the ride, the train has cranked up to 140 mph. Apartment towers, suburbs, and rice fields pass by in a blur. The nearly three-hundred-mile trip to Kobe is over before I finish reading my magazine.

IN the 1950s, the three-hundred-mile rail corridor between Tokyo and Osaka became so crowded with "rolling stock" (train-geek talk for "train cars") that there was no space left for additional traffic on the existing tracks. Demand for seats outstripped the supply. Something had to be done to ease the passenger crush.

The government began the early planning stages of a new high-speed, high-capacity line. They determined that the old tracks—designed for slower-moving trains—had curves too sharp for a bullet train moving at 130 mph or so. They also decided it would be impossible to build fancy new tracks alongside the old ones, because neighborhoods had nestled up around the old tracks and stations, leaving no room for fresh construction. An entire new system had to be laid out. New routes were carved and new station platforms were designed—accounting for the possibility that the slipstream of a bullet train whooshing by at full speed might sweep a bird-boned bystander off her feet.

The first Shinkansen trains (the Japanese term for them) opened to the public in 1964, in time to be showcased during the Tokyo Olympic Games. Almost from the start, they were a smashing success. On the old trains, it took six and a half hours to get from Tokyo to Osaka. On the Shinkansen, it took four hours. One year later, it was down to three hours and ten minutes. Bullet train ridership doubled within a few years, and doubled again after a few more. Soon, Shinkansen lines were being extended to reach new cities.

In his charmingly oddball memoir, *If There Were No Shinkansen*, former railway chairman Shuichiro Yamanouchi imagines life in Japan without bullet trains. He begins his thought experiment with these basic facts: On the Tokyo-to-Osaka Shinkansen line, each sixteen-car train carries thirteen hundred people, and a new train leaves from Tokyo every five minutes. This stipulated, he asks: Could

Japan possibly replace these trains with buses, airplanes, and automobiles?

To carry all those Shinkansen passengers on forty-seat buses, the buses would have to run all day at ten-second intervals. To use planes would necessitate an air route nine times more crowded than the busiest air route in the world (which happens to be between Tokyo and Sapporo, a city on the northern Japanese island of Hokkaido). As for cars, Yamanouchi-san quotes *The Economist* theorizing that "if the hundreds of millions who travel on these express [Shinkansen] lines each year switched to car travel, there would be at least 1,800 extra deaths and 10,000 serious injuries." By contrast, in the entire history of the Shinkansen the only passenger fatality happened when a person was killed by closing train doors. There has never been a passenger death due to collision or derailment.

Yamanouchi-san doesn't ask this question, but I will: Why has high-speed rail not taken off in the United States as it has in Japan? Some theories blame Amtrak's underwhelming performance on the fact that it's government run, or on the notion that its unionized workers are too intractable to allow a much-needed revamping. But Japanese railroads have seen their share of bitter labor disputes. And it's worth noting that Japan didn't privatize its railroads until the 1980s—long after the Shinkansen had built up its expansive infrastructure and huge ridership numbers.

To be fair, Japan's geography has clearly been conducive to high-speed rail development. Many of Japan's largest cities—including Tokyo, Osaka, Kobe, and Hiroshima—form a densely populated stretch along the main island, allowing one straight shot instead of a branching tree of connections. Similar geography has helped

Amtrak's semi-high-speed Acela service achieve a modicum of success in America's crowded northeast corridor.

In the end, though, the most important factor is likely cultural. Trains are a group-oriented form of transportation. In exchange for wonderful efficiency, they put limits on our autonomy, personal space, and self-expression. The Japanese are comfortable with this, as am I. It seems most Americans are less so.

Practically speaking, it might well make a ton of sense to build a high-speed rail line from, say, Los Angeles to Las Vegas. But then people would miss out on that epic road trip through the desert. Would you rather emerge from a Las Vegas train station as part of a faceless, thousand-person blob? Or would you prefer to gun your convertible down a stretch of open highway, stop for a burger at a roadside diner, and then cruise the Vegas Strip with the ragtop down, announcing your uniquely ass-kicking arrival?

One is more sensible. The other more American.

KOBE is a port city of 1.5 million wedged between a mountain range and a harbor. It has waterfront promenades, lots of high-end shopping, and a relaxed vibe. To foreigners, Kobe is perhaps best known as the site of a massive 1995 earthquake that killed more than five thousand people. A museum here shows video of the quake, including some harrowing silent footage taken from a security camera in a convenience store. (A customer is reaching for an item when suddenly everything on the shelves leaps into the air—as though the store were inside a roughly shaken snow globe.)

The city's other claim to fame is its world-renowned steak. Kobe beef is deliciously marbled, perhaps because the pampered Wagyu cattle are regularly massaged and fed large quantities of beer. They have a life I wouldn't mind for myself—right up until that abrupt final moment.

For the dedicated surface traveler, though, clearly the most compelling attraction here is the Kobe Maritime Museum. Upon our arrival in the city, we make it our top-priority destination. And we are not disappointed. To our tremendous excitement, there is an entire exhibit here on containerization.

Kobe's container port, built in 1967, was the first in Japan. By 1973, it was the busiest container port in the world, exporting Japanese cameras and hi-fi systems by the literal boatload. It's fallen down the rankings a bit since then. The earthquake didn't help, as it disrupted operations and damaged trucking routes leading into the city. Still, Kobe's port remains a major shipping center—fully worthy of the maritime museum's light-up diorama and accompanying low-budget educational video.

The video—dubbed into English, if you can find the right button to press—explains how a celery stalk harvested in California can come to appear inside a child's lunchtime bento box in Kobe. We watch as the celery stalk gets loaded into a refrigerated container in America, floats on a container ship across the Pacific, and gets unloaded onto a waiting truck in Japan. Hosted by the animated Professor Container, and his little robot assistant, the short film is captivating. But I'm not sure why it was necessary to show the robot getting sloppily drunk after he pilfers sake bottles out of an unattended container.

In the basement of the museum is an area called Kawasaki Good Times World. This sponsored exhibit details the exciting history of the Kawasaki Heavy Industries Group. (Founder Shozo Kawasaki established a shipyard in Kobe in the late 1800s.) Next to all the Kawasaki motorcycles, airplanes, and Jet Skis here, there are also pictures and models of Kawasaki-designed rolling stock. Kawasaki in fact manufactured the original 0 Series Shinkansen back in 1964. The exhibit includes a full-scale replica of that first bullet train, which was nicknamed for the appearance of its rounded-off nosepiece.

For me, the highlight of Kawasaki Good Times World is without doubt a video game called Let's Go by Train! 2—which presumably builds on the popularity of the original Let's Go by Train! Your mission in this game is to pilot a Shinkansen down a stretch of track and then bring it safely to a stop at a crowded station platform. I do just fine on the open rail, but when it's time to stop I always come in too hot and compensate by slamming hard on the brakes. An animated Japanese woman whiplashes her head forward and screams, while the screen flashes some Japanese characters that I assume say "Game over! Let's all try harder not to occasion mass casualties!"

THE typhoon has passed. According to Rebecca's evaluation of multiple online weather radars, the next couple of days ought to be clear sailing. We figure we'd better seize our chance to catch a ferry back to mainland Asia.

The China Express Line runs a once-a-week ship out of Kobe. The passage takes two days and ends at a spot on the Chinese coast about a hundred miles southeast of Beijing. Using the English-language page on the company's website, we book ourselves into a private cabin, having learned our lesson about the perils of shipboard group accommodations from our Estonian ferry's room of despair.

Who takes the ferry from Kobe to China? The practical reason to travel over water is usually that you're bringing something heavy with you (e.g., a car—or multiple cars, as those Russian guys were doing on the Fushiki–Vladivostok run). But this particular route may be the rare case where it's actually cheaper for a luggageless passenger to go by ship instead of by plane. Airfare between Japan and Beijing is surprisingly expensive. A family of five or six—and I'm seeing a lot of big families as I look around at the other passengers waiting in the ferry terminal—could save hundreds of dollars by opting for the slow boat to China.

Our ferry, called the *Yanjing*, is roughly the same size and vintage as the Russian ship we took from Vladivostok. It's infinitely cheerier, though. The staff greet us with wide smiles as we board, and they've festooned the main deck with red paper lanterns. The Russian ferry was all filthy, threadbare burgundy carpets, while the *Yanjing* is all brightly polished yellow linoleum.

After pulling away from the Kobe pier, the ship threads a path beneath massive suspension bridges and between the lushly hilled islands in Japan's Inland Sea. At one point, a half-submerged military submarine creeps up behind us. It approaches close enough that I can see the faces of the Japanese sailors standing on its small parapet. I snap a few pictures before the sub speeds silently out of sight, leaving barely a ripple of wake behind it.

We spend the afternoon watching freighters and tankers passing by us in the shipping channel. At precisely 6:00 p.m., a Chinese woman's gentle voice wafts from the public address system, speaking first in Mandarin and then in a lilting, inflected English. "Good evening, ladies and gentlemen," she begins. "The sun has set and the evening is coming. We hope a nice dinner will refresh you from the day's voyage." Her tone is so relaxing and her sentiments so soothing, it's like we've checked ourselves onto a floating sanatorium.

When we get to the dining room, there are about thirty other passengers already seated, eating the mushy chicken and gloopy rice that's served cafeteria-style in steam trays. Of these passengers, four are westerners. Three sit together at a central table. The fourth—a gaunt, older man with a ponytail and sideburns—eats alone in the far corner of the room, gazing out the window.

I'd love to be sitting at one of the tables full of Chinese people. They're all multigenerational families, with adorable kids scurrying under the tables, and tiny infants getting bottle-fed by grandmas. But no one seems to speak English, and to plop down among a family uninvited would be a bold move—probably awkward, and possibly unwelcome. We resign ourselves to eating with the trio of whiteys.

They turn out to be friendly, standard-issue backpackers. The outdoorsy Aussie couple is on a three-week vacation through Asia and is treating this scenic ferry ride as a relatively low-cost alternative to a cruise. As for the third paleface, a nerdy young Brit, she's just wandering around, fresh out of university. Behind her wire-rimmed glasses lurks a look of total aimlessness. Her budget ferry ticket grants her a space on one of the dozens of padded tatami mats laid out neatly on the wooden floor of a lower deck. She tells us the other mats are filled with Chinese families like the ones around us now. Some of the smaller children are already down there in their pajamas, set for bedtime. Sounds like a far cry from the room of despair.

We enjoy a pleasant meal with our dinner companions, but I find my attention keeps drifting to that older white dude in the corner. He's wearing an elegantly battered linen suit and a pair of leather sandals. There's something haughty in the cut of his mustache, the tilt of his head, and the careful braidwork of his ponytail. At a break in the conversation, I nod toward this fellow and ask the table quietly: "What's up with that guy?"

The British woman sneaks a quick glance over her shoulder. "I talked to him for a moment, earlier," she says. "He's an American. Not especially friendly."

Once dinner is over, the ship immediately turns into a ghost town. The Chinese passengers all retire to their rooms. We buy cans of beer out of a vending machine (vending machine beer is a terrific perk of Asian travel) and convince the Aussies to have a drink with us before we call it an early night.

How quiet a ferry can be when there are no Russians aboard.

AT 8:00 a.m., the woman's ethereal voice drifts from the ceiling-mounted speaker in our cabin. "Good morning, ladies and gentlemen. It is a new day that begins. It is said that breakfast is a healthy part of any good day."

The ship is rounding the southern tip of the Korean Peninsula now. It will enter the Yellow Sea, pass Pyongyang and Dalian to its starboard, and then push farther west into the Bo Hai Gulf. Tomorrow we'll dock at the Chinese port town of Tanggu.

The sky is clear and the ocean calm. Many of the older Chinese folks on board spend the whole day puttering in laps around the deck, wearing polyester Bermuda shorts and plastic shower sandals. The younger Chinese adults and the little kids watch an endless string of martial arts movies on a TV in the lounge.

While looking through the binoculars for seabirds, I catch a glimpse of the mysterious ponytailed man. He's lounging in a deck-chair, reading a weathered old hardback book. Surreptitiously aiming the binoculars his way, I make out the title: *The Myth of the Machine*, by Lewis Mumford. Apparently a 1967 treatise on the interplay between society, language, and technology. Erudite. Obscure. The intrigue continues.

By the next day, the water has turned sandy colored, the shipping lane has grown crowded, and the Chinese coast has come into view. We're entering the country through the back door—arriving not at an airport gate or a railway station, but at a lonely ferry dock in an industrial port.

We don't speak the language at all. It would be nice to have some wingmen to help us find the way to Beijing, but our backpacker bud-dies are all headed south toward Shanghai. On the plus side, this gives me an excuse to at last approach the mysterious, aloof, pony-tailed American.

He's reading his book in the main lounge, his scratched-up suit-case on the floor beside him. "Excuse me," I say. He lifts his eyes from the book and takes a moment to silently appraise me. "Will you be taking the train to Beijing?" I ask. He nods. "Perhaps we could travel together," I say, waving my hand vaguely toward Rebecca to encompass the three of us in this endeavor.

He spends another moment in silent thought. And then he assents—with the air of a man who'd much rather be reading his book in peace. He introduces himself as Lachlan. He says he's made the trip from Tanggu to Beijing many times before and tells us we're welcome to tag along with him if we'd like.

Not long after, the engine goes quiet and the ship settles to a stop alongside the pier. There's no real ferry terminal here—after a customs check on board the ship, we step down off the gangplank directly onto a concrete parking lot. At the moment our feet touch the ground, we're assaulted by a throng of hectoring cabdrivers.

"We'll need a taxi to the Tanggu railway station first," Lachlan says calmly, coming down off the gangplank behind us. He wades into the fray, suitcase in hand, and begins to shout in Chinese and wave around his free arm.

He's soon squared off with a middle-aged woman. She's negotiating on behalf of her husband, who drives the cab. She flashes numbers with her fingers in rapid succession and yells a lot. Lachlan yells back. (I don't even think he speaks fluent Chinese—it's just the universal language of haggling.) When she makes her final offer, Lachlan laughs loudly and turns his back on her. "This is a very disagreeable woman," he murmurs to us, looking at his watch. She's now jabbing the back of his elbow.

After several more skirmishes, they come to an agreement. We toss our bags in the taxi's trunk and sit three in a row in its backseat. The woman and her husband sit up front. The woman looks miserable. We assume Lachlan has negotiated masterfully, saving us a considerable amount of money.

"What was our final price?" I ask him, as the cab turns out of the parking lot and onto a roadway.

"Six dollars total, for the three of us," he says, not bothering to conceal his pride. "She wanted eight! Positively absurd."

THE Tanggu train station is packed to the gills. Lachlan weaves his way to the ticket window as we obediently hold his suitcase for him. He comes back with three tickets and the news that the train won't leave for another hour.

The waiting room is a warehouse-sized kaleidoscope of chaos. Shrieking children. Groups of men sleeping. Families engaged in elaborate picnics in the middle of the floor. Lachlan takes a quick peek inside and shakes his head. "It does no good for my Latin humanism to be in a room with fifteen hundred Chinese," he says. "They are a people very in touch with their bodies. The last time I took a taxi from a train station, the driver spat, farted, and lit a cigarette before he started the engine."

So we leave the station and walk to a nearby town square to wait. Rebecca goes off to explore a grocery store across the street. Lachlan and I find a bench to sit on. Attempting to make some casual conversation, I ask his thoughts regarding recent U.S. politics.

"Oh, I detest talking politics," he says. "It all just comes back to Plutarch and Machiavelli, doesn't it?"

Things go downhill from there. Sifting through his pretension, I manage to learn that Lachlan's lived in Hanoi with his Vietnamese wife for the past few years. Before that, he was living in Thailand. He hasn't been back to the States in two decades.

Whenever travelers and/or expats encounter each other abroad, as Lachlan and I have, the parties will swiftly sort themselves into a hierarchy. Lowest on the totem pole are the vacationers—the people on two-week or three-week breaks. They enjoy taking holidays, but never leave home long enough to truly abandon their workaday lives.

One rung above the vacationers are the restless wanderers. I'm in this camp. We knock around for several months at a time, perhaps even a year or two, and consider ourselves far more grizzled and worldly than the vacationers. Still, there's a gossamer tether that, in the end, always reels us back to a relatively sane existence. We restless wanderers look down our noses at the vacationing squares, but in turn we are looked down upon by the apex predator of the travel jungle—the permanent drifter.

The permanent drifter leaves home in a profound, spiritual sense, never to return. These adventurers, hedonists, and enlightenment seekers have no attachment to their roots. They've trimmed their roots clean off. They anoint themselves citizens of the universe, floating far above any petty notions of regional affiliation.

Lachlan has paid his dues as a permanent drifter. I can feel him looking down his aquiline nose at me—at my less-developed conception of human existence and purpose. The thing about permanent drifters, though, is that they all have to fund their wandering somehow. You can't bum around forever without turning into a . . . bum.

When I ask Lachlan's profession, he says, "I'm an artist," and avoids elaboration. Later, he makes reference to growing up on the

Upper East Side and spending his formative years at the shmancy-pants Dalton School. When he mentions his "monthly conversations with my lawyer," I put it all together. I'm fairly certain that Lachlan is a fifty-something trustafarian.

IT'S nearly time to board our train. Rebecca returns from the grocery with snacks for the ninety-minute ride. As we thrash our way through the teeming station, backpacks bumping everyone and everything around us, we get separated from Lachlan and eventually lose sight of him. I catch a final glimpse of the back of his faded, cream-colored suit, drifting away down the platform. We find a train car with a few empty spots and climb aboard. The train's seats are hard wood, and we're elbow to elbow with our neighboring passengers.

It's just after sunset as we arrive at the railway station in Beijing. We take the subway a couple of stops and pop up above ground in Tiananmen Square. The first thing we see is the iconic thirty-foot-tall portrait of Mao in his proletarian shirt-jacket. We make our way on foot to our hotel, just outside the high walls of the Forbidden City.

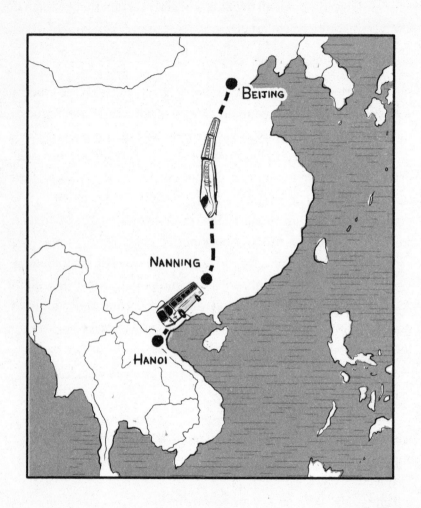

Chapter Five

Beijing to Hanoi

T HERE'S no point in traveling to another country if all you do when you get there is sit in your hotel room and stare at the television. At the same time, I'm a fierce proponent of sampling a smidgen of TV wherever you go. I assure you the locals are watching the tube, and it's worth it to check out what exactly is getting beamed into their living rooms each night. Treat it as a sociological study, and an intimate glimpse into a culture.

The TV set in our Beijing hotel room receives the state-run channels and little else. Much of the programming on the English-language channel is mild propaganda: news footage of Communist party leaders cutting ribbons, pinning medals on model citizens, and praising each other. Sometimes between the shows there are preview trailers for new Chinese movies coming out in the theaters. I'm pretty sure the government has also had a hand in producing these movies, because amazingly the films' plots always seem to revolve around a state-funded civil engineering project. There's a film about dredging a harbor. Another about building a railroad line to Tibet. Based on their trailers, it looks like these movies have high-gloss production values and attractive actors. Imagine George Clooney starring in *High Tension: Building a Suspension Bridge in Tulsa*.

One evening, in between all the movie promos and ribbon-cutting footage, something grabs our attention. It's a news report about a British man named Jason Lewis who has just completed a human-powered circumnavigation of the earth. No motors. No sails. Just pedal boats, kayaks, bicycles, Rollerblades, and his own two feet.

It's hard enough circling the earth without airplanes. I'm finding it hard to imagine making the circuit without the aid of any engines whatsoever. Even Lewis himself seemed to underestimate the difficulty and sacrifice involved. He'd thought the project might take him a couple of years. It took thirteen. He began when he was twenty-six and finished when he was forty. At times he was forced to put the expedition on hold, flying home to get more funding or to recuperate from injuries, and then returning to the geographic point where he'd left off.

Some of Lewis's accomplishments are truly staggering. He Rollerbladed over the Rockies. He pedaled a boat for seventy-three days, from Hawaii to an atoll in the center of the Pacific—during which time he fended off an aggressive shark; battled opposing currents that had him pedaling in the same spot for weeks; contracted blood poisoning from a strange oceanborne pathogen; and briefly developed a multiple personality disorder that stemmed from crushing loneliness. He was also attacked by a saltwater crocodile while kayaking in Australia, broke both his legs Rollerblading in Colorado when he was hit by a car, and got detained by the Egyptian military as a suspected spy.

Despite all this drama, Lewis's toughest challenge turned out to be simply getting along with another human being. The original plan had Lewis making the circumnavigation together with his friend Steve Smith. But on their very first leg, pedaling a modified canoe westward across the Atlantic, they got sick of each other's company and had a falling-out. I suppose things like this can happen after eighty-four straight days on open ocean, stuck in a small boat with one other person. When they reached land in North America, Smith quickly quit the project and went back home.

I think Rebecca and I can empathize, to a degree. We've now spent two months on the road together, locked at the elbow day and night. We've shared train cabins, ship's quarters, and the occasional bare patch of floor. We rarely leave each other's sight while in transit, for fear of getting separated on a crowded station platform or a busy street. When we tell people about our journey, they often ask—as delicately as possible—if we're getting along. Our pal Lachlan asked, somewhat less delicately: "At each other's throats yet?"

Any long-haul partnership will have moments of strain. The proximate causes of the arguments are often minor ("Did you lose the map?" "No, of course not! Wait. Maybe. . . ."). Meanwhile, the true conflict takes place deep below the surface, where the tectonic plates of two different personalities—pressed together in constant contact—occasionally grind.

Spending fifty straight hours in a shared railway cabin, or nine days together on a cargo freighter at sea, presents a much greater test of commitment than spending six hours sitting in adjacent seats on an airplane. Both joy and tension will be heightened, and it's vital to choose your travelmate with extreme care. I've chosen wisely: Rebecca has not abandoned me en route—even though I left the contact lens solution on the ferry from Kobe.

THE first thing we notice about Bejing is the pace of development. There's already more unbroken, polished plate glass in the three-block radius around our hotel than I think I saw in the entirety of Russia. There are cranes everywhere, and a new skyscraper seems to go up every half hour or so.

The morning after our arrival here, we decided to take the subway to the new Capital Museum on the other side of town. We checked the map to figure out which subway stop to get off at, and Rebecca noted that the system should be a breeze to navigate because there were only a couple of lines. After touring the museum, we took the stairs back down into the subway station. A team of workers there was in the middle of pasting up a revised system map. They'd literally opened a whole new subway line while we were strolling through the museum exhibits.

At this point, when we go out for the day, I half expect that by the time we return to our hotel we'll find a sparkling new monorail humming past the rooftop. Perhaps a streetcar line rumbling through the lobby. A small Kentucky Fried Chicken franchise operating out of the coat closet in our room. (They do love their KFC here. The menu's been tweaked for the Chinese palate and includes dishes like lotus root and preserved egg porridge. I wonder, is it mere coincidence that Colonel Sanders, viewed in just the right light, looks very much like an elderly Asian man with a Fu Manchu mustache?)

We've come here as preparations are heating up for the Beijing Olympics. There are sparkling new sports facilities all over town and a burgeoning excitement in the air. People seem to view the games as a coming-out party for modern China. The government is adamant about making a good impression on Olympic guests, so the state TV stations are airing public service announcements advising Beijing residents on how to interact with foreign tourists. The PSAs teach people to say "Welcome to Beijing!" in English. They also discourage mildly rude, locally accepted behaviors—like spitting in public.

Given the amount of loud, voluminous expectoration we've been witnessing around the city, I would deem the antispitting campaign a less-than-total success. Public spitting seems to be deeply ingrained in the culture. Anyway, I don't see the harm in a good spit, so long as you don't hit someone else's shoe tops or shins. I hope once the Olympics have ended and the tourist crush is gone, a new set of ads will pronounce it safe to start spitting freely again.

In addition to the loogie hocking, I've noticed a couple of other local behaviors of potential interest to a scholar of regional mannerisms. Both, coincidentally, are most often exhibited by elderly Chinese women:

1) In the midst of a conversation, older Chinese women will sometimes get angry and—without any warning—very suddenly boost the volume and the velocity of their speech. This has happened to us a few times now, mostly during exchanges with pushcart vendors when we're somehow screwing up the transaction. Since these

women are speaking Mandarin, which we don't understand, it sounds like: "Blah blahdy blah blah BLAH-BLAH-BLAH-BLAH-BLAH!" Executed with proper ferocity, that midsentence upshift is truly terrifying. I've been practicing it in my spare time, as I feel the maneuver might come in handy someday when, in the middle of an argument, I realize that in order to win, my only hope is to induce a massive heart attack in my opponent.

2) To get your attention, elderly Chinese women will sometimes clap their hands. Right in your face. With percussive force. I've also been practicing this technique, occasionally employing it on Rebecca. (For full effect, it's best if you follow your sonic-boom hand-clap with a frightening midsentence volume boost. And then spit on the ground.)

For her part, Rebecca's been most intrigued to learn that in Mandarin there is no easy way to say "no." It's just not in the language. To express a negative, you can use the word *bu*—the equivalent of "not"—coupled with the appropriate verb. So if someone inquires as to whether it's raining outside, you could answer, "Not is." Or if someone asks you if you want to go out to a movie, you could say, "Not want." Which, I would argue, sounds much harsher than an unadorned no.

Rebecca, in her endearing way, instantly cottons to this harshness. For a full afternoon, she adopts "not x" as her exclusive means of communicating with me. Rebecca, what time is it? "Not know." Rebecca, do you have the subway map with you? "Not have." Rebecca, this is sort of wearing on me. "Not care!"

*　　*　　*

TODAY is National Day, which commemorates the 1949 founding of the People's Republic of China. Thousands of people have gathered nearby in Tiananmen Square, beneath the giant portrait of Chairman Mao. Like bridge-and-tunnelers pouring into Times Square on New Year's Eve, all sorts of rubes fresh from the Chinese hinterlands have flocked here to celebrate the holiday.

It's pretty easy to spot the hicks. While most young Beijingers wear clothes that might not look out of place in an American city, the hayseeds are wearing fashions that seem thirty years past their prime. Lots of homemade stuff, too. Raggedly knit rainbow sweaters. Shakily hemmed, faded floral skirts.

The real tip-off is in the eyes. The country mice gaze slack-jawed at the skyscrapers, or at the hip city chicks sauntering by. The true urbanites will keep their focus locked on that rickshaw careening around the corner, headed straight for the crowded crosswalk.

Along with a flood of yokels, National Day ushers in the beginning of Golden Week. This week-long holiday (there's another one that coincides with the lunar New Year) is designed to allow everyone in China enough vacation time to visit relatives in distant cities. Or, alternatively, to go gambling with those relatives in Macao.

At least 120 million Chinese will travel during this Golden Week. Rebecca and I hadn't quite realized the magnitude of the holiday or how badly it would thwart our own plans. Yesterday we went to a railway ticket office and asked if there were any seats available on a train to Shanghai in the next few days. The man behind the counter actually laughed in our faces. He said something in Chinese to the coworker sitting next to him, and then that dude started laughing at us, too.

Every form of transport into and out of major Chinese cities is solidly booked. People have begun resorting to desperate measures. The *China Daily* has a story about a Beijing man who couldn't find a bus ticket to visit his family back home in Dandong, near the North Korean border. After trying everything he could think of, the exasperated man just gave up and bought a bicycle. He plans to ride it the entire six hundred miles home—an estimated nine-day journey. I don't fully understand his logic, since his vacation week will be over before he even reaches Dandong. But whatever. I guess what I'm saying is: Rebecca and I are stuck here in Beijing.

That guy's long-distance bike plan has us thinking, though. It might be liberating to ditch all these trains and boats and instead hit the open road on a couple of ten-speeds, wind rushing through our hair. We've been letting ferry captains and train engineers do the steering for us. Wouldn't it be empowering to take the helm for once? Even if it's merely the helm of a Schwinn?

It seems overly ambitious to just buy a pair of bikes and set off on a vague course toward Singapore. But we've managed to find a group bike tour that leaves from Hanoi a few days from now, headed south to Saigon. I'm generally allergic to package tours, as I hate the thought of being glued to a bunch of strangers. But this bike trip would provide us some much-needed exercise and also move us a few hundred miles nearer to the equator.

Given the difficulty of getting out of Beijing this week, there's a real risk we won't manage to reach Hanoi before the bicycle trip leaves without us. But we decide it's worth a gamble. We click to reserve the last two open spots in the tour group and cross our fingers that we'll get there in time.

*   *   *

THAT evening, while wandering the basement of a shopping mall (in search of cheap, knockoff Olympic souvenirs), we notice a restaurant packed with locals. It's not a particularly auspicious location, but the place is full of happy-looking families, and we're hungry for dinner.

It's love at first dish: green beans with Szechuan peppercorns. The Szechuan peppercorn was banned in the United States for a few decades, as it can carry bacteria that's harmful to citrus trees. Even now that the ban has been lifted, it can be hard to find the real thing in the States. When you do, there's no mistaking it.

Our green beans are loaded up with peppercorns, and they're activating taste buds we didn't know we had. A specific patch of my tongue, along the side, is radiating with a near-sexual pleasure. The name "peppercorn" is misleading, since it's not actually related to pepper. It's in fact the dried husk of a small berry. Whatever its origins, it's a magical substance—somehow numbing, warming, and spicy all at once. I swear it's narcotic, too. The more peppercorns I eat, the groovier the world gets. Rebecca's hip to it. "Hey—do you feel kind of high?" she asks with a sheepish grin. Sure do. Everyone else in the restaurant looks blissed out, too. It's like a culinary opium den.

Our next dish is stir-fried chicken. Unabridged. From the look of things, it's pretty clear that someone plucked the bird, laid it out on a cutting board, took a few desultory whacks at it with a cleaver, and then tossed the whole shebang into a hot wok. The dish reaches our table as a jumble of gristle, bones, and talons. On a normal evening, this might have occasioned mild squeamishness. Not tonight.

Under the disinhibiting influence of the peppercorns, we are at perfect ease with the grim realities of unedited poultry. Rebecca immediately grabs for the chicken's head, while I dig out its feet. We soon find ourselves employing them as props in a peppercorn-fueled, absurdist puppet show.

WE make another morning foray to the railway ticket window—having been negged the previous three times—and pray that the Golden Week rush has at last quieted down. The line is still long, but when we reach the window we're able to buy the last two remaining seats on an overnight train headed south. It will take us to Nanning, near China's border with Vietnam. From there, we can take a bus the rest of the way to Hanoi—or, if we must, pay someone to drive us.

As we're leaving the counter, clutching our tickets with relief, the lady railway clerk gives us one of those loud, attention-getting hand-claps. We turn around and she motions us back to the window. She grabs our tickets from us, pointing at the small print. We knew this seemed too good to be true. We're starting to fear we'll never leave Beijing.

But wait, she's smiling. She's directing our gaze to a silvery patch on the back of the tickets. Ah, a scratch-off component! We exhale and pull out a coin to try our luck. I've no idea what we might win, but I'm hoping it's a kilo of Szechuan peppercorns.

Once we've sanded away all the flaky silver stuff, it reveals . . . several Chinese characters. We expectantly hand our tickets to the clerk for interpretation. She squints at the characters, shakes her head, and hands our tickets back. Better luck next time.

I'd have liked to come out a winner, but still—you have to be impressed with China's unquenchable thirst for gambling. They manage to inject an element of chance into even the most prosaic of transactions. I wonder: Could this be the secret to reenergizing America's sagging public transport systems? Imagine you're deciding between a taxi and the subway. The taxi is faster and easier, but the subway ticket includes a scratch-off chance to win three hundred bucks. Turnstiles, here we come. Failing infrastructure: remedied.

THAT afternoon, we pack our bags and head for the Beijing West railway station. This is the busiest train station in Beijing, in a week when all of China is on vacation. We're about to become a part of what is literally, by my calculations, the most hectic holiday travel scene in the history of holiday travel.

The Beijing West station is a massive edifice topped by giant pagodas and surrounded by spiraling taxi ramps. Inside, it's like a shipping warehouse—that ships people. Every spot on the floor is covered by luggage or a Chinese family. The staircases and escalators are full at all times. Get caught moving against the flow of the crowd, and you'll take a fifty-yard detour before you're able to escape the current. If Rebecca and I get separated here, I think we'll just have to resign ourselves to never seeing each other again.

Our train's designated waiting room is filled to overflowing. The people inside have that beaten-down holiday traveler look you see at O'Hare on the day before Thanksgiving. The look that says, "Next year, Grandma and Grandpa are coming to *our* house." When an announcement in Chinese booms over the speakers after a few minutes, the room leaps to life. We follow the herd outside, where the platform is bedlam. The line of train cars stretches out of sight, and people are streaming into every open door. There will be easily more than two thousand people on board by the time we depart the station.

We hop on and begin moving down the train's length to find our assigned seats. In the spaces between cars, grimy groups of men squat on the floor, rolling dice and drinking liquor. We tiptoe around them, eventually finding our seats in the crowded scrum of a third-class car.

The wooden benches are arranged to face each other, and my knees are in firm, constant contact with the thighs of the old man who is sitting opposite me. He's shouting peevishly at his family—a bevy of kids and grandkids sitting together on the other side of the aisle—but his family is completely ignoring him, gabbing with each other or looking out the window. Soon after the train pulls out of the station, the old man gives up his hectoring, takes out a small pair of scissors, and starts trimming his fingernails. Over my lap.

Filthy fingernail crescents cling to my pants legs. I can't move, as I'm wedged between Rebecca and the guy sitting next to me—whose elbow is lodged in my rib cage. Meanwhile, I've noticed an odor wafting forward from somewhere in the back of the car. It's that nose-crinkling, high-toned tang specific to those who have urinated upon themselves. No one else seems to pay it any mind.

I'm trying to envision how I might have reacted if, a few months back, you'd plucked me off my comfortable couch in D.C. and set me down in the middle of this claustrophobic madness. Even though I've done a fair amount of challenging travel before, I'm pretty sure that my response to the sudden contrast would have been to freak out, jump off the train at my first opportunity, and hightail it for a luxury hotel.

Now, with seven thousand miles of railroad under my belt over the last two months—much of that involving Russians—I take a potentially overwhelming scene like this entirely in stride. It's not that I've grown to adore the chaos. It's just that it's expected, untroubling, and oddly invigorating. Yes, an adventure. The train is alive and different in a way a sterile airplane flight out of Beijing could never be.

And, fellow passengers aside, the train—if not fancy—is very nice in its way. It's clean and well maintained. It even has flat-screen TVs in each car. When we first boarded, these TVs played a loop of Chinese nationalist imagery, all set to a stirring orchestral soundtrack. Soldiers marching in lockstep. Military jets flying in formation. Footage of an ICBM test launch.

Now, though, the TVs have switched over to a blooper show. It looks like *America's Funniest Home Videos* (and the bumbling doofuses in the clips are all westerners), but there's something off. I could swear the show is using a batch of grade-D, subpar bloopers, packaged solely for the export market. It's like a blooper arbitrage scheme. Some savvy L.A. producer must have realized that the Chinese demand for bloopers was going unmet—and was also unsophisticated—so he threw together a reel of clips off the cutting room floor.

Sure enough, everyone around us on the train is cracking up at a clip of a toddler who simply falls over and starts to cry. Oh, the undiscerning palate of a developing nation. In America, a blooper like this wouldn't merit a chuckle, and it would never make it onto a televised show. One day, I expect the Chinese, too, will reserve their laughter for more refined and complex videotaped mishaps. Like, say, when an obese woman in a dress bounces awkwardly off a trampoline, exposes her underpants, and lands on a cocker spaniel.

WE'RE coming into hour two of a twenty-eight-hour train ride. I'm not sure I can spend the next twenty-six consecutive hours sitting upright on a bench, my knees and elbows jostling for space. I'm holding out hope that somehow, before sunset, we'll be able to talk our way into a pair of sleeper-class bunks.

An American friend we met up with for dinner one night in Beijing (a guy who works for a trade agency, greasing the gears of the Sino-American money machine) taught us the concept of *bupiao*. We understand this to be the Chinese word for "upgrade." Our friend instructed us to keep shouting it at every train worker within earshot until something good happened. He assured us—based on his own experience—that we'd eventually get lucky. We've taken his advice, shouting *"bupiao"* at anyone who'll listen, but so far we've nothing to show for it. Only apologetic shakes of the head.

At one point, Rebecca notices a crowd forming at the end of the next car, so she sallies forth to check it out. It's a five-deep crush of people, all waving their tickets in the air and screaming at a clerk who's standing behind a little counter. Rebecca assumes this must be a mad scramble for upgrades, because bunks have opened up when people disembarked at stops along the route. She wades in and manages to wriggle her way to the front. Once there, she shouts *"bupiao!"* with a victorious flourish and waits to be handed her new seat assignments. But again, nothing. The clerk meets her cry with a blank face. Was this mob gathered for some other reason? Perhaps another lotto drawing?

Rebecca returns, defeated. "I think we're going to have to tough this ride out," she says.

I can't face the thought of trying to sleep bolt upright. Ten minutes later, after the crowd has dispersed, I decide I'll approach the clerk again. This time, I'm prepared to offer an exorbitant bribe.

When I get to him, the clerk's still tidying up the mess of discarded paper scraps the crowd left behind. *"Bupiao?"* I ask, fully expecting a refusal—which I will counter with the thick wad of bills I'm gripping tightly in my pocket. But it never comes to that. Upon hearing my request, the clerk immediately punches a few buttons on his machine. It spits out two tickets. He hands them to me and goes back to his cleaning. We've been upgraded.

I have no idea what changed, or what the crowd that was here a few minutes ago was expecting, but I'm not going to stick around and ask dumb questions. I race back to Rebecca, who's still sitting dejectedly on our bench. *"Bupiao!"* I shout, waving our new tickets. Her face lights up. *"Bupiao!"* she shouts. We grab our packs and start walking toward our new berth.

It's a long march, through at least fifteen packed cars. When we get there, we find we've scored adjacent bunks—the upper pair in a six-bunk arrangement. Conditions in these bunks are still not ideal. There's not enough headroom to sit up. My feet droop over the edge of my bunk into the aisle, where they get smashed each time someone hauls down a suitcase from the nearby luggage rack. And, inches from our faces, embedded in the ceiling, are a bright fluorescent light (which stays permanently on, singeing our retinas) as well as a booming, distorted speaker (which frazzles our eardrums each time there's an announcement).

Nonetheless, we are thrilled. It's easy to forget how wonderful it is to find a flat piece of real estate when you need to fall asleep.

MUCH as she did on our ferry across the Baltic, Rebecca awakes to find there is a strange man staring at her face. This time, it's the toothless old fellow who's in the bunk below mine. He's sipping congee from a thermos, and when Rebecca opens her eyes, he wipes his lips and gives her a wide, gummy grin. She decides to take it as a compliment.

Our open-plan train carriage, with its sixty-odd bunks, is a hive of activity. Several multigenerational families have set up comfy homes away from home—with grannies tending infants, moms reading to toddlers, and packs of dads and uncles playing complicated card games. Food is shared. Laughter is everywhere. The mood on the Japanese Shinkansen was polite reserve. On this Chinese train, it's all hearty engagement with the stuff of life.

The train pulls into Nanning around 8:00 p.m. We fight our way through the crowd exiting the station, into the central town square. As usual, we've no idea where we're sleeping tonight, so when we get outside we look around to orient ourselves. I notice a large neon sign on a roof across the street. It reads "High-Class Hotel." Sounds like just the place for two high-class travelers like us.

Once inside, we surmise from its shabby lobby that this hotel is not quite as high-class as it would have us believe. It'll do for tonight, though. We check in, take the elevator to our room, and shower away the previous twenty-eight hours. As I'm drying off, I notice that the bath towels all say "High-Class Bussiness Hotel" (*sic*).

The implicit effort. The manifest failure. There is something so achingly sad about a typo embossed on a towel.

WE wake up early to catch a morning bus to Hanoi. At the depot, we run into a European couple also planning to catch this bus. "Do you know," asks the woman—she's French, I think—"where can we get the visa we will need for Vietnam?"

We break the bad news gently. Visas come from embassies. And all embassies in China are closed for Golden Week. This couple won't be crossing the Vietnamese border until at least three days from now. Questions about visas are something they probably ought to have asked themselves before they got to the bus station. I'm not one to judge. Left on my own, there's a solid chance I'd have made the same mistake. Lucky for me, I happen to be traveling with a logistical genius. Rebecca squared away our Vietnamese visas well in advance.

I occasionally wonder if Rebecca's travel-planning skills are *too* good. It might be rewarding to endure one of those mishaps that grizzled backpackers are always bragging about. ("So then I was stuck in Guinea for thirteen weeks because of the coup. Funny story—I briefly became undersecretary to the finance minister.") But Rebecca is forever four steps ahead of all possible pitfalls and minor political revolutions.

In the Internet age, it's become possible to prepare for any dodgy border crossing, planned rail strike, or imminent governmental col-lapse simply by reading the advice of others who've been there and done that. There are always a few gung-ho travelers out there who are eager to serve as guinea pigs and equally eager to boast about their exploits in real time—either on personal blogs or on the bul-letin boards of travel sites. Useful intel that could once be gleaned only by hanging out in expat cafés for days on end is now easily searchable and freely available on the Web. If the railway bridge col-lapses at a major Malaysian junction, that fact will be immediately noted online. And not long after, at least one traveler will post de-tailed directions for a viable detour.

We leave the crestfallen European couple behind and board our bus. It's comfortable and air-conditioned, and soon we're zooming down an empty highway. The road is wide, and freshly paved, but totally devoid of cars. The breakdown lanes are filled with bicycles and pedestrians, struggling along with heavy luggage. It seems China's preparation for a boom in automobiles has outpaced actual automobile usage.

WITHIN a couple of hours, we reach the border. The Chinese exit point is remarkably efficient. The clerk asks no questions and stamps our passports without any hassle. (By now we're collecting passport stamps like pocket lint.) When he's done, he points to a device on the counter in front of him. It has buttons with icons showing a smiley face, a frowny face, and two faces that lie somewhere in between. I realize, after a moment of confusion, that he's inviting me to rate his job performance. I press the smileyest face possible—on the theory that the frowny face button might open a trapdoor to a dungeon for malcontents.

Chauffeured golf carts ferry us through a few hundred yards of no-man's-land between the checkpoints. Armed soldiers stand along the road. When we get to the Vietnamese side, we enter what appears to be a small, decomposing shack. This turns out to be the border post. Outside, an old woman offers to sell us Vietnamese dong for our Chinese yuan—no doubt at an abusive exchange rate. Having no more use for the yuan, we make the trade.

Once our passports are cleared, we're sent to a counter labeled "Medical Check." The guy standing there says, "This is fee," and hands me a slip with a number on it. I pay the two thousand dong out of my brand-new stash (it's roughly twelve cents) and then apprehensively wait for some sort of medical check to occur. Will I be jabbed with a needle for a blood sample? Will someone beneath the table surprise me by whacking my knee with a reflex hammer? No. Instead, the clerk stares at me blankly. "Is there an actual medical check?" I ask, I feel somewhat reasonably. The clerk chuckles for a moment at my näiveté and then pushes me along with an irritated wave of his hand. We get through customs without anyone so much as glancing at our bags. Our connecting bus waits on the other side.

The Vietnamese bus is a bit rougher around the edges. Stuffing spills out of several seat cushions. The road is also much bumpier than on the Chinese side. Each of the countless potholes sends a jolt through our spines and coaxes a loud groan from the bus's suspension. Despite the ride, the scenery outside is growing ever more spectacular. It was getting chilly up in Beijing, as fall approached and the nights got colder, but now we're heading south into an entirely different climate. Palm trees line the road. All is green and lush. Limestone formations pop up here and there, where the rocky hills have eroded into tall, jagged towers.

We stop for lunch at a roadside stand. Rebecca and I are the only westerners on the bus, and our fellow travelers sweetly make sure that we understand the menu offerings. This is especially important because the most prominent items on display are preserved cobras— kept in large glass jars. I'd prefer not to accidentally ingest a plate of snake fried rice.

It's late afternoon when we hit the enormous traffic jam encircling Hanoi. Our bus crawls through the city streets for a full hour, a river of motorbikes flowing around us. At last we arrive downtown, hoist on our packs, and start walking to our hotel. Time to meet our bike tour group. We're no longer traveling on our own.

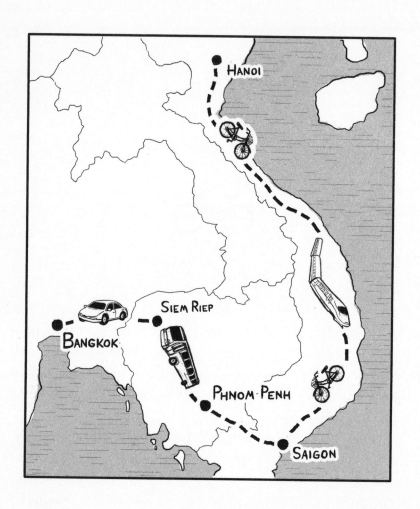

Chapter Six

Hanoi to Bangkok

THE streets of Hanoi are like gushing, white-water rapids—if you replaced the water with motor scooters. The motorbike is Hanoi's preferred vehicle, as few people here can afford (or have a place to park) a car. Endless torrents of scooters flow through the city's intersections and around its corners. The riders jostle shoulder to shoulder in a high-speed scrum. There are rarely any stop signs or crosswalks, and making it to the other side of a street can be a daunting proposition.

Your instinct is to wait for a small opening in the scooter traffic and then sprint across the street for all you're worth. But this would be suicide. As explained on a partly helpful, partly terrifying instructional sheet that's been posted in our hotel lobby—and is clearly an effort to preserve tourist lives—the proper tactic for crossing a Hanoi street is to wade in slowly and let the motorbikes flow around you.

You must free your mind of fear and step gingerly off the curb into the chaos. Making no sudden movements, you steadily inch your way across as the scooter drivers adjust to your presence. Please attempt not to notice the kilotons of metal and fiberglass whizzing by on all sides.

We're on our way to the orientation dinner for our bike trip. When we arrive (miraculously intact, after several near collisions with hurtling scooters), we take our places at a table filled with the other cyclists in the group. While knocking back a few crisp Vietnamese beers, we introduce ourselves to the folks we'll be casting our lot with for the next two weeks. There's a yuppie Canadian couple, a middle-aged Japanese man, two retired Aussie women, four young Australian blokes, and our tour guide, Scott—an Australian expat who's been leading bike groups through Southeast Asia for the last several years.

Ostensibly, the point of this tour is to experience Vietnam at the leisurely pace that a bicycle affords. We'll be at ground level, with no windows to separate us from our surroundings. We'll be moving faster than we would on foot, but not so fast that we'll miss any of the more visceral details. I can see, however, that in addition to the sightseeing, there will be a countersubtext on this tour: an underlying competition to be the fastest, fittest cyclist in the group. The buff Aussie lads are already comparing their workout regimens. And Yukihide, the Japanese fellow, has let it slip that he's an avid triathlete.

This is depressing news for Rebecca and me. The tour company's website recommended that we prepare for the trip with several weeks of strenuous biking, but it would have been hard for us to pedal a bike down the corridors of the trains and ferries we'd been riding around on. Besides, we couldn't quite bring ourselves to take this preparation advice seriously. A friend of ours used to lead bike tours through the French countryside, and she told us the people in her group (all of them older and wealthy) would generally dump their bikes on the side of the road after just a few miles, giving up in a huff and hailing the comfy support van. We'd imagined the people on our tour would also be plump retirees, and we assumed our relative youth would act as an equalizer. The unfortunate truth is that over the past year we've bicycled for a cumulative total of seventy-five minutes.

Sixty of those minutes came in Kobe, when we rented a pair of three-speeds and took a leisurely pedal around the city's flat, paved streets. The other fifteen minutes happened in Beijing, the day after we'd made the reservations for this bike trip. Thinking it might be a wise idea to get more practice in the saddle, we rented ten-speeds and set off on what we'd planned to be a full-day excursion. Things ended quickly: I tackled an incline with ill-advised gusto and popped the bike's chain. Luckily, there was a man with a bike repair stand on a nearby corner. (These stands are everywhere in Beijing, because everybody bikes.) The man pulled out his rusty box of tools and lubricants, fixed my chain, and then held up two grimy fingers to signal his price. I assumed he meant twenty yuan—which is less than three dollars. So I gave him a fifty-yuan bill and waited for change. He stared at the bill in bewilderment. It turned out that he'd in fact meant two yuan—which is roughly twenty-two cents. In American bike shop terms, I'd handed him five hundred bucks for a twenty-dollar repair job.

What a bargain, I thought, reaching back into my pocket for some coins. We rode off, and about a hundred yards later the chain popped again. I gave up and walked the bike back to the rental place. In retrospect, I suppose that repair job was worth almost exactly twenty-two cents.

Anyway, this was the sum total of our preparation. Tomorrow—as a little warm-up, to ease our way into the hard stuff coming later—we'll be cycling thirty-five hilly miles.

WE wake the next morning still feeling the effects of last night's beer. We all pile groggily into the support van. It drives us a few hours past the perimeter of Hanoi, to a spot where the roads empty out and the smog clears away. We retrieve our bikes from the equipment truck, hop on our pedals, and start the ride.

I'd confided in the guide my concerns about my fitness level, so after a mile or so Scott pedals up alongside me to check in. "Feeling okay? Is it all coming back to you?" he asks.

"Like riding a bicycle," I reply, with the flippant grin of a man who is due for a painful comeuppance.

The first ten miles leave me breathing hard, but mostly I'm just thrilled to be outside, working up a sweat. We've done so much passive sitting on this trip, as trains and ships carted us across the earth, that it feels ennobling to take the reins. After a quick break in the shade of some trees, we start the second ten-mile leg. I'm getting severely winded, but—to my surprise—I'm still chugging along.

At the next checkpoint, where we stop for lunch, Scott informs us that this final, fifteen-mile stretch will be entirely uphill. Rebecca judiciously decides to give up and ride in the support van. I (some-what less judiciously) choose to have a go at those hills.

I quickly, and miserably, realize that I must have been fueled by adrenaline for the first twenty miles. It's worn off now. Less than halfway into the final leg, I'm soaked in sweat and panting, mouth agape. My heart is thumping so fast that I can no longer distinguish individual beats. A heavenly white light is creeping in at the edges of my vision.

The stronger cyclists have zoomed far ahead, out of sight, and I find myself struggling at the back of the pack with the two retired ladies. Eventually the ladies run out of steam, dismount from their bikes, and wait by the side of the road to flag down the equipment truck. It's getting dusky out now. The hills are growing steeper. My quadriceps burn as though roasting over a six-burner gas range.

The truck eventually rumbles up behind me and flashes its head-lights. This is an established signal, which we'd discussed during the orientation. It means, roughly: "You appear to be having a stroke, sir. Please stop now. We fear for your life."

I'm so grateful for the excuse to stop pedaling that I ignore the humiliation and chuck my bike in the back of the truck. When we pull up to the hotel—a rustic, bare-bones lodge deep inside a jungle—we find the faster riders lounging on the covered front porch, showered and changed, well into their second bottles of beer.

The next couple of days go pretty much the same. I begin each morning vowing to keep pace with the lead peloton. We cruise along at a reasonable speed for the first few minutes, and then the stronger cyclists—meaning everyone but me, Rebecca, and the two older women—turn on the jets and leave the stragglers in their dust. Once

I've lost sight of this group, I revise the day's goal downward. New goal: Do not have a stroke.

My back and shoulders are sore from hunching over as I ride. My fingers are gnarled from gripping the bike's handlebars. And my ass is chafed to a pretty traumatic degree. I'm trying to think of muscles that aren't in agony, and all I can come up with are those tiny ones that regulate my inner ear. They seem to be doing okay.

On the morning of day four, though, an interesting thing happens. My heart settles into a steady rhythm. My lungs find a second wind. My ass firms up like a charred steak. Suddenly I'm able to pay some attention to the world beyond my body.

It turns out, when I at last look around me, that Vietnam is gorgeous—a tropical, emerald jewel. We're cycling through green hills and flooded rice paddies, speckled with villages of concrete huts. Along the roadside, a family of water buffalo munches at the grass. A small child, no older than seven or eight, stands atop the largest buffalo's back—holding a rope that's been looped through the animal's nostrils. Farther up the road, dozens of ducklings waddle behind their mothers toward a stream and then sploosh in two by two. It's the kind of thing you'd never see from a plane and you would speed past on a train. On a bike, you can roll to a stop and watch ducklings sploosh to your heart's content.

We watch them for a while, delighting at the sight of their teensy webbed feet, and then pedal back up to speed. Now that I can hang with the main pack, I discover the power of drafting. The cyclists at the front of our peloton act as an aerodynamic wedge, dragging me along in their wake. There are no cars around for miles, and we roll down the road in near silence. I hear only the whir of our tires on hard-packed dirt. The clicking of our chains and sprockets. The wind rushing past my ears.

IT'S downright shocking that the bicycle as we know it didn't come into existence until the 1860s. We'd already been riding on steamboats for several decades before that, and steam-powered trains had come to dominate American transportation by the 1850s. Photography, electromagnets, the telegraph—all these were invented before the bicycle.

It seems a simple and obvious idea: a mechanical, human-powered conveyance that could replace the horse as a means of personal transport. It's not exactly clear why it took so long to get the bicycle right, but part of the problem may have been the lack of practical surfaces to ride on. Smoothly graded roads were few and far between in the nineteenth century. If you've ever bloodied your knees learning to ride a bike, you know that getting started without falling over requires an immediate burst of momentum. On a rocky stagecoach trail, a primitive bike would be difficult to launch and even tougher to keep upright.

Still, an intrepid few strove to perfect the "mechanical horse." In 1817, a German baron created a wooden, two-wheeled "velocipede" that was propelled by kicking one's feet along the ground, Flintstone-style. Later, there were carriagelike contraptions powered by stepping on wooden treadles—like a mobile elliptical trainer. But most historians agree that the true progenitor of the bicycle didn't arrive until 1867, when a Parisian blacksmith named Pierre Michaux attached pedals directly to the front wheel.

Despite Michaux's breakthrough, the bicycle's popularity faded in and out over the next couple of decades. Michaux's front-wheel-drive scheme, upon encountering a bump, had the unfortunate habit of flipping the rider over the bike's handlebars. In 1866 Mark Twain, in his words, "traversed a brick" and toppled forward while riding his new bicycle in Connecticut. The bike went airborne and landed on top of him. "It was well it came down on us," he wrote, "for that broke the fall, and it was not injured." The early "boneshaker" bikes gave way to the "high-wheel" era of the 1870s. But these bikes, with a gigantic front wheel that allowed faster speeds, were still unwieldy and forced the rider to perch high above the ground.

The bicycle boom didn't take off in earnest until the 1890s, after the development of the "safety bike." This design used a chain to send the pedaler's power back to the rear wheel—as modern bikes still do—thus reducing the bike's tendency to pitch forward. Another vital innovation: In 1888, tire genius John Dunlop created an inner tube filled with compressed air. In 1891, Édouard Michelin made the tube detachable. Bike riding became smoother, faster, and more comfortable, and you could quickly fix a puncture with a replacement tube.

By 1893, a top cyclist using good tires could go twenty-five miles per hour. Cycling enthusiasts soon became legion. They began to lobby for better roads to ride on. At last, the horse had met its match—in a machine that needed no food or water, could be housed in a compact space, and, with proper upkeep, might never die.

IN the United States, automobiles eventually overtook the bicycle as the favored means of personal transport. Now only 1 percent of all excursions Americans make are by bike, while 84 percent are by car. Even in the Netherlands, the Western world's bicycling capital, 30 percent of all trips are by bike and 45 percent are by car.

In the poorest parts of Asia, where cars were simply out of reach, bikes were a godsend. Bicycle use was limited only by the fact that the bikes themselves remained a luxury item well into the twentieth century. The elite used pedicabs (bicycle-powered carriages, pedaled by servants—which had replaced the rickshaw setup in which the servant simply jogged along while pulling the carriage), but owning a basic bicycle remained beyond the means of the average person. As late as 1978, less than 8 percent of Chinese could afford a bike. Families scrimped and saved to buy a single bike they would share.

In a culture where owning a car or motorcycle was only for the rich, a bicycle meant freedom for working-class people. Suppose, for instance, that you were living in one of these rural Vietnamese villages we've been cycling through. Access to a bicycle would hugely expand the radius of places you could get to, and back from, in a reasonable amount of time. Most humans walk at about three miles per hour, but a cyclist can comfortably travel at three times that speed without too much exertion. On longer journeys, this adds up dramatically: The current record for running across the United States is forty-six days, while for a bicyclist it's eight days. Even over the course of a couple of hours, traveling by bike can make an immense difference. It allows a far greater range of choices about where to buy things, where to sell things, and where to make friends or meet a spouse. It literally broadens your horizons.

Our tour group has at this point shared the road with scores of Vietnamese cyclists, and I find their attitude toward biking radically different from ours. The Vietnamese tend to pedal at a comfortable, steady pace, aiming to reach their destinations without soaking themselves in sweat. They wear their everyday clothes to go biking in. Their bikes are old and cheap and look oft repaired. (I haven't seen any child-sized bikes, either. Vietnamese kids learn to use adult-sized bikes by riding while standing up—often pedaling in bare feet, with a smaller sibling or two perched on the handlebars.) Meanwhile, my tour group brethren and I tend to pedal as fast as we can and sweat profusely. Some of us wear tight-fitting "athletic" clothes in primary colors. We have gleaming new bikes with twenty-four-gear transmissions and flashy paint jobs. Frankly, we look like a bunch of kitted-out buffoons.

By contrast, the Vietnamese emphasize the humble utility of bikes. During the American War—as it's called here in Vietnam—bikes were a vital military resource. Soldiers could load them up with supplies and ammunition to be ferried between battlefields. Even now, bikes often function as cargo carriers. On this trip, I've had bikes pass by me stacked high with piles of scrap metal. I've cycled up behind a haystack that appeared to float magically down the road—and then drawn alongside it to reveal the cyclist hiding underneath. Terrifyingly, I've passed a woman with a large, rusty scythe lashed across her handlebars. It slashed inches from my eye as we both coasted down a hill at 30 mph, trying to avoid loose gravel.

But my favorite was the woman with two live ducks in her handlebar basket. They quacked with every turn of her pedals. It was like she was repeatedly squeezing a pair of loud, irritated bike horns.

*   *   *

THOUGH Rebecca and I have begun to adjust to the physical demands of the bike trip, the social transition has been less smooth. We've gone from us-against-the-world—or at least us-around-the-world—to spending most of our waking minutes as part of a collective. The tour group made an overnight ride in shared cabins on a Vietnamese train (skipping over some ground we could never have covered quickly enough on bikes), and most mornings we're crammed together in the close quarters of the support van as we head to the start point of our next cycling leg.

After the first few days, the group splits into cliques. The two older Aussie women stick together. The four Australian lads form a frat boy posse and take Yukihide the triathlete into their fold.

Meanwhile, Rebecca and I have hit it off with the Canadian couple, Tim and Kim. They're about our age, and they're clever and funny traveling companions. Kim's a doctor; Tim's a photographer. They're both excellent cyclists, and Kim keeps pace with all the boys despite the fact that she insists on biking in flip-flops. We generally sit next to them at meals and when we ride in the van, and we'll sometimes double-date when the group is in a larger city and splits up for a night on the town.

Thus we're a bit chagrined when, halfway into the trip, we board the van one morning and find the two of them seated far apart. "Do you not like each other?" Rebecca asks. (Rebecca views tact as a confusing obstacle. Best to trample right over it and see what happens.) The estranged couple replies with awkward murmurs, looking out their separate windows. They utter not a single word to each other for the rest of the day.

This continues into the next day, and the next. We get no explanation. The tension between them is uncomfortable for the group, but we can only imagine the couple's own discomfort—forced to sleep in a shared bed each night, yet unwilling to talk to each other all day. We see contempt in her eyes and acute embarrassment on the tips of his ears.

When we happen to be biking alongside each other one afternoon, out of earshot of Kim, I delicately ask Tim what's going on. Cycling side by side is a wonderful context for a conversation—staring out together at the road, matching your sentences to the rhythms of the pedals—and Tim and I have chatted a lot over the course of the past few days. But today, all Tim will say is, "I tried to bury the hatchet, and it got buried in my back."

And then it ends, as mysteriously as it began. One morning we board the van and Tim and Kim are sitting together again, laughing as though the rift never happened. That night, at an expat bar in Hoi An, our tour guide, Scott, sidles up to Rebecca and me just as we're finishing kicking ass in a foosball match against a pair of Israeli backpackers. "Do you know what the deal was with those two?" he asks in his Australian drawl. He nods toward the Canadians. We glance over and see them happily canoodling in a booth on the far side of the room. "No clue," I say to Scott.

Scott proceeds to regale us, a bit too gleefully, with tales of relationships gone awry on his tours. One poor fellow was planning to propose while on a tour with his girlfriend, and even enlisted Scott's help in setting up a romantic sunset dinner. Then the chap learned that his gal had been secretly getting it on with another guy in the tour group.

Rebecca and I have had occasional arguments since we left D.C., but they've all been trifling and brief—generally over in the course of an afternoon. Still, I'm glad whatever flare-ups we've endured have occurred far outside the hothouse atmosphere of a package tour. The group dynamics of these things are strange enough as it is.

Which gets me wondering about Scott. He's been leading these tours for ten years now and lives his whole life inside their bizarre bubble. It seems like a job that, if you do it too long, might permanently warp your conception of travel. A classic permanent drifter, Scott tells us he hasn't been home to Australia in years. He also says he hasn't taken a single day off from guiding in the past six months.

On the plus side, he gets to ride a bicycle through various beautiful destinations, date cute Vietnamese women, eat delicious food, and go out on the town night after night. All of which seems delightful, if exhausting.

Every two weeks, though, he's forced to meet a fresh batch of total strangers. He must immediately befriend every one of them—whether he likes them or not. Because they're paying him.

As a result, Scott has developed an ability to be all things to all people. He flatters each of us in targeted ways. When he finds himself in conversation with the yuppie Canadians, he dusts off his trove of information about Vietnamese history and culture. Later that night, when he's out with the Aussie blokes, he morphs himself into a hearty drinking buddy—talking sports and matching the lads beer for beer.

He's not allowed to show boredom, though he's done this exact same trip at least six times before. He's never allowed to be tired, cranky, or unsociable. He's on stage every moment of the day.

By the end of the tour, his scatter of strangers will have transformed into a flock of friends. In fact, it's happening right now. We've stopped for the night in an old French colonial guesthouse. Tim has lit a fire in the cozy library on this chilly evening, and one of the Australian boys has produced a bottle of whiskey. We recount some of the vivid moments we've shared. We realize we've grown fond of each other's quirks. It's a lot like summer camp. We even promise to keep in touch when we return to our real lives.

But this *is* Scott's real life. At the end of the two weeks, he'll say good-bye and promptly wipe us from his memory. The last night of the tour will be a warmhearted, maudlin affair. And then morning will come, a new group will arrive, and Scott will start from scratch—with a stilted icebreaker dinner where he'll strive to learn everyone's name. The next day, he'll take the tour group to the Ho Chi Minh Museum and pretend like it's not the fifteenth time that he's been there.

The wonderful thing about extended travel—the whole lifestyle, with the come-and-go friendships and the rootless freedom—is that it breaks you out of ruts you've carved in your everyday life. But when you never stop traveling, travel itself becomes a rut. At some point, you're no longer gaining a richer perspective on your life. It's more like you're running away.

AS an American who's watched pretty much every Hollywood depiction of the Vietnam War, I find it difficult to gaze out on the rice paddies and thick jungles here without picturing a platoon of camouflaged soldiers marching through, or an olive green chopper chocka-chocka-ing down to pick up wounded. I'm trying to stop. Those things happened forty years ago. Vietnam is now one of the world's fastest-growing economies—a place where people look forward, not back.

Still, the history is all around. We've visited Ho Chi Minh's war bunker. We've cycled through Hue, the old citadel town that saw a brutal, monthlong battle in which more than two hundred Americans and five thousand Vietnamese died. We've been to China Beach, in Da Nang, where American servicemen took their R&R.

I've been reading a copy of Michael Herr's *Dispatches*—the ultimate you-are-there take on the Vietnam War, based on Herr's work as a correspondent for *Esquire*. (I bought it from a street vendor in Hanoi for about forty cents. It's a fake: a stack of photocopied pages bound together in a vague approximation of a paperback book.) There's a passage where Herr describes rolling into Hue in a military convoy. "Hundreds of refugees held to the side of the road as we passed," he writes, "many of them wounded. The kids would laugh and shout, the old would look on with that silent tolerance for misery that made so many Americans uneasy, which was usually misread as indifference. But the younger men and women would often look at us with unmistakable contempt, pulling their cheering children back from the trucks."

As we cycle through small towns here, the kids still laugh and shout at us. They come running out from their concrete houses to wave, shout "hello," and hold out their hands to slap us five. (Sometimes they miss and hit our handlebars, sending us wobbling off the road until we recover.) In one larger village, kids lined the road for a hundred yards or so. "It's like the bloody Tour de France," shouted one of the Australian lads as we sped through the gauntlet, acknowledging our fans.

Contrary to Herr's experience, the adults are also friendly. They smile warmly at us as we pass. When we stop to buy tea at roadside stands, people invite us to use the toilets in their little houses. It occurs to me that the middle-aged Vietnamese we see would have been children back when Herr was riding in that convoy.

"It's sort of surprising they're so nice to westerners, after everything that's happened," Tim reflected one day as we cycled along.

"Maybe it's because they won," I theorize. "No insecurities here. They whupped France, and then when France tagged out they whupped America, too. So they're, like, 'Hey, losers! Welcome back! Now spend some money.'"

WE'RE coming into the homestretch of the bike tour. I'm fitter and stronger—to the extent that I can now bike for ten miles breathing calmly through my nose. I have little trouble staying within hailing distance of the front of the pack so long as we're riding on flat ground. I've also discovered a cheat: I covertly take some pseudoephedrine-infused cold medicine before each ride, for an energy boost.

It's the hills, though, that separate the wheat from the chaff. I can't keep pace with the quicker riders when we hit an incline—even with the aid of my performance-enhancing substance. It's been galling me.

The Australian blokes go out drinking every night and stumble into the van each morning looking like corpses. "Where were you last night?" I'll ask them. "We were at this duuuubious bar," they'll drawl, "and then we met these girls...." The story goes on from there. I figure there's no way they'll be able to bike in this condition, but they always hop right on and start pedaling happily. At the day's first checkpoint, they'll smoke a cigarette. At lunch, they'll drink a couple of beers, toasting each other with "Up your bum!" and "Here's blood in your undies!" And yet none of it matters—I'm no match for them the moment we start climbing.

Our last big challenge is to bike over the Dran Pass, in southern Vietnam. It's fifteen miles of switchbacks up steep mountainside. I'm determined to make it all the way to the top without giving up, and to keep pace with the lead group.

Just halfway up, though, and already dropping behind, I have nothing left in the tank. I can see the pack of Canadians and Aussies five switchbacks above me. There are another ten switchbacks between them and the summit. I find myself whispering, "Right, left, right, left," as I pump the pedals. I'm in the lowest gear, moving slower than I would if I got off and walked.

When you're struggling on a bike, it's amazing how attuned you become to things like wind direction and velocity. Or small bumps in the road. Or tiny changes in the grade of the ascent. In a car, you don't notice this stuff at all. But each time the breeze shifts into my face, or the hill gets a tick steeper, I become acutely aware of the adverse effect on my quadriceps.

Three-quarters of the way up, the support van passes me with all the quitters inside. Rebecca leans out the window and waves. I'm expecting a "Way to go!" or a "Keep it up!" but instead she shouts, "It's really comfortable in the vaaaaaaaan!" as the vehicle turns a corner out of sight.

At this very moment, it begins to rain. A tropical rain with thumb-thick drops. My pedals and handlebars are getting slippery, but the rain feels wonderful on my scorching muscles. After a few minutes, the downpour stops. I glance around and realize that I've in fact climbed up through the rain cloud, and am now looking down on it from above. The valley below is filled to its brim with swirling fog.

When the summit comes into view ahead, the faster finishers are waiting there for me, cheering me on. All sensation in my legs has ceased. I am now pure distillate of will. It's not a race against the clock or an opponent—it's a race against loss of consciousness due to exertion.

At last I reach the peak, to a chorus of huzzahs. I manage to untangle my aching limbs from my bike just before the whole jumble topples over. I slump exhausted onto a stone wall at the edge of the road as one of the Aussies hands me a beer. He'd stashed them in a cooler in the van before we left this morning, declaring them a reward for any among us who conquered the mountain. "Good on you, mate," he says, clapping me heartily on the shoulder.

The beer is ice-cold. I swallow it down in about four seconds. It may well be the most delicious beer I've ever had. Or perhaps I'm just tasting my own endorphins.

We've covered a lot of ground making our way around the world. Yet none is sweeter than the ground I just covered under my own power. Again I'm reminded that when it comes to travel, the slower you go, the more you appreciate where you've gone.

THE traffic-choked roads that lead into Saigon would be dangerous and wretched for us to bike on, so for the final leg of our trip we ride in the van. As we creep deeper and deeper into the central city, the density of motorbikes becomes almost dizzying. We watch them zip past, swirl around us, and disappear down off-ramps and onto side streets.

I've decided my favorite make of motorbike is the Honda Super Cub, which I admire for its classic, utilitarian look. This iconic little 50 cc workhorse was first manufactured in the late 1950s. We've seen them all over Vietnam, new and old, shiny and rusted. Thanks mainly to its enduring popularity in Asia, the Super Cub has become the best-selling motorized vehicle of all time.

Tiger—the spritely, Saigon-born tour guide trainee who's joined us as Scott's intern for the last few days of the trip—tells us that he owns not one but two motorbikes. Most of his Vietnamese friends own two motos, as well. The first is a knock-around bike for daily use. "Made in China. Two hundred dollars," explains Tiger. The other is a formal, out-on-the-town bike. "For picking up girls. Or maybe for taking on a long holiday." Tiger says the fancier bikes are generally Japanese made and range in price from two thousand dollars up to nine thousand and beyond. Their owners touch up their paint every weekend to keep them looking tip-top.

Motorbike traffic in Hanoi and Saigon has become so overwhelming that Vietnam's Ministry of Public Security experimented with restricting the number of motos to one per person. The rule was eventually struck down, though, and in Saigon alone there are now one thousand additional motorbikes registered each day. A local magazine quotes a British expat describing the chaos that reigns on the streets: "I can never guess who or what will appear in front of my motorbike—another motorbike, a pedestrian, a dog, or even a buffalo."

If getting a bicycle means freedom in Vietnam, then getting a motorbike is the dawning of the Age of Aquarius. Compared to the 3 mph pace of a pedestrian, or the 10–12 mph pace of a cyclist, a motorbike that clips along at 35 mph is a warp-speed spaceship. And they're highly functional: Young families here treat their motos like station wagons. I've seen a mom, dad, and three kids all precariously balanced on a single 50 cc scooter.

I've also noticed that women solo-piloting motorbikes look incredibly fetching. It's that blank, aloof expression—suggesting icy confidence—as they focus on the road ahead. Also, their skirt hems rustle suggestively in the breeze. True, many female riders here wear surgical masks to combat the air pollution, but even this conveys a sort of sci-fi sexiness. It's like there's a zombie virus spreading through the city, and they're racing to meet their lovers in the quarantine zone.

THE final night of the trip, the whole group goes out for good-bye drinks. We quickly lose the Aussie blokes, who've split off in search of romance. The retired ladies are early to bed. It's down to Yukihide, Kim and Tim, and Rebecca and me. We order a last round on the rooftop of the Rex Hotel, not far from the Continental—the lovely French colonial grande dame where Graham Greene lived for a time, and which he used as the setting for several parts of *The Quiet American*.

Looking out from our rooftop perch onto downtown Saigon, we can sense the lingering differences between northern and southern Vietnam. Up north, Hanoi has the somber Ho Chi Minh memorials, and the city still feels like it's still not entirely at ease with capitalism. Aside from the western hotels, the buildings are for the most part simple and modest. And good luck finding much in the way of high-end retail. Meanwhile, here in the south, Saigon has blazed an enthusiastic course toward flashy modernity. Several tall towers spike out of its skyline, and there's oodles of brand-name shopping. I imagine this is what Bangkok must have looked like twenty-five years ago, as it began to mushroom into the metropolis it's now become.

We're all exhausted from the cumulative abuses of two weeks of cycling. And the alcohol isn't helping. When Yukihide nods off at the table, we decide it's our cue to call it a night. *"Ohayou gozaimasu,"* I murmur into Yukihide's ear ("good morning"), and he blinks his eyes open with a chuckle. We all pay our bill and stumble back to our hotel.

The next day, most of the tour group heads for the airport. Rebecca and I aren't sure where we'll go tomorrow, but almost everyone else in the group knows precisely where they'll be first thing tomorrow morning: back at their desks in Australia, battling culture shock and attempting to achieve a stable reentry into their lives. For a few nights after they get back home, the Aussie lads will give a Vietnamese-style *"Mot, hai, ba, yo!"* toast at the pub (translation: "One, two, three, in!"). But soon enough they'll revert to "Up your bum!" Within a few weeks, all will be back to business as usual.

Meanwhile, Rebecca and I—to the burning but good-natured envy of the others, who've only just found their traveling rhythm—will keep right on rolling. We're on a voyage, not a vacation. We've already memorized "hello" and "thank you" in Khmer, preparing for our arrival in Cambodia.

*　　*　　*

THE twelve-dollar bus from Saigon to Phnom Penh, the capital city of Cambodia, is quick and hassle-free. It's less than 150 miles between the cities. Our fellow passengers seem to be mostly local middle-class families. The bus driver handles the border crossing, taking our passports from us and expediting the process.

The moment we cross into Cambodia, the poverty becomes brutally evident. Where huts in Vietnam were often concrete blocks, here they're sticks and mud. Many huts are lifted high up on stilts, with brown floodwaters lapping at the ground beneath them. Naked children run through the puddles, their flanks smeared with dirt.

When we reach a river, Rebecca's GPS map indicates that there should be a bridge. But there is no bridge. It's washed away. Our bus rolls onto an incredibly dodgy-looking ferry, which floats us to the other side—along with at least a hundred motorbikes, pressed together in every open space on the boat's outside deck.

On the way into Phnom Penh, we pass one of the sites known collectively as the "killing fields." From 1975 to 1979, the Khmer Rouge government executed hundreds of thousands of Cambodians at places like this, burying the bodies in mass graves. The regime's aim was a return to "Year Zero"—a mythical, utopian age before ideas like capitalism and industrialization screwed everything up. Achieving this end apparently required the Khmer Rouge to murder most of their countrymen. Phnom Penh itself (being a city, and thus a symbol of evil modernity) was almost completely emptied as part of a forced evacuation of more than 2 million people. The city has gradually come back to life, and recently even turned into a bit of a tourist destination.

We arrive in Phnom Penh just before sunset and check into the Hotel Cambodiana. From our top-floor room we have a stunning view of a bend in the Mekong River. Tiny wooden fishing boats trawl the waters, powered by outboard motors or, in some cases, paddles.

Downstairs, the hotel's casino is hopping. We start placing bets on the roulette wheel. A waitress comes by with fruity drinks. We can't say no. All around us, packs of male Vietnamese tourists are gambling and chain-smoking with equal intensity. They're much richer than their Cambodian neighbors, and it seems the Vietnamese guys treat Phnom Penh as a sort of Tijuana.

Up on the stage, there's a Filipino cover band called Clyxx. Filipino cover bands—like eastern European sex workers—appear to be one of the world's few endlessly renewable resources. I've seen Filipino disco combos in Amsterdam, Dubai, Los Angeles ... wherever there's a call for bland Billboard hits, they will magically appear.

When Clyxx wraps up its performance, a man dubbing himself "Asia's Tom Jones" takes the stage. He is indeed Asian and indeed a dead ringer for Tom Jones. He wears a giant gold cross beneath his unbuttoned, flowing silk shirt. He of course opens his set with "It's Not Unusual." Rebecca, by now drunk on all manner of tropical beverages, glances around at the bloop-bleeping casino games, the shit-faced Vietnamese dudes, the skimpily clad Cambodian cocktail waitresses, and the creepy-looking European men who all look like police sketches of wanted pedophiles. She ponders the fact that this hotel, built in 1962, witnessed the exodus of the entire city some thirty-five years ago, and the subsequent return of human life to Phnom Penh.

"It's not unusual. It happens every day," sings Asia's Tom Jones.
"It's a little fucking unusual," mumbles Rebecca.

WE'VE traveled enough now that I'm growing inured to the exotic and shocking—the feral animals on the loose, the naked beggar children filling the sidewalks, the millions of moto-rickshaws careening around the streets. None of it fazes me anymore. The fact is, though, Cambodia is the least-developed country we're likely to visit on this trip. It's a bit of a wild frontier and, as such, tends to attract a slightly different flavor of western tourist. My amateur research reveals that the western crowd here comprises two main categories:

First, the backpackers. These budget travelers come in search of crazy-cheap accommodations, a taste of adventure, and—perhaps above all—marijuana. Strolling around the backpacker district in Phnom Penh, I'm approached at least three separate times by Cambodian dealers whispering, "Good smokes? I have good smokes."

There's a strange economy in the backpacker district. Rooms are two dollars for the night. Pot is essentially free, as it seems there's always someone passing around a joint. But a dog-eared, fifteen-year-old English-language Tom Clancy paperback will run you a whopping five bucks. I suppose it's just supply and demand.

The cheapest backpacker hostels are clustered on the banks of a swollen lake. We wander into the grounds of a two-dollar-per-night guesthouse and find them completely flooded. A small fish jumps out of the foot-deep murk, splashes back down, and disappears. A kid returning to his room has trouble opening his door because of the lake water stacked up against it. When he finally succeeds, he sends a thick, rippling wave coursing across the courtyard. On the veranda above, two blazed-out kids watch a Hollywood movie on DVD, smoking yet another bowl.

"Maybe they should call this place 'the chilling fields,'" I say to Rebecca. "You're going to hell," she says, taking my hand and leading me back toward civilization. The gin and tonic I later order at the Raffles Hotel—in an attempt to wash all tang of backpacker from my system—costs enough to house one of those stoned rangers in a fleabag hostel for a full two weeks.

As for the other class of tourist we've noticed here . . . How can I put this most delicately? They are pedophiles.

Just yesterday, on the TV in our hotel room, we saw a news report about yet another European pedophile getting arrested in Southeast Asia. It seems to happen all the time. I suppose they're attracted by the warm climate, the low cost of living, and the destitute, easily exploitable youth.

Granted, I can't prove that the western men we've been seeing around Phnom Penh are pedophiles. They could be honest business-men drawn to an emerging market. But my gosh, if ever anyone looked like a pedophile, it's these dudes we've been seeing lounging by the pool at our hotel and prowling the nearby shopping mall food court where the kids hang out. These guys have their own sort of uniform: dandruffy hair; thick plastic eyeglasses; socks with sandals; and nervous, darting eyes.

Back home in D.C., Rebecca and I will sometimes play the old "punch-buggy" game when we happen to spot a Volkswagen Beetle. There are very few cars in Cambodia, so it's harder to play the game here. But at one point, as we walk down a Phnom Penh street,

Rebecca jabs my shoulder. "Punch-pedophile," she whispers. I look up just as we pass another sketchy-looking dude slithering his way toward the shopping mall.

IT'S a six-hour bus ride to Siem Reap, home of the famed temple complex known as Angkor Wat. The passengers on the bus seem evenly split between western tourists and locals. A TV hanging from the bus ceiling shows a bizarre Chinese spy movie, dubbed into Khmer. Rain has turned the roadway into mush, and the bus driver swerves to miss cows, water buffalos, and bicyclists slogging through the mud alongside the road.

We tour Angkor Wat the next day on the back of a "remorque-moto." This is an ordinary motorbike rigged to tow a specially fitted carriage. (Though similar, it is not to be confused with the Thai "tuk-tuk" or Indian "auto-rickshaw," which are integral three-wheeled vehicles—not motorbikes with towing harnesses.) Our remorque driver, Darith, says he rents his vehicle from a central clearinghouse for two dollars per day, and then lets the tourist hotels book him out at twelve dollars per day. Subtracting his fuel costs, and the hotel's fat take, he takes home about one or two bucks each night. But that's before tips. A single generous tourist will sometimes more than double Darith's weekly income with a folded bill.

Which gives you some idea of how vital the tourism industry is to Siem Reap. With Cambodia emerging from its dark past, this UNESCO World Heritage site has blossomed into a trendy destination. Older, richer tourists have begun to flood in alongside the backpackers. Projections suggest that soon, Angkor Wat will host 3 million visitors each year.

Walking through these temples, hidden behind the vines of a misty jungle, it's easy to feel like an archaeologist stumbling upon a lost civilization. But as happens with anything wonderful that everyone wants to see, it's not enough simply to see it. There also needs to be a gift shop, and a nice upscale restaurant, and a five-star room to sleep in. Luxury hotels are encircling Siem Reap like the vines encircling the temples. A fancy golf course is now under construction at the edge of town.

Still, a bohemian, backpacker ethos has survived in some outposts. On Siem Reap's main tourist drag, there's an eatery called Ecstatic Pizza. The logo is a crazed, swirly-eyed face. Our understanding is that if we ask our waiter to bring us the "happy pizza," the pie will arrive with marijuana baked into the cheese.

"Happy?" asks the waiter when we order. "Or *happy* happy?"

"*Happy happy* happy," I answer without hesitation.

The other tables are all young westerners, and there's a mischievous camaraderie in the air. It feels like a den of thieves. Mellow, giggly thieves.

Cannabis is in fact a traditional element in Khmer cuisine (pizza, not so much) and our pie is delicious—especially all those clumps of fibrous, green matter. We finish up, pay the bill, and walk swiftly to our hotel. We're hoping to get home before the weed takes hold and scrambles our sense of direction. We'd prefer we not end up lost and stoned in the jungle at night.

The sensation hits soon after we get back to our room. It is wonderful. Rebecca eventually gets drowsy and drifts off to sleep, but I lie awake in bed with the warm night air wafting through the open window. My hazy thoughts turn to home, for the first time in a long while.

I miss friends and family, and I'd love to chat with them. But if I dialed them right now from the hotel phone on the nightstand, the conversation would be hopeless. My head space—heightened by the weed and the floaty mood of the traveler—would surely be too far removed from theirs to find a common wavelength.

I ponder what else I've left behind. After all this time on the road, living out of a backpack and drifting town to town, it occurs to me that I've begun to lose my attachments to things and places. The town I grew up in, the town I supposedly live in: They are becoming just two more dots on the map. The clothes, furniture, and mementos that we carefully placed in storage before we left D.C.: I wouldn't care one whit if they all burned to ash and blew away. With equal parts pride and concern, I realize I'm transforming into a juggernaut. I'm rumbling across the map, forever in transit. Motion is my new identity.

I don't remember falling asleep. Eventually, I dissolve into an almost comically symbolic dream. I'm in a car, driving on a wide highway into Washington. We have made it all the way around the earth, and these are the final few miles. But when I reach the city, I can't find a parking space. The lots are full, the meters all taken. I keep circling the car, around and around, until I wake up with a start.

It's morning. I hear a rooster crowing. The tinny horn of an impatient motorbike. Foreign sounds—but I can't for the life of me recall where I am. China? Vietnam? It's all beginning to pile up and blur.

It's not until I've limped into the shower and let the lukewarm water cascade over my skull that I manage to click things back into place inside my brain.

WE hire a car and driver to take us to the border with Thailand. It's ninety miles, but it takes a full three hours because of the road conditions. The highway is little more than a muddy blotch, ribboning its way through flooded fields.

(The backpacker rumor holds that local airlines bribe the Cambodian government to keep this road in disrepair. The airlines do a thriving business flying tourists in from Bangkok to see Angkor Wat. It's a relatively short, 230-mile trip, so if the highway were safer and smoother more tourists might drive or take a bus instead of boarding a plane.)

Our hired Camry sloshes back and forth between the ditches on either side of the road. There are people trudging through the mud, holding their shoes in their hands. There are animals everywhere. We are in grave danger of T-boning a cow.

When we come up too fast behind a stopped car, our driver slams the brakes. But we slide right into the car's rear bumper with a thud. The car's driver gets out to complain, but our own driver laughs and honks his horn. He chunks his shifter into reverse, disentangles us from the bumper, and then pulls around the shouting fellow and keeps right on motoring. Not long after, we approach a narrow bridge. A child beggar is blocking the entrance, his hands clasped in prayer. Our driver doesn't slow down one notch. The beggar kid matadors out of the way at the last possible instant, hands still folded.

A few miles later, we pull to a stop at the side of the road. The driver wordlessly opens his door, walks a few steps, and starts peeing into the ditch. (I keep expecting D.C. taxi drivers to pull this maneuver on K Street, but it's never actually happened.)

The demon driver drops us off at the border checkpoint, where the guards give us no trouble. I note a small pang of remorse at having left the chaos of Cambodia behind us. From here on out, the countries we pass through will almost certainly be tamer.

We find a Thai cabbie on the other side who's willing to drive us the remainder of the way into Bangkok. The roads on the Thai side are paved and wide, with painted lane markers and a median strip. Before long, we can see the city's evening skyline twinkling to life.

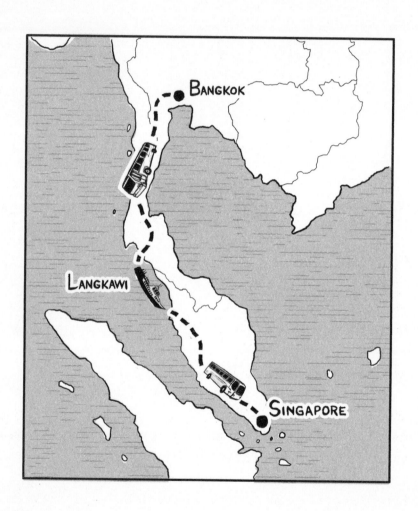

Chapter Seven

Bangkok to Singapore

T HE last time I was in Bangkok, several years ago, I accidentally stumbled onto a cockfight. A bunch of shouting men were betting money on the outcome. The roosters viciously pecked at each other's necks. I considered laying down a few baht on the larger rooster (he had the look of a champion about him) but in the end refrained out of a vague moral discomfort.

Bangkok still has its share of developing-world nuttiness. The knockoff street markets sell "Beebok" running shoes. The shantytowns in the vacant lots feature small-scale animal husbandry. There's an entire sex district catering specifically to Japanese men.

Having just come from Phnom Penh, though, Bangkok feels like Denver. Its grimier scenes are mostly hidden behind sleek new shopping malls and office towers. You might glimpse them from far above, as you whoosh by on an elevated light-rail line.

Given its plush environs and speedy broadband, Bangkok makes a perfect base for plotting the next legs of our trip. There's been no need to plan too far ahead when we're moving on dry land—since frequent train and bus services cover most of our route, and we could always rent a car in a pinch. The problem is, we're about to run out of land.

We can push another thousand miles south on terra firma— down to the bottom of the Malaysian peninsula. We can then cross a bridge to the island of Singapore. But there, all roads and railways end. We'll need to find ourselves a conveyance that floats.

We log on and start searching. It turns out that several shipping company websites track current locations and planned ports of call for active cargo freighters—a sort of digital edition of the shipping news. Sifting through them, we can identify most of the container ships scheduled to pass through Singapore's harbor in the next few months.

Very few of these freighters are equipped, or permitted, to handle civilian passengers. (Most online shipping sites are designed to help you send a container full of knitwear, not send yourself.) But we manage to find a freighter called the *Theodor Storm* that has welcomed aboard passengers in the past and will be sailing out of Singapore in a couple of weeks, bound for Brisbane, Australia. We send off an e-mail to Hamburg Süd, the 140-year-old German shipping line that operates the *Theodor Storm*, and request a cabin.

Next we look around for a ship that could take us onward from Australia. We spot a French freighter called the *Matisse*—operated by CMA CGM, the world's third-largest shipping company—that's sailing from Brisbane to Auckland. It seems remiss not to include a stop in New Zealand, which we've always wanted to see. We contact CMA CGM's head office in Marseille and book ourselves a cabin.

Once this French freighter has hopscotched us the fifteen hundred miles from Australia to New Zealand, we'll be nearly to the international date line (roughly the midpoint of the Pacific Ocean). But here things will get more complicated. New Zealand has less than one-quarter the population of Australia, and nowhere near the industrial output that moves through Singapore. As a result, it sees a relatively meager amount of container ship traffic. We'll be in a remote corner of the Pacific, and it'll be tough to find a freighter headed our way.

As for passenger liners: There aren't any useful eastbound ferries that depart from Auckland. Because where would they go? There's no bustling demand for a commuter service to, say, the tiny Pacific island of Rarotonga.

We start searching through international cruise line schedules. Cruises are meant to be self-contained vacations—not a practical means of getting from point A to point B—so most cruise ships run circle routes that begin and end in the same port. Still, we figure we might be able to sweet-talk our way onto some cruise ship for a partial segment of its journey.

Regent cruise line's *Seven Seas Mariner* makes port in Auckland and gets to Los Angeles about three weeks later. Seems like a great fit, but with two caveats: 1) The cruise ship departs Auckland only one day after our French freighter is due to arrive there. There's no margin for error, and freighters are notorious for delays—sometimes en route (due to winds or currents) and sometimes while they're still in port (due to snags in the container-loading process). There's a danger the cruise ship might be gone by the time we get to Auckland, and we'd have no way of catching up with it. 2) This is a super-high-end luxury cruise. Absurdly expensive. A budget buster.

Unfortunately there aren't many other viable options for crossing the Pacific that don't involve hopping on a plane. There are no useful-for-our-purposes freighters departing from Auckland in the next several months, and we can't just plan to walk out on a pier and hail a Maori outrigger canoe bound for Honolulu. So I gulp hard and enter my credit card on the cruise line site.

With this pricey leg of the journey arranged, we've now mapped out our basic route all the way to Los Angeles. The restless wanderer in me wishes we could leave our itinerary more open-ended, but long-haul travel over water doesn't lend itself to spontaneity. It turns out it's difficult, bordering on impossible, to hitchhike across an ocean.

BANGKOK'S been a pleasing blend of upscale elegance and scruffy hubbub. We've found a delicious hole-in-the-wall joint with the best tom kha gai soup Rebecca's ever tasted. Meanwhile, I've managed to watch my Red Sox win the World Series, catching the final game on satellite TV in the juice bar of a swanky fitness club. I had to beg the waiter to tune in the channel, and was the only person paying any attention to the game. The fashionable Thai women sitting near me—fresh off their treadmills, sipping pomegranate smoothies—glanced at me warily when I shouted and pumped my fist after a key home run.

But it's come time for Rebecca and me to start making some

progress toward Singapore again. We mustn't lose our momentum now. We zip up our packs, throw them over our shoulders, and put on our travel faces.

The Bangkok train station is nothing like the madhouse we encountered in Beijing. In fact, it's rather empty, which is refreshing. I'm envisioning a relaxing overnight ride to Malaysia.

And then a uniformed man sticks his face in mine. "Where you go?" he demands. "Train is canceled." This is suddenly less relaxing.

The man's uniform's a bit shabby, and I convinced myself he's running some sort of scam. Having persuaded us there's no train, he'll offer us a ride to Malaysia in his cousin's minivan. For a fee.

We ignore him, step past him into the station's main vestibule, and head for the ticket window designated for foreigners. It now becomes clear that this is no scam. Several other uniformed men are breaking the bad news to other travelers. The woman at the ticket window informs us that there's a rail workers strike.

There are no Thai people waiting in the train station, which makes sense, seeing as how all the trains have been canceled. As for the western backpackers in the station—slowly coming to grips with the fact that they won't be toking up on a Thai beach before the sun sets tonight—they've congealed into a miserable-looking glob. They've sprawled out on their bags in the middle of the hall and appear to be waiting for someone to rescue them.

Rebecca and I find a table at the station's café and begin poring through our guidebooks to figure out the Thai intercity bus system. An American nearby overhears us plotting and pulls up a chair. He's a laid-back Texan, also headed for Malaysia, and he seems to consider the rail strike a delightful opportunity for improvisation. "We just need to beat that crew to the punch," he drawls, nodding at the puddle of sad backpackers. "Or there won't be any bus tickets to go around."

We determine that the southern Bangkok bus depot is the one we want, and the three of us share a taxi that whisks us there in minutes. At the depot, we find the chaos that was unexpectedly absent from the train station. Hundreds of Thais, and a handful of in-the-know westerners, are desperately attempting to replace their canceled trains with comparable buses. We quickly lose our Texan in the teeming crowd.

The harried clerk at the ticket window speaks no English, but I manage to buy two tickets on a bus I believe to be headed south. My key tactic was to point to Malaysia on a map I pulled out of my backpack. But now I realize, as I look at the map again, it's possible that I was actually pointing to Myanmar. If our bus gets stormed by protesting monks, we'll know what went wrong.

BUSES are perhaps the least romantic mode of surface transport. Ships and trains maintain a classic allure. The automobile has its passionate cult. But you rarely hear anybody rhapsodizing about a bus trip. You're far more likely to hear bus-related horror stories.

My own: While traveling in Ecuador I caught a rural bus headed for a tiny beach town on the Pacific coast. There was no room left inside—people were sitting on laps and standing hip to hip in the aisle—so the driver directed my friend and me to a ladder on the back of the bus. We climbed up onto the vehicle's roof, where we rode atop an enormous pile of strapped-down luggage. The bus rumbled along dirt roads at 40 mph, and we clung for dear life to random suitcase handles. I couldn't see through the dust and was nearly decapitated when we passed beneath a low-hanging electrical wire.

Traditionally, the reason to go by bus—besides the wild thrill of unpredictability—is that buses are much cheaper than a train or plane. In exchange for this inexpensive fare, you accept a markedly lower quality of life. Most bus companies cram more seats into the cabin than seems physically practicable. There's no room to cross your legs, and barely room to possess legs at all. No matter how far you sit from the rear restroom, your nostrils will at some point make you acutely aware of its presence.

It's true that flying economy class on a plane is not much less claustrophobic. But the average airplane interior is cleaner and brighter than the inside of a bus. And if you've ever spent time in a Greyhound depot on a Saturday night, you'll agree it's a significantly seedier scene than the one going on at the airport. I'm sort of afraid to use bus station vending machines for fear of catching gonorrhea.

As for trains, there's no comparison at all. Most trains' seats are roomier, their aisles wider, and their ride smoother. You can walk a train's length if you're feeling restless—a move that, while possible on a bus, proves far less satisfying.

None of which is meant to condemn the bus. It's still a noble chariot. It conveys the masses cheaply and to places that trains and planes can't or won't access.

Once upon a time, buses were even vaguely fashion-forward. Famed industrial stylist Raymond Loewy—who would later design the interior of the Concorde and the paint scheme for the exterior of Air Force One—conceived the Greyhound logo and the look of the company's 1950s-era buses. Dubbed "Scenicruisers," these elegant land yachts featured stewardesses pushing drink carts up and down the aisles.

Consider this assertion from a Smithsonian exhibit on the history of American transportation: "Americans who rode intercity buses in the 1930s and early 1940s were using one of the most convenient, modern, and comfortable forms of motor transportation of the time. Advertisements, movies, and on-board amenities made bus travel seem glamorous and modern. Streamlined design and art deco bus stations added to the allure."

The film *It Happened One Night*, which won the Academy Award for Best Picture in 1934, takes place in large part aboard a Greyhound bus motoring from Miami to New York. While it's made clear that Claudette Colbert's character, an heiress, is traveling well beneath her station (she's trying to go incognito while on the lam from her angry father), the movie depicts an overnight bus ride rife with camaraderie and romantic possibility. The whole bus joins in a sing-along (I challenge you to try this the next time you ride Greyhound), and Colbert ends up fighting for a seat with the hunky Clark Gable.

By 1969, times had changed. Middle-class people generally owned their own cars. Buses—the mode of transport for those too poor to afford a car—came to signify something much grungier than they had before. That year's Oscar winner was *Midnight Cowboy*, which concludes with a bus trip from New York to Florida that's a sort of counterpoint to the cheery bus ride in *It Happened One Night*. This time the mood is less Clark Gable and more Dustin Hoffman. His character—a greasy, tubercular bum named Ratso Rizzo—dies aboard the bus, in the back row of seats, in the arms of a male hustler.

Things may have come full circle of late, as the bus seems poised to enter another golden age. Several recently launched bus lines—including BoltBus, operated by good old Greyhound—now offer cheap but comfortable service up and down America's northeast corridor. The key selling point remains price, as these bus tickets are hundreds of dollars cheaper than the equivalent fare on a train or plane. But there's something else: an attempt to rebrand bus travel for a new generation. These newer bus lines have attracted a more youthful, upscale passenger by including amenities like wireless Internet access and electrical outlets for laptops. Nationwide bus ridership actually increased from 2006 to 2008—marking the first uptick in forty years.

The bus we're riding on now, going from Bangkok toward Thailand's southern border, boasts an even more radical reimagining of bus possibilities. It's a luxury coach. Each seat features a personal video viewer stocked with current Hollywood films. The seats themselves are spacious and sumptuous and almost fully reclinable. The other passengers on board seem to be a mix of young Thai businessmen traveling for work and middle-class Thai families setting off on vacation.

We should have no trouble falling asleep on the overnight ride. Our only real concern is for our safety. There are no seat belts (as on most buses), and we're sitting at the extreme front end of the double-decker, on its upper level. There's nothing in front of us but a wide pane of glass.

"If we crash," says Rebecca, "please tell my parents I loved them."

"If we crash," I say, "you can tell them yourself. You're going through that windshield, and you're not stopping until you land in Sarasota."

THE bus arrives early the next morning in the town of Satun, on the Thai west coast, just north of the Malaysian border. From the bus station we take a *songthaew*—a taxi fashioned from a pickup truck, with benches welded onto the bed—a few miles to a boat dock. Here we catch a small, empty ferry that plows southwest through the choppy waters of the Andaman Sea. After a ninety-minute passage, it docks at a marina on the Malaysian island of Langkawi.

Langkawi has powdery beaches, a jungle interior, and five-star resorts. With plenty of time to relax before we need to catch our freighter down in Singapore, we decide to settle into this quiet paradise. On the porch of our hotel room, we pop open two bottles of beer and gaze at the ocean.

Within minutes, a squadron of macaque monkeys interrupts us. They storm our porch railing, begging us for food. I swear they're strategically shoving their cutest baby monkey front and center to win our affection. And it's working: Rebecca can't resist tossing them a few crackers from the minibar.

As soon as they scamper off, another band of primates swings into some trees overhanging the beach. The hotel's guest pamphlet identifies these as "dusky leaf monkeys" and says they are a constant presence around the resort grounds. They're small (about the size of a terrier) and covered in soft black fur—save for a white monocle around each eye, and a wispy white Mohawk. They quietly munch the leaves off the branches they're sitting on. They watch us with placid, curious expressions and are far too dignified to beg us for food like those shameless macaques did. Once they've had their fill of leaf munching, they all swing out of view.

That night at the hotel's outdoor bar, the parade of adorable mammals continues. We notice something leaping between the trees in the lighted grotto. Not quite leaping, though—more like floating. Closer inspection, and further research, reveals that they are small flying critters called colugos. They jump from a high branch, extend their arms and legs to unfold membranous flaps that act like wings, and then glide for what seems an eternity. When they reach a tree seventy-five feet away, they slam on the air brakes and gently alight on the side of its trunk, hooking in with their little claws. They glide back and forth all night, as though doing it purely for our entertainment. It's like watching a troupe of tiny, furry acrobats.

IN the morning, I rent a moto for forty ringgits from a guy in a concrete hut on the side of the road near our hotel. He has just one moto that he rents out—his main business is doing tourists' laundry—and unfortunately the bike doesn't have an automatic transmission. I'm forced to quickly learn how to kick the shifter pedal into the next gear while not toppling over.

I soon get the hang of it, and before long I'm buzzing down a narrow road between coast and jungle, squinting in the wind, occasionally whapping the big, soft leaves that dangle into my path. I lean hard into the curve of a roundabout and take it at top speed. I coast for a moment to read a road sign and then pop into a lower gear and crank my wrist to gun the accelerator. I feel like Steve McQueen—if, instead of a badass, chromed-out motorcycle, Steve McQueen rode a purple, 50 cc scooter.

As our ferry chugged into the harbor yesterday, I'd noticed a posh little marina tucked away in a nearby cove. It's called the Royal Langkawi Yacht Club, and it's where I'm headed now. My mission is to ingratiate myself with any yacht owners I can find there. Rebecca and I have time to work our way slowly down the Malaysian coast, and I'm wondering if I can find someone with a sailboat who's willing to take us partway to Singapore. Maybe as far south as Kuala Lumpur. There's a lot of leisure boat traffic passing through these waters, so perhaps some skipper can be convinced to take on a pair of friendly, able-bodied deckhands.

I park my moto on the sidewalk and step into the yacht club. A young Malaysian woman stands behind the front desk. I ask her—halting and stumbling, because I'm not quite sure of the protocol—if it's okay for me to, like, wander around the yacht club's docks and talk my way onto a boat. "No problem," she says with a smile. "You should talk to my friends. They're on the *Lady Kathleen*." She gives me the slip number.

I walk past ketches and catamarans before arriving at a gray sloop, about forty-five feet long, with "Lady Kathleen" painted on its hull. Two young dudes are hanging out on the deck. The blond guy's strumming an acoustic guitar; the brown-haired guy's doing an effortless set of push-ups. Both are shirtless and deeply tanned.

"Excuse me," I say, interrupting them. "Do you know of anyone sailing south?" After I introduce myself and explain my situation, they welcome me aboard and offer me a seat in the yacht's cockpit, in the shade of the bimini top. The blond one disappears belowdecks then reemerges moments later to hand me a mug of Vietnamese-style coffee with condensed milk.

Mike (the blond-haired guy, who looks about twenty-three) and Forbes (the brown-haired guy, who's a few years older) are both Vancouverites who've been traveling around together in Southeast Asia. They found their way to Langkawi a few weeks back and, soon after arriving, met the American fellow who owns the *Lady Kathleen*. The guy works in the oil industry in Indonesia. He keeps the *Lady Kathleen* berthed here in Langkawi but spends much of his time at a house in Jakarta. When he left Langkawi a few days after Forbes and Mike met him, the oil guy invited them to live on his empty sailboat. They accepted, and ripped up their plane tickets back to Canada.

Now they spend their days lounging on the deck of a yacht—fixtures in this weird little community of marina dwellers. They occasionally pump out the *Lady Kathleen*'s bilge or make light repairs to her rigging. Sometimes they crew in sailboat races at regional regattas. But mostly they play guitar, do push-ups, and get tan.

Forbes was an experienced sailor before he came aboard this boat. His father designed and built a schooner, back in Vancouver, and Forbes himself has refurbished a yacht. While he can't offer to pilot me south on the *Lady Kathleen*—he doesn't want to push his luck by asking the owner for permission—he thinks he might be able to help me by making some introductions. "Come on," he says, "let's take a walk around the docks and see what happens."

Barefoot, still shirtless, a tumbler of iced tea in his hand, Forbes leads me up and down the finger piers. He offers a running commentary along the way, pointing to various boats and exclaiming, "That one is sooooo seaworthy" or "Look how they've got that autopilot rigged." He's hoping to find me a spot on a beautiful trimaran that's been docked here a couple days, but the Canadian guy who owns it says he doesn't feel like going anywhere.

Further efforts are similarly fruitless. Everyone's very cordial—they always invite us aboard their boats and offer us cold beers—but no one's in the mood to, you know, sail. They seem more in the mood to drink. One guy emerges from his yacht's cabin exhibiting visible alcoholic shakes. It's a troubling scene. At this point, Forbes suggests I come back tomorrow to see if I have better luck.

I return the next afternoon, this time bringing along Rebecca on the back of the moto. We shoot the breeze for a while with the boys on the *Lady Kathleen*, and then Forbes and I take another stroll around the marina. Again it turns up nothing. Out of curiosity, I start asking folks if I can pay them a fee to sail me south. Nobody's interested. Chances are, if you're lounging on your yacht in paradise, money's not a major need.

More than that, though, people just don't want to leave. They're having waaaay too much fun. Langkawi has duty-free beer and, as best I can tell, half the boaters here are soused day and night. As Forbes and I head back to the *Lady Kathleen*, we dodge a man riding a fold-up bicycle down the docks. He's just returned from the liquor store, and he's carrying a case of beer under one arm and a bottle of booze in his free hand. As he passes a row of boats, people look up from their paperbacks and wave hello. "They come here not intending to stay," says Forbes, "and then they look up and it's three months later."

We hang out on the *Lady Kathleen* awhile longer, and some other young folks join us—a Brit, an Aussie woman, and a Langkawian who does boat repairs around the marina. We're having such a lovely time that we invite them all back to our hotel for sunset cocktails.

Rebecca and I take the moto—getting caught in a brief tropical downpour, raindrops stinging my eyes—and the rest of them show up in a cab a little later. We call room service and order up a bucket of beers, a bottle of rum, and some plates of food. Everyone's getting tipsy. We spot a hornbill in one of the trees near the porch, and Lee, the Langkawian, tells us he sometimes hunts them with a slingshot. When he gets one, he eats it. "But they mate for life," he says, "so if you kill one, you have to kill the other. You don't want it to be lonely."

"How many piercings do you have?" somebody asks the Aussie woman. She touches one ear and counts, "One . . . two." She turns her head to touch the other ear. "Three." She pauses thoughtfully for a moment, looking downward. "Seven," she says with finality.

The British kid, whose dad owns a yacht berthed at the club, pulls a baggie full of weed from the pocket of his shorts. "This is very bad news here," he says, rolling a joint. "Death penalty." He sparks it up, takes a long toke, and passes it around.

The yachting vibe is infectious. Rebecca and I start fancifully discussing whether we should blow the remainder of our life's savings on buying a boat. We could cruise around from one tropical port to the next. Or just slowly dissipate here in Langkawi. Boats up to forty feet can berth at the marina for three hundred bucks a month. That's a fraction of the price of a nice one-bedroom apartment in D.C.

Forbes is surfing the Web, looking at sailing-related online bulletin boards to see if anyone's seeking crew. He hasn't given up. "I'm gonna get you on a boat!" he says, a bit wild-eyed. When he takes a break to get another beer, I run a quick check of my e-mail.

There's a message from Hamburg Süd in my in-box. The *Theodor Storm*—the freighter we're planning to take from Singapore to Brisbane—is having mechanical problems. It needs to bring engineers on board to fix them. It can't take us to Australia.

This is utterly disastrous news. It plunges me back into reality. We shelled out nonrefundable deposits for the freighter that goes from Australia to New Zealand, and also for the cruise ship that will take us from New Zealand to Los Angeles. It was all lined up in a tight row. But with the first domino fallen, I'm not sure we can catch the next two ships. If we do miss them, we'll be out a truly painful amount of money. (Like, a two-door Japanese hatchback amount of money.) And we'll be stranded halfway across the world from D.C.

I crack another beer and put on a brave face. But I'm panicking inside. The simple truth is that we cannot afford to miss those ships and eat the expensive deposits. If we don't find a surface route to Brisbane in time, we'll have to get there using . . .

It's unspeakable. The entire quest would be ruined. Just the thought of walking through the airport security gate and down that jetway, slumped in defeat, is making me nauseous.

THE next morning, we cut short our Langkawi idyll and hit the road with determination. There's zero time to waste. It's imperative that we find a ship departing from Singapore by the end of this week.

We catch a ferry out of Langkawi to Penang, about eighty miles south down the Malaysian coast. The skies are rainy and the seas are rough, and I'm still hung over from last night's party. A loud Chinese-language action movie plays on a TV bolted to the ship's wall. I'm trying to keep my eyes fixed on the horizon to stave off seasickness, but out the porthole all I can see is rolling gray swells.

In Penang, we head straight for the bus depot. There's just time to scarf down some fried rice from a steamy little stall in a corner of the station before we board another overnight coach. This one calls itself "executive class" and touts its comfy "snoozer seats." They're indeed roomy, but it doesn't matter: I can't fall asleep. My mind is racing, searching for solutions. There must be some good way to get across the Java Sea to Australia.

We arrive in Singapore early the next morning and hit the ground running. I start methodically calling every single port agent in town. Port agents are the folks who sit in little outbuildings down by the docks, managing container ship traffic in and out of the harbor. They know which freighters are in town right now and where the ships are headed next.

Sadly for us, none are going our way. A port agent with a thick Indian accent tells me he only handles ships bound for Calcutta. Another agent only deals with freighters that shuttle north to China. A third guy says he has a ship that goes to Australia, but it gets there too late to catch our freighter out of Brisbane. (In the course of every call, there comes a moment when the agent asks, "Why don't you just fly?")

And then a glimmer. A port agent named Lucy tells me there's a freighter called the *Kamakura* leaving for Fremantle on Sunday. That's the opposite coast of Australia from Brisbane, but we might make it work if we can drive across the Outback at furious speeds. "I need to get on that ship," I say into the phone, trying not to let desperation creep into my voice. Lucy says she'll see what she can do.

Fifteen minutes later, she calls back. It turns out the *Kamakura* is owned by a Japanese firm—the Hachiuma Steamship Company, whose owners have been in the shipping business since 1878. Lucy tells me she spoke to Hachiuma's head office in Kobe and explained the special nature of my request, but it didn't matter. Strict security rules: No civilian passengers. No exceptions.

More calls to port agents, more dead ends. Half the time I can barely understand them through their thick Cantonese accents. I try phoning a few of the big shipping companies in Europe to see where it gets me. But it gets me nowhere. The woman at Hapag-Lloyd cuts me off four words into my spiel. "We don't take passengers," she says, in a stern German accent. "We never take passengers."

I've filled a sheet of paper to its edges with scribbled phone numbers, names of agents and freighters, dates and destinations. I'm losing track of it all. "Alex in Port Kelang. *Bunga Teratai*—chemical tanker." I can't even remember why I wrote this down.

And then, another glimmer: A port agent—about the fifteenth I've called—tells me the freighter *Cape Preston* is leaving from Singapore for Australia in two days. It's owned by Columbia Shipmanagement, based in Cyprus.

Moments later, I'm on the phone long distance to Cyprus. A man named Mr. Borbe patiently listens to my story. I'm at the end of my rope by now, and make an emotional final plea. A few seconds of silence, and then Mr. Borbe says, with great solemnity: "I will try to do this for you." He tells me he'll call back after he's consulted other executives at the company.

I have an excellent feeling about this. There was a warmth that ran through the phone line between us. Mr. Borbe understood me. And I think I like Cyprus. There's that Cypriot tennis player, Marcos Baghdatis—I've always liked his game. Lots of variation and flair. Yes, I think this is going to work.

But Mr. Borbe calls back an hour later with bad news. "I'm so sorry, Mr. Stevenson," he says with deep sympathy. "We can't be doing this."

WE'VE now inquired about pretty much every single freighter in Singapore Harbor, with no luck. We've also looked for cruise ships, public ferries, anything that might take us across the water. Nothing's panned out.

Phileas Fogg dealt with problems like this by throwing money at them. When he's stuck in India, he buys an elephant. Later, he buys a steamship. We lack the necessary scratch to purchase our own freighter, so we'll need to get creative.

After posting the message "Need boat from Singapore to Australia, can anyone help?" on my Facebook page, Rebecca and I take the Singapore metro to a stop by the water, near one of the swankier marinas. A sign there says only members are allowed on the docks, but we hop the gate.

By now, there's no point in even looking at sailboats. They're too slow. At typical speeds of seven or eight miles an hour, they couldn't possibly get us to Brisbane in time. Our only hope is to find someone with a muscular cabin cruiser. A few large powerboats in the marina could do the job, but none of their owners seem to be around.

We take a cable car to Sentosa, an island in Singapore Harbor that hosts a couple of posh yacht clubs. We hop more gates, walk around more docks, but it's a lost cause. Even if we found a fast private boat, the odds are slim that we could convince the owner to taxi us the two thousand miles to Australia, burning a fortune in fuel along the way. I briefly consider stealing a boat—and then remember that I am in Singapore, where spitting your gum out on the ground will basically get you executed.

And so, having exhausted every idea I can generate, I give up. It's over. The quest has failed.

As we take the cable car back from Sentosa, Rebecca looks down and notices a cruise ship moored directly below us in the harbor. There's a Web address printed on its smokestack. She asks me for a pen and writes the URL on her hand.

"We already looked up all the cruise ships on the web," I say, dejected. "None of them work."

"I don't remember seeing this one," she says. "And you never know."

REBECCA goes to look up the cruise ship online while I wallow in our hotel room. I've resigned myself to buying us a pair of plane tickets. I figure we'll fly to Brisbane, finish out the rest of the trip as planned, and then come back at a later date to redo the missing Singapore-to-Australia leg by sea. I tell myself I can save it for later in life, as a project to look forward to. But I know it won't be the same. It will eat at me forever.

Just as I'm about to make a sad shuffle down to the travel agency to ask about flights, Rebecca bursts into the room. "It goes to Australia!" she shouts. "It goes to Australia!"

The ship, called the MV *Van Gogh*, is operated by a small British cruise company. Rebecca's written down the phone number for the booking office in London. The woman there who answers my call tells me she isn't allowed to sell me tickets because Singapore's a way station for the cruise, not an official embarkation point. (This also explains why the ship never popped up in our earlier online searches.) She says we'll need to speak to someone on board the ship and see what they say.

"When does the ship leave harbor?" I ask her.

"Not until tomorrow," she says.

I decide we might as well pop down to the pier right now to get this sorted out, since it's our last chance. Rebecca tosses our passports in her purse, in case we might need them to buy tickets. "Come on!" I bark, hustling her out the door. "I like your sense of urgency," she says with a grin, as we begin our swift walk to the metro and catch a subway train back to the harbor.

When we get to the cruise ship terminal, we get in line with the final few passengers reboarding the ship after having spent the day ashore. A security guard stops us at the metal detectors because we don't have tickets. "I need to talk to someone on the ship," I say.

He takes out his cell phone. "I'm calling Phil, the operations officer." After punching in some numbers, he hands me the phone.

When Phil answers, I immediately launch into my spiel—for the umpteenth time today—noting how far we've come, and what a tragedy it would be for everything to fall apart now. "So," I conclude, "I just really hope we can get on the ship tomorrow."

"Tomorrow?" says a confused Phil, in a crisp English accent. "We leave right now. In fact, we were meant to leave fifteen minutes ago. Anyway, we don't have any empty cabins. I'm sorry, but I'm going to have to hang up now, because we're honestly just about to depart."

"Wait!" I scream. "We have to get on this ship! There has to be some way to let us on this ship! We're right here!" I can see the ship through the terminal's glass window. I squint in an effort to pick out Phil somewhere on deck.

"Well, you can try the London operations office," Phil says doubtfully. I take down the number and then use our cell phone with its local SIM card to call England. I note that the phone's battery is running low. I want to punch myself in the spleen: Not bothering to charge up the phone this morning could be the difference between circumnavigating the earth successfully or not.

Meanwhile, Rebecca realizes that if we're going to get on this ship tonight, one of us must deal with our abandoned luggage sitting back at the hotel. She tells me she's going to catch a taxi, make the ten-minute ride to the hotel, grab our bags while the cab waits outside, and then race right back. I wish her Godspeed. "Wait," I say, as she's turning to go. "You'd better give me my passport. And kiss me good-bye. Just in case." And then she's on her way.

When a man answers at the cruise operations office in London, I pour my soul out through the phone to him. I have never been more earnest in my life. "Please," I conclude, "I hope you can find it in your heart to help me." Somehow, this doesn't sound sappy. He asks me to hold for a moment and then clicks back on.

"Someone's coming for you now," he says.

I hang up. A minute later, I see a vision from on high: a man in a pressed, white cruise ship uniform with golden epaulets. He's jogging toward me from the other side of the security checkpoint. I wave at him. "Mr. Stevenson! Come with me!" yells Phil. "Quickly!"

I pass through the metal detector, hand the immigrations clerk my passport—thank God Rebecca remembered we might need them—and meet up with Phil, who's by now panting heavily. "We've got to run!" he says between breaths. His walkie-talkie crackles: "Phil? Where are you?! We need to go now!"

I push to keep up with him as he sprints down a carpeted hallway, around a corner, and then onto the long, narrow gangway. I'm stumbling over my flip-flops. I hear the cruise ship's horn blow—it almost sounds like it's angry. When we reach the edge of the deck and step aboard, two terminal workers immediately lift the gangplank away behind us.

Phil and I lurch to a stop in the middle of the deck, doubled over, gasping for air. After a few moments, I feel the ship moving.

Phil begins to get his breathing under control. "That's the strangest embarkation I've ever seen," he gasps. "I've never done *anything* like that."

"Neither have I," I say, my heart still racing.

He appraises me for a moment. "Where's your luggage?" he asks.

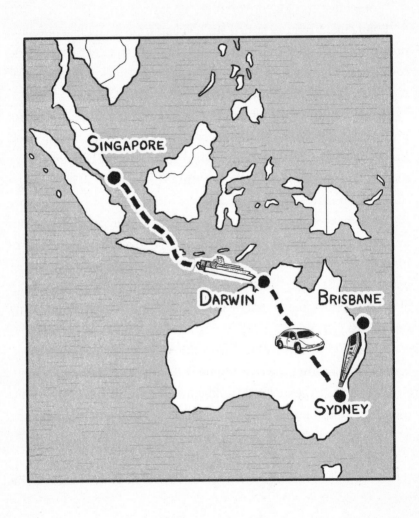

Chapter Eight

Singapore to Brisbane

I'M still catching my breath on the main deck of the *Van Gogh*— with Phil, the cruise ship's operations manager, huff-puffing beside me—when my cell phone rings. It can only be Rebecca, who is no doubt back at our hotel room packing up our bags. I hit the answer button and say, "Hello?"

The phone immediately dies. Out of battery charge.

This is a problem. As far as Rebecca knows, either I didn't get on the ship at all or she'll soon be joining me on board, having retrieved our luggage from the hotel and brought it back to the pier. I smack the back of the cell phone hard against my palm and try to power it back up. As it blinks to life, it immediately rings again.

"Where's our next stop?" I ask Phil, calculating quickly.

"Bali," he says. "Three days from now."

I press to answer the phone and, with not a moment to waste on greetings, yell: "Meet me in Bali!"

"What? I can't hear you!" shouts Rebecca over the scratchy connection. The phone dies again before I can say another word.

"Here, give me your SIM card," says my new best friend Phil. As he pries the back off his phone and subs in my card, he warns, "You don't have a lot of time before you'll lose all signal." I look around. The *Van Gogh* is pulling steadily out to sea.

Phil repowers his phone, my SIM card in place, and there's yet another ring. "I have good news and bad news," I tell Rebecca, once we've established that we can hear each other. "The good news is, they let me aboard the ship."

"I can't believe it," Rebecca says excitedly. "I thought there was no chance! I'm almost done packing our bags—I'll catch a taxi to the terminal now!"

"See, this is the bad news part," I say, watching the docks slowly recede into the distance, an expanse of water filling the space between.

Reader, you may think me a terrible person for abandoning Rebecca alone in Singapore. With all our luggage. (Particularly since it was her sharp eyes that spotted the *Van Gogh*, and her dogged research that determined it was bound for Australia.) I admit I feel twinges of guilt, even now.

But for her part, Rebecca bears no ill will. She considers this a team effort. If one of us makes it around on the ground, we've both succeeded.

As the cell phone signal begins to fade, I wish her a safe flight to Bali and arrange to meet her on the docks there when the *Van*

Gogh arrives. It will be three days at sea for me, three hours in the air for her.

ONCE we've caught our breath, Phil takes me to the ship's administrative desk to get me squared away as an official cruise passenger. Several crew members who'd witnessed our chaotic sprint across the gangway now scurry over, eager for an explanation. Phil and I recount our adventure. Though we met but six minutes ago, we already have the makings of a fine comedy duo—trading riffs, interjecting asides, prodding each other into increasingly animated tale telling. As more crew members gather, we start over from the beginning. My audience is gobstopped by the fact that I've boarded the ship with nothing but the clothes on my back, my wallet, my passport, and the cell phone.

The purser has me fill out a few forms and then hands me the key to my new cabin. She tells me it's the only empty cabin on board. It became available this afternoon—in a miraculous, if slightly macabre, stroke of luck for me—when its elderly inhabitant took gravely ill and was forced to disembark and check in to a Singapore hospital. It turns out this ship is filled almost entirely with British retirees. In the corridor on the way to my room I pass a steady stream of wheelchair-bound passengers.

The cabin itself is a windowless, interior cubby—dim even after I've flipped on the fluorescent ceiling light. I'm still jittery and wired from from my battle to get on board the ship and from the lingering anxiety that I'd be forced to fly. The velocity of those last few crazed minutes has now abruptly downshifted, leaving me feeling caged.

The ship chugs along at its own pace, oblivious to my zappy neurons and fluttering heartbeat.

THE next three days are a bleak interlude. After getting used to having Rebecca at my elbow every day for four months, I suddenly find myself very alone. Traveling solo can be romantic and energizing—the lone traveler moseying down the dusty road—but there's nothing romantic or energizing about a budget cruise ship for old people. I feel untethered without Rebecca here to help me put my thoughts into context, and to assist me in ridiculing these fogeys.

The cruise itself doesn't offer enough distraction to pull me out of my own head. It's a small ship, without many amenities, so there's little to do but lounge in a deck chair all day long. I order a sucession of cold beers from the outside bar and try to drink myself into a nap.

When I'm not sleeping, I watch for green Indonesian islands on the horizon or scan the ocean's shimmering purple surface for schools of flying fish. A dozen of them at once will all suddenly spring from the sea together. They glide through the tropical air for several seconds—their pectoral fins acting as wings—before they knife back into the side of a swell. It tickles me to think of them briefly escaping the watery confines of their universe. I imagine the exhilaration of the unfamiliar air, and the disappointing splashdown into normalcy. (Yes, it occurs to me I may be anticipating my own reentry into real life.)

As I won't be reunited with my luggage until Bali, I've had to buy a toothbrush and other sundries from the ship's small convenience store. Tragically, this store does not sell underwear. I wash out my one pair each night and pull them back on, cold and a bit damp, each morning when I wake up.

With nowhere to buy new clothes, meals are a sartorial fiasco. The dinner dress code calls for jacket and tie, but I am of course still wearing the outfit that I boarded in: flip-flops, battered khaki trousers, and a T-shirt with the word "Cambodia" printed in large letters on the front. (This last was bought in Phnom Penh during a particularly acute laundry shortage.) The first time I arrive at the entrance to the restaurant, the tuxedoed maitre d' recoils at the sight of me. He ponders for a moment and then reluctantly leads me to a table at the extreme rear corner of the room.

The other passengers aboard this U.K.-based budget cruise line are mostly working-class British pensioners. Lots of outdated fashions, lots of chain-smoking. A whole lot of terrifying dental situations. Across from me at the dinner table the maitre d' has chosen for me is a man with a distinctly alcoholic pallor and a tattoo of his wife's name—Brenda—etched onto his forearm. As I sit down, he's bragging about the price he got on a bottle of whiskey at a Singapore liquor store. "He'll drink the other half of it tonight," says Brenda with affection, patting his shoulder. "Oh, he'll be off his head, he will."

I introduce myself to the table and end up again recounting my madcap gangway sprint. When I explain that my ultimate goal is to circle the earth, my tablemates are intrigued—but not overly impressed. This is an around-the-world cruise, starting and ending in

England. By the end of the three-month journey, every geezer here will have circumnavigated. Which slightly deflates my sense of accomplishment.

In classic cruise-ship style, the *Van Gogh* has assigned restaurant seating. This means that once the maitre d' has chosen a place for you, you're stuck at that table for all eternity. Breakfast, lunch, and dinner—with the same set of people—day after day. My tablemates have eaten every meal together for the past several weeks, and the strain shows. One evening, the white-haired man who sits to my left suddenly lifts his head from the paperback novel he's been reading at the table. "How long do we have left on this cruise?" he asks no one in particular. "Eight weeks to go? Jesus Christ, it's like a prison sentence!" When he gets uncomfortable looks in return, he ducks back into his book.

THOUGH it's only three days, I swear it takes weeks for the ship to finally reach Bali. My heart leaps like a flying fish when I sight Rebecca standing on the dock.

As we carry our bags onto the ship, I ask her what it felt like to be in an airplane. But it turns out she doesn't remember at all: She got plastered at the Singapore airport bar in an attempt to subdue her crippling fear of flying. She landed in Bali late last night, somehow drunkenly found herself a hotel, and then caught a cab this morning to meet the *Van Gogh* at the pier.

At dinner that evening, the table buzzes over two new developments. 1) Rebecca has joined us, raising the overall beauty and vivaciousness of the group by orders of magnitude. 2) With my luggage back in my possession, I'm wearing a new outfit for the first time in nine meals.

Group conversation is aided by Rebecca's wise decision to order two bottles of wine and freely share them. The oldest fellow at the table, clearly in his cups, reveals to us (with no small amount of pride) that a few years ago he legally died on a hospital operating table. He had a cardiac arrest and then surged back to life. "It's true," says his wife. "Ken died." She tells us she bought insurance for their tickets on the cruise "in case he doesn't make it the whole way round."

Rebecca and I pass the next few days sunning together in adjacent deck chairs, maintaining a constant, low-level alcohol haze. Dinners continue to blur the line between deadpan hilarity and awkward horror. "I used to be a dancer," undead-Ken's wife says, during a conversation about the jobs we'd all worked at before we retired. "I had trouble getting work because I was too skinny." Attempting a comment on changing societal ideals and representations of the female body, I say to her, "That wouldn't be a problem these days, I guess." Hearing this, she looks down at her plump torso with a hurt and baffled expression on her face. Before I can explain the misunderstanding, another man interrupts to tell us about his time in the British military. Later, there's a round of disquietingly racist comments as the oldsters agree that "England just isn't for the English anymore."

Though Rebecca's attitude is infinitely brighter than mine, she agrees with me that we must exit this cruise at the earliest possible instant—before we ourselves morph into a wrinkled, humpbacked, perpetually sloshed British couple. My original plan was to take the cruise all the way to Brisbane, where we're catching our freighter, but I no longer find this option acceptable. A ride to Australia is all we needed from this ship, and that's all we'll take from it. Hanging out with barely motile geezers has bruised our sense of adventure, and we need to escape.

When the ship makes a brief stop in Darwin—a sun-roasted town of 120,000 on Australia's forbidding northern coast—we run back down that gangplank I was so thrilled to sprint across in Singapore. Once on shore, we don't look back. I'm eternally grateful to the *Van Gogh* for letting me aboard and for ferrying me across the Java and Timor seas. But I now feel as though I've been liberated from a floating nursing home.

I haven't driven a car since we left the States and I've been itching to get behind a wheel. A drive across the Outback seems like potentially the best road trip available on this planet. Granted, we don't have a car. Nor do we have any clue as to the possible perils involved in crossing the Outback. But we've managed to get ourselves three-quarters of the way around the world so far. We're feeling cocky.

Our initial hunch is that renting a car will be pricey. (After all, we'll be asking the rental agency to let us drive their vehicle across an endless expanse of desert doomland before we ditch it on the other side—thousands of miles away.) But it turns out that one of Darwin's rental outlets is offering a relocation deal. They need to quickly ship a sedan to a sister franchise in Sydney. If we can drive the car there for them, and complete the journey in four days or less, they'll give us a massive discount on the price. Total rental cost: one dollar per day.

We can't believe our fantastic luck. Until we hit the road and look at a map. "Hmmm," says Rebecca, sitting in the passenger seat of our newly acquired Toyota Camry as I drive us south toward the dead, empty center of the continent. She's studying the Australian road atlas that we bought at a bookstore on our way out of Darwin. "It's come to my attention that Australia is very large," she observes.

To make it from Darwin to Sydney in our allotted time we'll have to cover about six hundred miles a day. We've tied ourselves to waking up at sunrise, getting in the car, and then driving without much pause until dusk. (We daren't drive at night on these dark, lonely roads—for fear of breaking down, leaving the car to seek help, and being devoured alive by a pack of ravenous dingoes.)

We now understand why the rental car cost us only four dollars. It's because we're not customers. We're hired help. We're doing a difficult, demanding job, and we've been tricked into paying a small fee for the privilege.

No matter. It's worth it. I'd forgotten the amazing rush of driving fast down an empty two-lane highway. Sure, we've had a measure of autonomy with other vehicles on this trip: our bicycles in Vietnam, the scooter in Langkawi. But there is nothing like a car. The private, mobile world of its cabin. The picture windows front, sides, and back. Point the grille in any direction you please, depress the accelerator, and feel the freedom. With an Australian country song blasting from the radio, we begin eating up the miles.

*　*　*

DARWIN on its surface appears to be an unremarkable suburb—the type you might find anywhere in heartland America. But its generic, two-story buildings and sleepy culs-de-sac belie its freakish setting. It is in fact an outpost. A fragile fortress surrounded by the most brutal forces of nature. On one side is a deadly, unswimmable sea. ("Don't worry about the sharks," a taxi driver reassured us. "They've all been eaten by the saltwater crocs or poisoned by the box jellies.") On the other side is the barren, pitiless Outback.

Within a half hour of exiting the rental car company's parking lot, we leave all hints of human existence behind. There is nothing out here but red dirt, lime green scrub, and a broiling orange sun. The deeper into the Outback we go, the more desolate it gets. We can drive for forty-five minutes without passing a single car and go hours without seeing a house or a building of any kind. No gas stations. No billboards. It's a startling emptiness—an *absolute* emptiness—of a sort that is difficult to find in America these days. Which makes sense, given that Australia is nearly as large as the continental United States but is home to 20 million people instead of 300 million.

At one point, we drive past a massive brush fire burning not a hundred yards from the side of the road. The flames are ten feet high. There's not a single soul in sight. We're the only witnesses to this hellacious, raging inferno. With nothing to block the wind, a fire like this can suddenly sweep across the plain, inhale all in its path, and breathe out a wispy trail of ash. During a recent set of fires near Melbourne—one blaze stretched sixty miles long—survivors spoke of having twenty seconds from the time they heard a crackling roar approaching until the moment the flames overtook them.

The overwhelming impression I get is that this continent hates living things. It's like a part of earth that refuses to assimilate. The creatures that make it are forced to get by either on their wits (as humans have) or with bizarre, weaponous mutations. Basically half the animals you encounter here are capable of killing you in a matter of seconds. And only Australia could produce the platypus—a venomous, egg-laying mammal, which naturalists at first thought must be a prank some trickster was playing on them. Or the kangaroo—whose ridiculous, propulsive hopping, sometimes with an infant roo peeking out of an onboard pocket, seems to have been a prank played on the animal by its creator.

We've already seen dozens upon dozens of dead roos, lying in the road and in its ditches. But it's not until our second day of driving that we spot our first live one. And now we understand why: Kangaroos have a death wish. They hop in packs along the roadside, and as our car approaches at least one roo will invariably gauge our speed, gather his hoppy momentum, and zag across the pavement directly into our path.

I don't blame him. Australia is a constantly menacing environment, and no doubt there comes a time when you're just ready to give up the fight. So far we've managed to swerve around these suicidal roos—mostly because we've learned to hit the brakes at the moment a troop comes into sight. I sometimes shout out my window at the roos, preemptively: "Don't you do it, Matilda! You've too much to live for!"

The other cars on the road all have beefy front grilles, designed to buffer a roo collision by deflecting the tawny-colored limbs and crimson guts over and around the windshield. Most cars are also equipped with exhaust snorkels that extend above their roofs, presumably to allow the vehicle to drive through chest-deep floods. The sight of all these rugged armaments has left us feeling less sanguine about our own naked-grilled, nonsnorkeled, factory-issue family sedan.

When we (very occasionally) pass another car, its driver will always wave. Initially, we'd assumed our brights must be on or that we were dragging a roo carcass or three from our undercarriage. But then we realized these friendly hellos are just an effort to forge an ephemeral moment of human contact. You take it any way you can get it out here. And you never know when you'll run out of gas one hundred miles from nowhere and need to siphon from a friendly Samaritan.

OUR first night on the road we stop in Renner Springs. It's a speck in the middle of the desert with some gas pumps, a pub, and a rambling one-story motel, all surrounding a mudhole. Our room is home to a feathery cockroach the size of a badminton shuttlecock and a pair of grasshoppers with legs like chopsticks.

On our second night we reach Kynuna. Population: eighty-five. We eat dinner at a roadhouse called the Blue Heeler. Standing on its porch, we see no other evidence of civilization in any direction, up to the horizon.

We end up drinking with a trio of local cowboys—or "jackeroos," as they're called here. They tell us they spend all day herding ("mustering") cattle. These days, instead of riding on horses, they use 400 cc motorbikes to patrol the rocky ranchlands and steer the animals into line. "Roped a huge fella today," says the youngest jackeroo with pride. "Had his balls still on him. Never seen a white man before. I had to pull him down and get him by his back legs."

Another of the jackeroos is getting liquored up and maudlin. He confesses that he misses his girlfriend when he's out here at the cattle station. "Can't even get no cell phone signal to call her. I got my mate to hoist me up in the cherry picker once, to wave the phone around and get some bars. 'Where are you?' she asks me. 'I'm up in a bucket!' I say."

When it's time to call it a night, they invite us to go shooting with them tomorrow. It's their day off, and they're planning to make money on the side by killing kangaroos. They tell us they get paid by the kilo, for the meat. "I'll have about thirty in the back of my ute by the end of the day," one of them says. "You have to be a marksman, though. Can't sell it unless it's a clean head shot."

We politely decline. Partly out of revulsion. Partly because I'd be more likely to shoot myself in the ankle than make a clean head shot on a hopping kangaroo at one hundred yards. Besides, we have no time—we're still up against the clock in terms of getting this relo car to Sydney. We retire to our room, which is four corrugated metal walls and a cement floor with a bed in the middle and a sink in the corner.

AFTER the kamikaze kangaroos, the biggest menace on an Outback highway is a road train. Road trains are giant trucks that have—

instead of just one trailer linked to the cab, as most semis on American roads do—three or four trailers stretching out in a long line. Sort of like a train. But on a road.

Passing one of these things is a real knuckle-whitener. You pull out onto the wrong side of the highway and gun the gas, and then time seems to stand still. This ain't no wussy eighteen-wheeler you're overtaking. You've got sixty-something wheels you need to put in your rearview mirror. Even at top speed, you'll be driving alongside the beast—and praying you encounter no oncoming traffic—for a full mile or two.

On top of this, we're still not comfortable with having the steering wheel on the wrong side of the car. In America, as in the great majority of the world (including ships at sea), we stay to the right when passing an oncoming vehicle. I've yet to find any satisfactory answer as to why some countries insist on doing it differently.

One theory holds that in the age of the horse, everyone kept left—so that the right hand (the dominant side for most people) would be in position to greet, or clash swords with, an oncoming rider. A second step to the theory is then required, and it goes like this: Napoleon, being left-handed, preferred to ride on the right side of the road. The diminutive tyrant insisted that his soldiers, and everyone he conquered, follow his lead.

This of course does not explain why countries such as America and China drive on the right (unless I'm forgetting that time when Napoleon invaded the New World and then kept marching onward toward Asia). But there are myriad other theories, including one about American wagon configurations and another about ladies' sidesaddle etiquette.

In 1913, an international committee concluded that the whole world should settle on one side, for uniformity. This counsel obviously went unheeded. Still, several countries have made a switch over the years. For instance, Sweden did it in 1967. At 4:50 a.m. one night, all traffic stopped. Everyone carefully switched their cars to the other side of the road and then, ten minutes later, resumed driving. Astonishingly, it worked.

Whatever the history, this nonstandardized traffic stuff is a source of angst for anyone forced to switch back and forth. Since we got to Australia, I've been looking the wrong way every time I pull out onto the road. And Rebecca has not once managed to flash the turn signal without first pulling the lever that activates the windshield wipers. "The turn signal should really be over here on this side!" she complains, to no avail—as another roo gears up to ram our fender with its head.

HOUR after hour we drive, yet the scenery never changes, and our spot on the map never seems to progress much. It doesn't help that the only thing on the radio is a cricket test match—which as best I can tell has no beginning and no end, though they sometimes take "tea breaks." We stop the car every once in a while just to stretch our legs. When we get out, it feels like someone has aimed a blow-dryer at our faces and switched it to high. (Also, the blow-dryer was filled with black flies.)

At last, on day four, we make it over the Blue Mountains, marking the end of the Outback. The signs of civilization are everywhere now. We know we've reached the end of authentic Outback when towns start labeling themselves "Outback towns," with hokey Outback-themed billboards and signs. A true Outback town never needs to point it out. It's evident—because all you see, in every direction, is Outback.

When we get to Sydney, we drop the car off at the rental agency office, near the airport. We take a final look at our trusty chariot. Its hood, front fenders, and windshield are a riot of animal matter. We see bird feathers, enormous insect wings, and pasty green guts of unknown provenance. "I want to do DNA testing to see how many species we have stuck to our car," says Rebecca. "I wouldn't be surprised to find a fully intact roo head lodged behind the grille."

The cheerful woman at the return counter asks where we're headed next, and we tell her we need to get to Brisbane. "Oh, easy, just an hour's flight," she says, assuming we're headed to the airport right now. When we tell her we're actually taking the train, she looks stunned. "Why? You see nothing but trees!" she laughs. "Trees, trees, and more trees!"

WHEN you're traveling long distances without airplanes, and trying to see everything in between, you'll by necessity gloss over a few places that you really wish you hadn't. Such is the case with Sydney. A world-class city, and yet tragically we can spend just a single day here if we're going to catch our freighter up in Brisbane. There's only time enough to take a ferry around the harbor, past the legendary opera house, and then to visit the spectacular zoo. (The zoo's captive roos have a crazy gleam in their eyes, as though they're looking for car wheels to jump under.) A quick walk around the stately downtown suggests it's what might result if you scraped up a few square miles of London and plopped them down in Santa Monica.

To figure out the train schedule to Brisbane and make reservations, I call an automated phone line. It asks me to speak my answers to its questions, but the computer doesn't recognize my words when I talk American. I scramble to imitate an Australian accent, and quickly find the key is to use the extreme rear-upper reaches of my mouth. It all flows from there. Once I slip into a dead-on Crocodile Dundee impression—"foive a'claawk"—I have no problems.

We catch an overnight train out of Sydney in the afternoon. It's still light out, and as we clackalack along we're treated to a rolling panorama. Far from just trees, as the woman at the rental car counter had suggested, we're seeing lakes surrounded by rocky hills, and grassy fields full of frolicking horses. It's gorgeous countryside. On a plane, we'd never see all these details far below beneath the clouds. And the train moves at a civilized amble that invites us to gaze aimlessly, to let our minds drift, and to ruminate on where we've come from and where we're going.

I'm congratulating myself yet again on having hewed to the earth's surface, when I get a sudden, jarring reminder that it cuts both ways. A strung-out, junkie-looking woman and her tear-stained daughter board the train after sunset and sit right behind us. The woman starts zombie-shuffling up and down the aisle, her pupils dilated like hockey pucks. Her daughter is restless, and the woman can't handle it. "Alexis, lie down!" she yells over and over, slurring her words in a thick Australian accent.

The junkie mommy is keeping the whole car awake with her shouting. If we were on the plane, this ordeal would have been over in an hour (and likely never would have happened—I'm fairly certain this woman is in possession of hard drugs, which is why she didn't want to go through airport security). On the train, with its accursed gentle pace, the misery lasts all night.

When we at last reach Brisbane at 5:00 a.m., I'm woozy and miserable. And, to my horror, I sort of wish I'd flown.

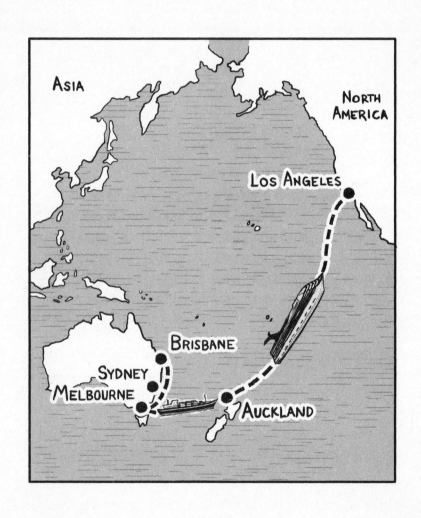

Chapter Nine

Brisbane to Los Angeles

A T the Port of Brisbane, waiting to board our freighter, we pass the time drinking beer in the seafarers' center. It's a little wooden shack dwarfed by the surrounding gantry cranes and container stacks. Most ports have an outpost like this that caters to the crews of the merchant vessels passing through the harbor. They're a sort of home base, where deckhands on shore leave can gossip, check e-mail, and make long-distance phone calls. There's a foosball table in the corner. Stacks of evangelical pamphlets. Groggy seafarers napping on the musty couches. No one questions our presence here, perhaps because by now we look like a couple of old salts.

At last our ship, the MV *Matisse*, radios over to the seafarers' center to tell them we've been cleared to board. The port's shuttle bus scurries us across a big container yard and alongside a massive hull.

We climb a steel ladder hundreds of feet up to the ship's deck and follow a cadet to our cabin.

Soon enough, we're back down below in the mess room, eating an overboiled dinner from another Filipino cook. The good news: Because this is a French-owned ship, our meal is served with a bottomless carafe of red wine. The bad news: Because it's a rusting old cargo freighter, this wine verges into the realm of subpalatability. No matter—we manage to down two quick glasses before we're summoned to the crew lounge for the mandatory safety lecture.

It turns out the *Matisse* is staffed almost entirely by Romanians. This makes for a stark—and ultimately pleasing—contrast with the starchy, by-the-book professionalism of the German officers on the freighter we took across the Atlantic. For instance, Lucian, the first officer here, seems to view his safety lecture less as vital information than as an opportunity for an open mike comedy routine.

I wish I could convey Lucian's accent on the page. Imagine a man speaking with a half-pound of cabbage lodged in the middle depths of his throat. "First thing," Lucian begins. "Drugs not allowed on board. But eez okay as long as we're not seeing you with them." Through his inch-thick corrective lenses I see him wink a highly magnified eye.

"Second thing: Don't be falling in ocean. I don't think you are surviving this." Here Lucian chuckles in a manner that suggests he would be curious—in a detached, analytic sort of way—to see what might transpire if we did in fact fall into the ocean. "You can shout for help, yes," he muses, "but ship is moving at fifteen meters per second. So by time you shout you are already behind us. Maybe if you fall off bow we can get you—but then maybe you are sucked into propeller, and you are turned a little bit sushi."

We're led on a quick tour of the ship. It's significantly larger than our previous freighter was—nearly one hundred feet longer—and able to carry far more containers. It's also dirtier. While the German crew maintained a shipshape sheen, the crew aboard the *Matisse* seems not to mind a few stray cigarette butts, muddy decks, and paint-peeled railings. Also, where the Germans established strict rules regarding which times we could visit the bridge, Lucian intimates that we, as the only two passengers, can basically pop in and hang out on the *Matisse*'s bridge whenever we want.

OUR first full day on the water, we'd expected to hit the open ocean and make serious progress toward Auckland. Not happening. For unclear reasons (though we suspect it has to do with keeping us on board the ship longer, and thus charging us more money), nobody informed us in advance that the *Matisse* first makes stops in Sydney and Melbourne, loading and unloading cargo, before it departs to New Zealand. Meaning that our miserable, sleepless, thirteen-hour overnight train ride up to Brisbane was in fact completely unnecessary. I must tell you, there is a unique flavor of frustration one feels when one backtracks over bitterly earned surface miles.

Upon berthing in Sydney, we attempt to leave the port and spend the afternoon downtown, hoping to see some things we missed during our last, brief stay. This is no simple task. Escaping the port itself involves walking through interstitial zones that are jumbles of concrete, chain-link, and abandoned dock equipment. These days, cities spend millions of dollars to tailor the experience of travelers coming into and out of airports. No such efforts are expended on behalf of container ship passengers. Our transition from transport to destination is unsanitized and unsocialized. We're never routed through a duty-free shop. Even after we leave the port (flashing the laminated crew IDs provided by the *Matisse* so we won't be arrested for trespassing inside the container yard), it's not clear to us how we should get into the city. We're alone on an empty road in an industrial wasteland.

Eventually, we spot a bus depot in the distance. It turns out this is where Sydney's city buses begin their day—with the drivers arriving for work, fueling up, and heading out on their routes. There's no actual bus stop here, so we just wave our arms and shout as one of the big buses pulls out of the gate. The driver slows hesitantly, opens the door, ascertains that we're not trying to hijack him, and then lets us aboard without making us pay the fare.

Returning to the ship after a few pleasant hours in downtown Sydney isn't any easier. Our taxi driver has no clue where the port is. "Somewhere near the water?" we suggest. He gets lost multiple times before accidentally stumbling upon it.

By the time the *Matisse* has chugged down the Australian coast, and made it in and out of Melbourne's port, we're able to identify and differentiate several types of commercial marine vessel. There are the low-slung tankers that hold oil or chemicals. The tall, flat-sided Ro-Ros that allow wheeled vehicles to roll on and roll off through the giant doors set in their hulls. The small, freelance freighters with their own deck-mounted cranes. And of course the container ships, arrayed in long queues that stretch clear across the harbor—the equivalent of airplanes circling above a landing strip. Some of these appear to be following the same cargo circuit as us, and we find them tied up and waiting each time we arrive at a new pier.

We can also recognize, from hundreds of yards away, the various shipping company logos painted on the containers. Hapag-Lloyd uses an eye-catching orange. Hamburg Süd favors a deep brick red. Maersk employs a utilitarian all-caps, sans serif typeface.

I can't even guess at how many individual containers we've seen at this point. There are two thousand aboard our own ship, another couple of thousand aboard each ship we pass, and what seems like millions, stacked in endless rows, crowding the docks whenever we approach shore. Once you become attuned to the ubiquity of containers, you spot them in the backs of department store parking lots, along the sides of train tracks, and everywhere else. They are the empty husks discarded by global commerce.

IT'S three days at sea from Melbourne to Auckland, and the crew is anticipating heavy weather. "Be ready for three days of hell," says Lucian with a cackle. He says he wouldn't be surprised if we lose some containers. When the ship rolls steeply, they can wrench free a dozen at a time and topple into the ocean with mushroom-cloud splashes. Apparently, the most sought-after freighter captains are the ones best able to read weather systems and chart a course through calm seas—thus preventing these occasional container losses and, more important, saving fuel that would otherwise be spent battling headwinds and powerful waves.

We're concerned the bad weather might slow us down and force us to miss our connection with the cruise ship in Auckland. We're also not looking forward to severe seasickness. But the storms never come. Instead, we just hang out on the bow with the Romanians and watch for whales. "Is most peaceful place on ship," says Andrei, a bearded engine-room technician. "Far from engines," he notes, flicking a cigarette butt over the rail. "You can think about lot of things here."

Our vigil on the bow eventually pays off when we spot a pod of twenty or thirty humpbacks a few hundred yards off the port side. Plumes sprout from their blowholes at percussive intervals. It's like a toneless pipe organ.

Fleeting moments like this are one of the perks of a life at sea. Lucian gets positively poetic, for instance, when he describes what it's like to pass through the world's major canals. "When you go through the locks in Panama," he says, "you can reach out and touch the walls. Maybe meter away. But Suez is my favorite. If you get off and walk into the desert, and then look back, it looks like the ships are floating across the sand."

The sailors have also experienced less magical maritime moments. Lucian tells us that the *Matisse* got pirated a few years back, not far from Singapore, as it crossed through the bandit-infested Strait of Malacca. Due to some engine trouble the *Matisse* had slowed to half speed, and "this made ship very good for boarding," as Lucian explains.

The pirates threw grappling hooks over the rails, scrambled aboard, and brandished knives. They went straight for the captain's room and forced him to unlock the ship's safe. Once they'd stolen all the money and valuables inside, they rappelled back down their ropes. "They are gone so fast," says Lucian, "most of the crew had no idea it happened. They thought it was joke when captain says we are pirated."

Generally, the crew members are quiet at meals, wolfing down their food in silence. (Which could be a coping strategy: The *Matisse*'s menu is heavy on indistinguishable, rubbery meats, served in gloopy stews. Rebecca has decided it's the inevitable outcome of putting a Filipino cook—named "Cookie," as the cook is on every freighter—in the galley of a French-owned ship, and then asking him to cater to the taste buds of Romanians. The result is a sort of watered-down, global hash.) At dinner one night, though, an engineer named Doru introduces himself and starts chatting with us in perfect English. Doru is ruggedly handsome, speaks five languages, and at all times carries around his neck a large, expensive-looking camera—which, based on my observations, he uses solely to photograph port installations. Given all this, I think there's about a 40 percent chance that he's a spy.

When I ask Doru to share any nightmarish tales of life at sea he might have, he recounts the time, seven years ago, when he was working on a freighter in the Mediterranean. His first indication that something might be amiss came when he realized that the ship had no working radio. Its only means of communication was to get close enough in to shore that the captain could use a cell phone. One night, shortly after docking at a port in Italy and beginning to load cargo, the captain mysteriously left the ship, offering no explanation. The next morning, customs agents raided.

The entire crew was handcuffed, arrested, and held for questioning. It seems they'd unknowingly loaded aboard four tons of unlicensed cigarettes. Doru—along with several equally innocent Pakistani deckhands—got locked up in a jail in southern Italy. He was occasionally bused, wearing shackles, to hearings at a local courthouse. He wasn't freed for thirty-two days.

THE *Matisse* is running behind schedule, due to long delays getting in and out of the crowded Australian ports. There's not much we can do about the slow pace. My constant nagging of Lucian doesn't persuade him to goose our speed.

Phileas Fogg, in danger of exceeding his allotted eighty days and losing his bet, opted to tie up a ship captain, seize the helm himself, and start burning structural parts of the ship as fuel to stoke the engine fires higher. It would be difficult for us to replicate these tactics (and anyway this freighter is made out of metal). So we'll just have to pray we get to Auckland in time to board our cruise ship. As it stands, we're due to arrive almost precisely when the cruise ship is due to depart.

When Auckland's port finally comes into view, we're enormously relieved to see the giant white cruise ship still at the pier, just a few berths away. We jog over as soon as we clear customs and disembark from the *Matisse*. The cruise ship workers out in front of the gangway tell us the ship will be departing in about two hours.

Luckily, the port is very near the city center. Unluckily, the entirety of our experience in New Zealand involves running around downtown Auckland's toothbrush-clean streets, searching through clothing stores for bits of attire presentable enough to wear on the cruise ship's scheduled formal nights. When we return to the pier, the ship's porters can't quite bring themselves to believe that we're actually boarding with nothing but our backpacks and a couple of small shopping bags. They politely inquire as to when the rest of our things will be arriving. All around us, rolling dollies groan under the weight of elaborate, twelve-piece matched leather luggage sets.

Our cabin, on one of the middle decks, gives an indication of why this cruise is so expensive. We're in the cheapest tier possible, and yet the cabin is nicer than anywhere I've ever lived. A king-size mattress with the approximate thickness of forty stacked phone books. A walk-in closet that looks completely empty even after we've unpacked our tiny allotment of clothing. A large television with a DVD player and satellite channels. Most thrillingly, we have a balcony with sliding glass doors. It now offers a close-up look at a ship in an adjacent berth, but we anticipate expansive views of the South Pacific and a taste of clean, salty air—enjoyed in the comfort of our lush, ship-provided terrycloth bathrobes. One more lovely touch: On our small dining table is the first in an endless string of complimentary shrimp platters.

We are joining the cruise on the final leg of its Grand Asia Pacific tour, which went up the U.S. west coast to Alaska, across the Bering Strait to Russia, and then down Asia's eastern coast—stopping at ports of interest along the way. Passengers who've been on board for the whole megillah are referred to as GAPpers, and have paid something like seventy thousand dollars each for the privilege (and much more if they're residing in one of the ship's two-thousand-square-foot luxury suites). The only reason the cruise is remotely affordable for Rebecca and me is that this last segment is a "repositioning." It makes only a few stops and its principal mission is simply to get the ship back to Los Angeles so a new loop can begin.

IN "A Supposedly Fun Thing I'll Never Do Again"—probably the funniest essay ever written in English—the late David Foster Wallace wrote about the week he spent on a giant white cruise ship puttering around the Caribbean. Though he had all the food he could eat and all the sunshine he could absorb, Wallace felt sharp pangs of despair. In part, this was a reaction to his tacky fellow passengers. But Wallace also had the depressing realization that, no matter how pampered and spoiled he was on the ship, the grasping infant inside him would remain unsatisfied, forever demanding greater degrees of luxury and ease.

I've done my time on one of those Caribbean cattle-car cruise ships. I grew disgusted at the sight of the buffet line, which was peopled by an obese and sunburn-prone cross-section of middle America. The buffet food itself was abundant, but boring. My room was cramped and had one undersized porthole that I could barely see the ocean out of. The casino was packed to its bleep-blooping gills at all hours of day and night. We made port in a series of soul-crushing tourist hellholes like Cancún and Cozumel.

After spending a few days aboard the *Seven Seas Mariner*, though, it occurs to me that perhaps I was just on the wrong cruise. Once you get behind the cruise industry's velvet rope (in this case, staggering prices that are beyond the realm of affordability for all but a few), life is much different. Regent ranks high among the top-drawer luxury cruise lines, and the *Mariner* carries only seven hundred passengers instead of the four thousand that get crammed onto those waterslide-equipped cruise behemoths. The *Mariner* is filled with accomplished retirees who are generally smarter and fitter than I am, and who are for the most part clothed in attractive, understated fashions.

I've enrolled in an onboard yoga class, in which the other students are all sinewy fifty-something women who look like they own multiple NPR tote bags. I've been attending fascinating lectures about the history of the Middle East, delivered by the retired Beirut bureau chief of the *Washington Post*. I never miss afternoon tea— served in dainty porcelain cups on the rear observation deck, as a live jazz combo plays quietly in the background. Rebecca and I have even double-dated with a charming retired couple from Beverly Hills, discussing art and politics over dinner in the ship's gourmet French restaurant.

Granted, not all of the *Mariner*'s passengers are cultured sophisticates. We've eavesdropped on our share of shipboard conversations, and most have centered on the following topics:

1) Elective surgery.

2) Nonelective surgery.

3) Bridge. There is an ongoing, seemingly endless bridge tournament, which everyone on board besides us participates in. Each morning's bridge results are dissected for hours afterward in every public (and presumably private) space on the ship. The main tone of these discussions lies somewhere between ill-concealed envy and open, snarling resentment. For example: "The Shapiros won

again today," says a dour-faced woman to her dour-faced friend as they sit near us at teatime. "That's a shame," says the friend. "Because they are not nice people."

4) How poorly certain other passengers have been treating the crew. This is without a doubt everybody's preferred topic. Upon witnessing another passenger acting rudely toward a crew member, people will positively sprint to tell their friends. Then they'll tut-tut together, barely suppressing their pleased smirks. They'll agree that the best sort of people—meaning themselves—would never treat the staff with anything less than the utmost kindness and warmth. My fellow passengers so clearly relish these conversations, and bask so luminously in the glow of them, that it seems like it might almost be worth it for me to arrange a fake scene with a bartender or waitress, in which I'd purposefully play the cad— thereby providing conversational fodder and dramatically boosting the overall satisfaction levels of the shipboard population.

Some passengers get particularly hung up on enforcing the ship's exclusivity. One evening, in the Horizon Lounge, we overheard a jerky fellow complaining that "every time they offer one of these repositioning discounts, it lets on the riffraff." His ire had been enflamed when he noticed someone committing a minor dress code violation in one of the ship's restaurants. It might have been me.

These dress codes are presenting a real challenge. "Informal" nights mean jacket and tie. "Country club casual" seems to also mean jacket and tie—but the tie can be more daring. As for "formal" nights, Rebecca and I have taken to just hiding in our cabin.

Even during the day, when anything goes, we feel out of place. Everyone else's clothes look newly bought from high-end department stores. Meanwhile, our clothes have stains and broken buttons, and look pretty much exactly as you'd expect clothes to look after they've circled the earth inside a backpack.

IN a stroke of incredible luck—or possibly because I mentioned that I was a journalist when I booked our cabin—Rebecca and I have been invited to dine with the ship's captain at the Compass Rose restaurant. Dining at the captain's table is the rarest of cruise ship privileges, coveted by all on board. In honor of the occasion, I have ironed my one nice shirt and donned the ill-fitting cotton blazer I bought in Auckland during our madcap rush to find grown-up clothes.

After inviting us to sit down and pouring some wine into Rebecca's glass, Captain Alfredo Romeo—and truly, one could not invent a better name—tells us that he began his maritime career on cargo freighters. After a few years, he switched over to passenger ships. It's easy to see why he'd make the change: In his present role, he is combination rock star and monarch.

Captain Romeo enjoys remarkable job perks. (Tomorrow, for instance, once he's anchored us near a small island in the South Pacific, he'll be taking the afternoon off to go scuba diving with the ship's resident naturalist—a beautiful, lithe blonde woman who works for the Cousteau Society.) He eats gourmet cuisine at every meal. His staff is obliged to treat him with deference, and the passengers beam when he deigns to walk among us.

The ladies, especially, light up in the captain's presence. I should mention that Captain Romeo is a striking figure in his dress whites, epaulets, and captain's hat. He is a tanned, barrel-chested man, with close-cropped hair the color of gunmetal. He also works a three-months-on, three-months-off schedule and lives in an Italian villa when he's not commanding a ship. If Rebecca left me for him, I suppose I'd just nod and get on with my life.

The other side of the coin: Should anything at all go wrong on this voyage, the blame falls squarely on Captain Romeo. And so very much can go wrong. For instance, elderly passengers often fall ill. If you've been on a cruise, you likely heard the term "Code Orange" spoken over the loudspeaker at least once. It indicates a health crisis—such as a cholesterol-addled old man keeling over in the dining hall, streaks of marinara sauce still dripping from his cheeks and lapels. When emergencies like these arise, the captain must immediately decide whether to divert the ship to the nearest proper hospital facility (thereby ruining the expensive vacations of the seven hundred other guests) or to trust the shipboard medical staff to handle the treatment (thereby risking calamity and/or a lawsuit).

Of course, the spine-chilling, ever-present fear for any captain is that he might let his ship go down. Less than a month before the *Mariner* left Auckland, a cruise liner called the MV *Explorer* was off the Antarctic coast when it hit an iceberg, cracking open its hull. At three a.m., the captain issued the order to abandon ship. Passengers spent five harrowing hours shivering in open lifeboats, making nervous *Titanic* jokes, before a Norwegian cruiser arrived to rescue them. Captain Romeo read news reports about the incident and he tells us it was a minor miracle that everyone survived. Had a storm kicked up, and lifeboats toppled into the icy Antarctic water, the outcome could have been far grimmer.

Captain Romeo's own personal nightmare seems to involve rogue cargo containers (the kind Lucian warned us of), which can dislodge from freighters in storms and be left adrift. "They float just far enough below the surface that you can't see them," the captain tells us. "And they don't show up on radar." He has a piece of steak skewered on the end of his fork, and he waves it ominously in the air before him. I believe the steak—which he has sliced into an approximate rectangle—is meant to represent an invisible container lurking somewhere out there in front of us, waiting to punch a hole in our hull.

Earlier in this loop of the Pacific, while crossing the Bering Strait, the *Seven Seas Mariner* got caught in a wicked storm. Down in the hold, the food supplies sloshed around. Pallets of eggs were smashed into yellow goo. Tins of tomato sauce exploded into bloody splatter patterns. This would have posed a problem for the ship's restaurants— had any of the passengers not been too seasick to eat.

Even when things run smoothly, captaining a cruise ship has its hassles. Half the time, you're more a hotel director than a sailor. And you're completely divorced from the simpler pleasures of a life on the waves.

A day after dining with the captain, I chatted with one of the ship's navigational cadets. He's a seventeen-year-old British kid named Richard, and this assignment on the *Mariner* is a required internship arranged by his maritime school. His previous internship placement had been aboard a cargo freighter. Even though the freighter's "drunk Russian cook" served the same viscous soup for every meal, and even though one of Richard's shipmates shattered a bone while out on deck when a wave leaped over the bow and crushed his leg, Richard says he vastly preferred living on a freighter to living on this cruise ship. Cruise ships, in his eyes, have almost zero to do with actual seafaring. He'd never in a million years want Captain Romeo's job.

"Way too many people bothering you," he says. "I want to be a freighter captain, and to do as little as possible. Just suntan up on monkey island"—the roof above the bridge, at the very pinnacle of a container ship—"and maybe read a book, or look at the sky."

I'm with Richard.

IN the ship's small, leather-armchaired library is a book titled *The Only Way to Cross*, in which author John Maxtone-Graham describes the glories of the great ocean liner age. It's hard to imagine it now, but in 1920 an oceangoing steamer left the port of New York every twenty minutes. Some were affordable means of transport, which returned from Europe full of newly arrived immigrants. Others were elegant, floating social parlors, with huge Roman baths and Empire-style ballrooms.

After World War II, shipping companies competed to build ever more opulent, ever more powerful passenger liners. The zenith came in the summer of 1952, when the massive liner *United States* set a new transatlantic speed record. She made the eastbound crossing in three days, ten hours, and forty minutes—an average of nearly forty-one miles per hour.

The *United States* was a tremendous success. And by 1969, she was out of service. The airplane had killed her.

It all began with the *Graf Zeppelin*, which in 1928 became the first commercial passenger airship to cross the Atlantic. Though it presaged a revolution in long-haul travel, this blimp posed no immediate threat to the ocean liner industry. It made the journey from Germany to New Jersey in 111 hours—more than a full day longer than it took the *United States* to get from New York to Great Britain—and it could only carry forty-three crew and twenty passengers.

In the 1930s, the improved designs of planes like the Douglas DC-3 made air travel cheaper and faster. But by 1939, airplanes still represented only 2 percent of all American commercial passenger travel. And a transatlantic flight still lasted a rather bumpy twelve hours.

The Boeing 707 was the airplane that changed everything. It cut the transatlantic crossing down to only six or seven hours—a far more tolerable amount of time to be trapped in a cramped, vibrating cabin. The 707 debuted in 1958. That same year, for the first time, more passengers crossed the Atlantic by air than by sea. By 1960, airplanes owned 70 percent of the transatlantic passenger business. By 1970, it was 96 percent.

These days, there's not a single year-round transatlantic passenger service by ship. The *Queen Mary 2* still offers a functional (though, at five and a half days, somewhat leisurely compared to the *United States*) crossing between New York and Southampton most weeks of the spring, summer, and fall. But each November, Cunard sends her south to run a bunch of pleasure jaunts around the Caribbean. She's forced to moonlight as a tawdry cruise ship to make ends meet.

The final chapter of *The Only Way to Cross* laments the sad fates of the grand old liners. The original *Queen Mary* was turned into a floating museum in Long Beach, California. On her final cruise—from New York, around the horn (because she was too fat to fit through the Panama Canal), and on to the West Coast—"the ship passed through tropical latitudes for which she'd never been designed," writes Maxtone-Graham. You can feel his prim embarrassment for her when he adds that on this final voyage "scandal erupted on board—a swarthy Latin-American beauty was put ashore at Rio, surrounded by shocked whispers of prostitution."

The *Queen Elizabeth* met an even crueler fate. She was neglected for a stagnant few years in Fort Lauderdale, got sold to a millionaire who changed her name, and was eventually destroyed by a fire in Hong Kong Harbor. Her successor, the *Queen Elizabeth 2*, is slated to become a floating hotel off the coast of Dubai.

Captain Romeo, during our dinner with him, recalled that in the early 1970s he worked on one of the last functional long-haul passenger liners. It served mostly to carry working-class emigrants from Italy to new lives in Australia. The Italian families brought all their worldly possessions with them—even pieces of furniture, which got stored in the cargo hold. Music played and streamers unfurled as the ship left the dock, and with tears rolling down their cheeks people waved good-bye to the loved ones they were leaving behind. It's a scene that just doesn't exist on the docks anymore. Today's poorer immigrants say good-bye to their families at airport gates, ride in the economy sections of jumbo jets, and bring with them only as much luggage as the airlines' draconian policies will allow.

* * *

THE South Pacific is vast and barren. There's just not much land between New Zealand and Los Angeles. We're covering sixty-five hundred miles on this cruise—longer than the distance covered by the Trans-Siberian railroad—and for almost all of it, we're chugging through empty ocean.

Our only real shore time comes in French Polynesia. We've stopped in Bora-Bora and Tahiti. We've also anchored in the bay of an island named Mooréa. It is a place with emerald hills and turquoise waters so achingly beautiful that I recommend you never look at a single photo of them unless you can commit yourself to visit, as the sheer sight of them will make you ill with longing. I'd also add that most of the tourists in French Polynesia are, not surprisingly, French, which equates to tastier food in the restaurants, trendier fashions in the boutiques, and skimpier bathing suits on the beaches.

After Polynesia, the only geographic point of interest we meet up with is the equator. Our crossing is celebrated with a goofy ceremony held out by the pool deck. It's commemorated with embossed certificates that are delivered to all the passenger cabins the moment we nose into the Northern Hemisphere. (With no tattoo parlor on board the ship, we can't mark the occasion the way old-school sailors might have.)

We also pass through the international date line, which is a mind-bender. According to the ship's calendar, we wake up on December twelfth, live through the whole day, go to sleep that night—and then wake up on December twelfth again. This freaks me out.

It freaked out Magellan's sailors, too. They'd kept careful track of the passage of days as they circled the earth westward. They were incredibly confused when they got back to Europe and found it was one day later than their records suggested. The date line also threw Phileas Fogg for a loop. In *Around the World in 80 Days*, Fogg is convinced he's lost his bet when he gets back to London. But because he's circled eastward it's in fact one day earlier than he'd realized.

I couldn't wrap my head around the date line paradox for the longest time. Would I be one day older than a twin brother who'd stayed at home, I wondered, because I've lived through the same day twice? The key to understanding it is to remember that each time Rebecca and I have crossed a time zone moving east, we've set our watches ahead and lost an hour. (When we've moved swiftly over ground, we've actually experienced minor train lag and ship lag.) Now we're getting each one of those twenty-four hours back—all at once.

AFTER we leave Nuku Hiva, in the Marquesas Islands, the next stop is America. But getting there means six full days across the ocean with no land in sight. And here the despair begins to creep in.

Aboard this ship, I live a wholly unnatural life. All food is free, including twenty-four-hour room service. At any moment I wish I can order a filet mignon, or whatever gourmet dish I please, delivered directly to my cabin.

All liquor is also free. I pick up the phone, ask the porter to send a glass of scotch to my room, and ... ding-dong, there's the door, and here's my scotch. As a result, my alcohol tolerance has grown frightening. Rebecca and I generally hit one of the ship's bars for a drink before dinner, order a bottle of wine with our four-course meal, and then drink at another bar until we stagger back to our cabin at the end of the evening. To enhance the ritual, I tend to pick a random signature drink each night—white Russians on Wednesday, champagne cocktails on Thursday, cognac on Friday.

The ship's amenities are amazing. There is a full-service gym with on-call personal trainers a mere four hundred feet from my cabin. Satellite Internet in the computer lounge. Trivia quizzes and sports challenges all day. Professional entertainment every night in the theater.

And yet I want nothing more than to be off this ship. I wouldn't stay aboard the *Mariner* past Los Angeles even if my passage were free. It might be hard to understand that from where you're sitting—assuming you're sitting in a place where people don't bring complimentary shrimp platters and champagne to your door twice a day. But I can assure you it is possible to grow resentful of comfort.

In part, I've been put off by the chilling vision of human nature that the ship has offered me. When people—and even more so, smart, wealthy, accomplished people—are thrown together for two intense weeks in a bounded space, they inevitably form cliques. They cultivate enemies. They look for ways to entertain themselves by stirring up conflict. (Often under the guise of partner-based card games.) It's not pretty to watch, and I've had my fill of it.

There's also the depressing realization David Foster Wallace put his finger on. That however many awesome things we have, we will forever crave the next awesome thing. And that even when all discomfort is eliminated, and life is "perfect," less-than-perfect emotions will persist in our stubborn brains. Which calls into question just what the fuck it would take to make you happy. Try pondering that sometime when you're on your seventh free mojito in the harbor of a South Pacific island, and perhaps you'll know how I feel.

THE last night of the cruise, the ship takes on a loosey-goosey, end-of-high-school vibe. Though I wouldn't have previously imagined it possible, people are accelerating their gluttony into the home-stretch—eating and drinking at new, uncharted levels of excess. We've also all gotten suddenly social, emboldened by the knowledge that after tomorrow we'll never need to see each other again.

Somewhere toward midnight, Rebecca and I find ourselves drinking mai tais at the bar in the disco club. We're chatting with Max, the very cool drummer from the ship's jazz combo. Max wears a Hawaiian shirt and a pair of hipster eyeglasses. He's twelve to fourteen drinks ahead of us, but we're catching up fast.

Max tells us he took this job at sea because it gives him a steady paycheck, so he doesn't have to struggle for wedding reception and nightclub gigs from week to week. When we ask him for some juicy, inside cruise ship gossip, he obliges by describing the never-ending feud between the *Mariner's* staff (who sleep in stacked bunks down in the bowels of the hull, observe a curfew, and eat in a staff-only cafeteria) and its entertainers (who, though they're likewise getting paid to be here, live like passengers). He also points out two older women shimmying out on the dance floor. He tells us they propositioned one of the other musicians with an offer of a Xanax and a threesome.

Across the room, I spot the only two passengers aboard the ship who are younger than Rebecca and me. I've been curious about them the whole time, as I've seen them around the bars and restaurants and at the evening shows. They're in their early twenties, pretty obviously gay, and even more obviously rich. The skinny one is handsome, with twinkling eyes and pants that seem tighter than is medically advisable. The pudgy one wears loafers whose buttery leather, even from thirty feet away, smells pungently of boarding schools, country clubs, and inexhaustible trust funds.

"What's the deal with those two?" I ask Max.

"Yeah, those guys," he says. "They're a couple. The rumor is the fat one is the heir to a huge fortune and he and his boyfriend just ride cruise ships all year round. They never work, or spend a day in the regular world. Come on, let's go say hi."

Max leads us over and introduces us. "I hear you guys really like cruise ships," I say, with about four quarts of rum on my breath. "I'm curious—what is it about them that appeals to you?"

"Oh, we just enjoy it," says the skinny one.

"It's relaxing," says the pudgy one.

And with that, they give a silent, nearly imperceptible, and yet unmistakable signal that the conversation is done. We follow Max back to the bar.

"It's really hard to talk to them," says Max, apologetically. "They treat the nonrich as another species. They're curious about us, but they don't understand us, and ultimately they can't be bothered with us."

Social chasms aside, I'm appalled that anyone would choose to spend his days floating in a cruise ship bubble. That goes not just for these two young dudes, but for the retired couples on board who take five or six cruises a year. They wear sweatshirts and windbreakers emblazoned with the logos of the other cruise ships that they've been on. They openly refer to themselves as "hard-core cruisers" (a vaguely pornographic locution I take pains to avoid) and claim they're never happier than when they're at sea on one of these bobbing wedding cakes.

Living as a hard-core cruiser would quickly prod me into suicidal urges. Just a few days ago, sitting out on our balcony on a moonless night, I found myself tempted—in an abstract way—to tip over the railing and let the inky Pacific envelop me. It's strange, but the ocean seems to call to you in moments of spiritual emptiness. It offers an escape into something so incomprehensibly enormous that your own petty troubles are small and meaningless by comparison.

"I know exactly what you mean," says Max, when I tell him about my dark night of the cruise ship soul. "There's a numbing quality to being on a cruise. It starts to drive you batty."

"It's a way to slowly, comfortably die," Rebecca chimes in, bolstering her point by waving her drink at all the white hair and wrinkled faces in the room.

She's right. The elderly people on board are very obviously fading into the sunset. Each day of pampering aboard the *Mariner* is another painless step closer.

And now we're starting to get at what so disturbs me about cruises. It's that cruise ships are, fundamentally, a lie. A charade.

When airplanes stole passenger ships' reason for being, the ships had to reinvent themselves. The ocean liner companies scrambled for answers. Cunard, the proud shipping name behind the *Queen Marys* and the *Queen Elizabeths*, changed its slogan to "Getting There Is Half the Fun"—implicitly acknowledging that the getting there, while perhaps fun, took twenty times longer than it did on an airplane. Ships were forced to pitch themselves as a more romantic, less convenient option.

Eventually, all pretense of functionality got dropped. And thus was born the cruise ship. Most people on board are literally going in a circle, embarking and disembarking at the same place. The ship may look like one of those old-time passenger liners—the kind that took people where they needed to go. But a cruise isn't a form of transport. It's a way to kill time.

IT'S a clear, crisp December day as we chug into Long Beach. The sea lions lounging on the harbor buoys bark at us as we pass. People fire up their cell phones when we get into signal range and begin making calls.

"End of cruise blues, my friend," says a man to his buddy as they sit at an outdoor bar on the top deck. They're enjoying their last two glasses of gratis liquor.

Once the ship has docked, the line forms to disembark. It's calm and orderly, but slow. The old, wheelchair-bound, apparently senile woman behind us throws a hissy. "I've never seen such chaos," she says. She sounds like Margaret Dumont in a Marx Brothers movie.

At last, we step onto dry ground. I can see Max up ahead, with the rest of the band, his arms raised in triumph. "Freedom!" he shouts back to us.

We hail a cab and throw our backpacks in the trunk.

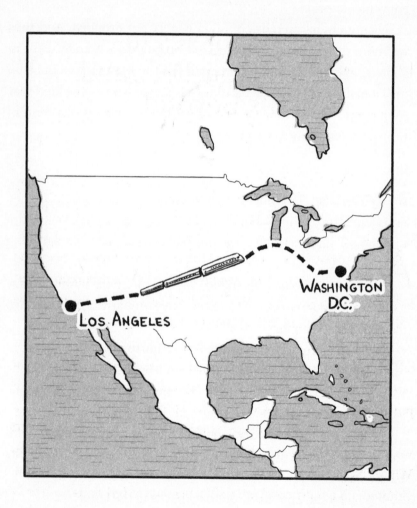

LOS ANGELES

WASHINGTON
D.C.

Chapter Ten

Los Angeles to Washington, D.C., and Points Beyond ...

As we've made our way around the world, we've always been one step ahead of the cold. We slid south just as autumn arrived in Beijing. We crossed below the equator as summer began in the Southern Hemisphere. We've lately been meandering through tropical island chains where the temperature is idyllic year-round. All in all, it's been a hands-on education in how the earth's curvature and orientation can dramatically affect regional temperatures. More important: I haven't needed long sleeves in months.

Now our voyage has made its sine wave turn back north, and we've been dropped into the late-December chill of Los Angeles. Winter has caught up with us—or perhaps we've caught up with it. Granted, it's a mild, southern California winter, but there's a bite in the air that we are unequipped for. Our first mission on land is to buy jeans and warm sweatshirts at an army-navy surplus store on Sunset Boulevard.

A few days ago, from aboard the ship, we'd e-mailed a friend who lives in L.A. and asked if we could crash with him. It turned out he was going to be out of town, but he very thoughtfully left the keys to his Silver Lake apartment in a flowerpot near its front door. The place is high up on a hillside, with a wide wooden balcony gazing out on the downtown skyscrapers. Rebecca and I get there in time for the final rays of the afternoon. As evening falls we watch the twinkling city lights, contemplating the adventures we might get into out here. We could stay for a week, look around town, maybe even rent a car and motor up the Pacific coast. Fend off the real world just a little bit longer.

But we won't. This trip feels distinctly over. We're back in America, and there's not a ton of mystery or challenge left. What's more, we're tired. For the first time since we left, I've become exhausted by the concept of motion. My fantasies right now involve a couch, cable TV, delivery Thai food, and a month of stagnation. I just want to touch my toes to the ground in D.C. and—at long last—decelerate myself to a final, triumphant stop.

The next day, we walk out onto Sunset and hail a city bus headed for Union Station, L.A.'s beautiful railway terminal. Built in 1939, it arrived just as trains were on the cusp of being outmoded by the automobile. It turned out to be the last of the classic old stations.

Today is Christmas Eve. We celebrated Thanksgiving at a bar in Brisbane, and once again we will mark a holiday without friends or family—another casualty of life on the move. A few of the passengers waiting inside Union Station's central hall wear jaunty red Santa caps and carry wrapped gifts.

AMERICANS once dreamed of a water passage across the country, through rivers and lakes from one coast to the other. This was before Lewis and Clark made us aware of a minor obstacle called the Rockies. It's tough to navigate your steam-powered paddleboat straight up a mountain stream or through the rapids of the Grand Canyon.

Plan B was cross-country train service, which met with far more success. The final spike in the transcontinental railroad was driven in Promontory, Utah, in 1869. News of the accomplishment spread immediately by telegraph, and Americans rejoiced. It was a modern marvel. Once supplies and people had taken months to cross the country. Now it took a mere four days.

And 140 years later, it still takes four days. (Well, three nights and significant parts of four days.) Which is par for the course when it comes to modern American train travel. Many routes are now actually slower than they were fifty or sixty years ago when they were the preeminent way of getting around. It used to take nine hours to get from New York to Montreal by train, but now it takes nearly twelve. Chicago to Minneapolis used to take less than five hours, and now it takes more than eight.

It's absurd that American rail is so slow. Japan can run bullet trains at well over 100 mph through densely populated urban corridors. Yet even in the empty scrublands of New Mexico, our Amtrak locomotive won't match this pace.

Somewhat embarrassingly, our train also won't travel on dedicated passenger tracks. From L.A. to Chicago, we'll be rolling on rails owned by the Burlington Northern and Santa Fe Railway Company—an operator of freight trains. This is one of the reasons Amtrak trains move so slowly: Tracks designed for freight don't have the kinds of railroad ties, road crossings, and signals that would be necessary for high-speed journeys.

Why doesn't Amtrak have its own rails? Blame the automobile. The first cross-country car trip was in 1903, and by 1930 more than half of American families owned a car. We absolutely loved the things. Given the choice in the middle of the century, we chose to invest in our interstate highway system instead of an efficient rail network. Even now, as the government makes some noise about boosting efforts on the high-speed rail front, most of the country seems to greet the news with a disinterested yawn.

Amtrak's modest pace would be okay if the trains were luxurious or the tickets were cheap. Neither is the case. Our "roomette" on this three-night trip is costing us about as much as we were paying for a month's rent in our D.C. apartment. And it's the size of two conjoined phone booths. By day, our seats face each other, knee to knee. At night, the porter transforms them into a pair of stacked, narrow bunks.

There's limited dining car seating and many hungry people. Each time we enter the car for a meal we're assigned to a booth we share with strangers. So far we've been placed with a young Japanese tourist, a shy academic, and a fiercely right-wing retiree. We try to steer each conversation to safe ground: the wonders of train travel. We learn that the academic is here because she's scared of flying, that the retiree is a borderline-delusional railroad fetishist ("I ride Amtrak whenever I can," she says, "because it's always so delightful"), and that the Japanese tourist seems to have been under the impression that American trains are as fast and comfortable as those in Japan. (He's discovering the unfortunate truth. And he seems a little bitter about it.)

AT dinner on our second night, the maitre d' seats us with a younger man and an older woman. They turn out to be mother and son. Both are already drunk.

He's knocking back beers. She's sipping a tumbler of rum and Diet Pepsi. As our salads arrive, she pulls a little plastic bottle from her purse, shakes a pill into her palm, and snaps a third of it off with her teeth. "Valium," she tells us, though we haven't asked. "I just like to nibble on a little throughout the day."

"See, this is why I can't get a girlfriend," says the son, apropos of we're not sure what. "And when I do get a girlfriend," he laughs, "she tries to kill herself." We assume this is a joke, since he's smiling, and we force ourselves to chuckle along with him.

"Oh, honey, I don't think she tried to kill herself," says the mom reassuringly, downing another gulp of her drink and chomping on an ice cube.

"No," says the son, dead serious now. "She did try to kill herself."

Long, awkward pause. "So," says Rebecca brightly, "where are you guys traveling to?"

When they disembark the next morning (terrifyingly, they had shared one of the tiny roomettes), we overhear two Amtrak porters gossiping in the hallway. "Did you see that mother and son who just left?" one porter asks the other. "Mmmm-hmmm," answers the second porter. "She done *messed* him up!"

DESPITE all this—the cramped living quarters, the poky pace, and the bizarre companionship—the train is still sort of wonderful. It's that view out the window of an ever-changing American landscape. You just can't top it. You wake up in the morning when the sun hits your face, and after rubbing your eyes you look up to find yourself in the middle of unspoiled Arizona cactus desert. The tracks have meandered far away from the highway, and the land is devoid of any human presence. It feels like a theme park ride through an exquisitely tended replica habitat.

To escape the tight confines of our roomette, we spend most of our waking hours in the observation car. It's like a rolling greenhouse, with windows for walls and broad skylights for a ceiling. If there's one discovery I've made on this trip, it's that there is nothing more meditative than a long, quiet journey on a ship or a train. The shooshing bow waves and clacking tracks seem almost engineered to induce a fugue state in our brains. The expansive view of the horizon seems to set our thoughts free to roam far and wide. Consider that Walt Disney conjured Mickey Mouse to life while aboard a cross-country train between New York and Los Angeles—and then ponder whether he'd have mustered the same intense concentration if he'd been watching an in-flight movie on a 747.

The dusty western cities and towns roll by, one after another. San Bernardino, Barstow, Flagstaff, Gallup. In Albuquerque, the train makes an hour-long service stop. We get off and take a stroll through the city's thin air and thinner sunshine. It's Christmas Day now. The stores are closed and the streets are deserted. A few old Native American women sit shivering behind folding card tables on the train platform, selling handmade jewelry.

We rumble north through the dark of night, then cross the iced-over Mississippi the next sunny morning. The towns run closer together now. We see backyards, loading docks, parking lots. We move into the culs-de-sac of the Chicago suburbs and then into the grid of the city itself. There's a layover of a few hours here, giving us just time enough to meet an old friend for dinner in the Loop. And then we're back at the station, boarding a new train, gearing up for the very last leg of our journey.

As a thought experiment, I imagine what it might be like to catch a cab to O'Hare right now and board a plane to D.C. Compared to the train, the flight would save us twelve hours of transit time. But how miserably buzzy and enervating that flight would be. I can feel my lungs gasping at the dry, recycled air. My legs cramping in my tiny seat. My mind recoiling at the abrupt transition between the two cities, at the inelegance of the conveyance, at the bloodless practicality of plane travel.

This is my final step back into my real life, and I find I'm clinging fiercely to the eccentricity of an overnight train ride. I've grown addicted to the calming clackety-clack of the wheels. It's like a rolling decompression chamber. It's acting as a buffer—between the quirky, whirlwind travels I'm leaving behind and the static, wearying responsibilities that lie ahead of me.

*   *   *

FIFTY years ago, an American tourist on vacation might well have taken a ship to get to Europe. Fifty years before that, it was not unusual to ride in a stagecoach. For someone growing up in the first half of the twentieth century—watching the automobile and the airplane evolve into everyday conveniences—it must have seemed that humankind's advances in the field of transport were only just getting started.

But then, sometime around the mid-1960s, the progress stopped. Air travel had its golden age in that era, and since then flying really hasn't improved. With notable exceptions like the now-defunct Concorde, the jets never got much faster. Meanwhile, they did get a whole lot less comfortable, as airlines crammed in more seats and cut out the amenities.

Whatever romance may have existed up there in the clouds, once upon a time, it's long gone now. These days, the experience is relentlessly drab. Still, there's no puzzle as to why people continue to fly. Airplanes equal convenience. They get us places faster—orders of magnitude faster.

I wouldn't want to deny people the option of flight. At the same time, I think it's fair to acknowledge that progress comes with trade-offs. Yes, we've gained convenience. But along the way we've deprived ourselves of some extremely wonderful things. The starry skies of an Atlantic Ocean crossing. The bleak beauty of an old Russian train chugging its way through Siberia. The jaunty freedom of a road trip with a carful of friends.

And there's no going back. Along with the ability to cross an ocean or a continent in six hours comes a societal expectation that you'll do so. Your two weeks of summer vacation time are predicated on the assumption that you'll *fly* to Italy for your honeymoon—not take a full week to float there, look around for an hour, and then take another week to float back.

As a result, when people think about travel these days they think purely of destinations. They barely give a nod to the actual . . . traveling. The problem with this isn't just that we lose out on the pleasures of trains, ships, bicycles, and all those other terrific modes of rationally paced, ground-level transport. I think we also dim our experience of the destinations themselves. We've forgotten the benefit of surface travel: It forces you to feel, deep in your bones, the distance you've covered; and it gradually eases you into a new context that exists not just outside your body, but also inside your head. (It eliminates travel sicknesses, too: Rebecca and I never once got ill as we moved slowly and steadily between clusters of regional bacteria.)

Teleporting from airport to airport doesn't allow for the same kind of spiritual transformation you undergo whenever you make an overland trip. When you take a seven-day vacation bookended by flights, I would in fact argue that your soul never completely leaves home. You've experienced it, I'm sure: Your airplane has landed in Quito, but your heart and mind are still stuck back in Boston. The sudden, radical change in your surroundings sparks a glitch in your processor. You know you're physically standing in Ecuador, yet the sensation is more like watching a really immersive television documentary *about* Ecuador. And then, at last, when you begin to feel whole again, your feet firmly planted in the foreign soil (no longer some hollow seedcase that's been dropped, weightless, into an alien world), it's time to teleport straight back to the comfortable familiarity of home.

I acknowledge that for most of us, it's no longer feasible to take an ocean liner to South America on our summer holiday. But that doesn't mean we wouldn't have a better, richer experience if we did. So my advice to you is this: The next time you want to travel—I mean really travel, not just take a vacation—please consider getting wherever you want to go without taking a plane.

I promise you will look at that globe on the shelf in your study in a whole new light. You will run your finger along the curve of the sphere and think: I know what this distance feels like. What this ocean looks like. What it means to trace the surface of this earth.

THE train leaves Chicago after dark. We're asleep as it makes middle-of-the-night stops in South Bend, Sandusky, Cleveland, Pittsburgh. We wake up in West Virginia, just a few hours outside D.C.

In these final moments, I feel less triumphant than lost. I did it—I circled the earth. But now the journey is done. And what will I do without the imperative of motion? Where am I going if I am not going anywhere?

Our arrival in Washington is an anticlimax. No cheering crowds at the station to herald our accomplishment. No confetti in our hair. We're two more commuters getting off the train. I want people to notice the wear on our backpacks, the swagger in our walk, the steely glint in our eyes, and have them wonder where exactly we've come from. I want to grab someone by the lapels and shout, "Motherfucker, I just circled the earth! Ba-boww! What did *you* do?"

I do not grab anyone. We walk calmly through the station and out the exit. We crash at a pal's place that night because we have no home to come home to.

We bump around for the next few weeks visiting family and friends. It's as though we can't bring ourselves to slow to a full stop. Eventually, having exhausted the hospitality of others, we're forced to sign a lease on an apartment. I feel a deep pang of sadness looking at the clutch of keys in my hand—front door key, mailbox key, deadbolt key. I haven't carried keys in six months, and their weight in my pocket feels a lot like an anchor.

Our first night in our empty new place, we sleep on an air mattress we bought for fifty bucks at a local discount store. Lying awake, I catalog my regrets. We never rode on elephants or behind a team of sled dogs. We never sailed on a yacht. We've so much more traveling left to do!

But in the morning, it hits me full force: For the first time in forever, there's nowhere to go next. I haven't the energy or resources to continue this adventure. I'll sleep in this same room again tonight, and the night after that, and the night after that.

The readjustment is brutal. The little victories and losses of day-to-day existence seem ridiculous. When we get our furniture and clothes back from the storage company, I'm almost physically repulsed by the sight of them. It feels like someone else's possessions. Why on earth did we ever buy all these things, and, worse, take the

271

trouble to preserve them while we were away? Everything I need, I now know for sure, I can fit into a backpack.

But of course the fierceness fades. Week by week, I grow softer. Comfort and routine begin to creep back in. We need to make money, so Rebecca finds another law firm job, and I start writing for magazines again. We trade out our air mattress for a real bed and get a flat-screen TV and an Internet connection. We go out to the same bars and restaurants that we did before. We're right back in the thick of it, carving new ruts.

One day, though, a few years down the line, I know we'll blow it all up again. Perhaps we'll be walking along a beach and we'll see a sailboat, out past the breakers. I'll catch a little gleam in Rebecca's eye. And we'll both be thinking: I wonder how far away we can get in one of those.

ACKNOWLEDGMENTS

I owe my journalistic life to *Slate*. Wherever I may roam, it has always been my home port and safe harbor. I want to thank all my wonderful friends and colleagues there for making it so. I owe particularly massive debts of gratitude to Jodie Allen, David Plotz, Michael Kinsley, Jack Shafer, Jacob Weisberg, and Julia Turner. Very special thanks go to June Thomas, *Slate*'s travel editor, who has repeatedly shipped me off to some strange corner of the world on only the shakiest of assurances that I'd bring her back a story.

Zoë Pagnamenta, my agent, navigated a first-time author through the sometimes frustrating, occasionally baffling world of book publishing. Zoë would be an excellent cargo freighter captain: reassuring, always in command, and able to pilot past the dangerous shoals toward the fair seas beyond. Many thanks, as well, to everyone at Riverhead—and especially to my editor, Laura Perciasepe. Like a speeding Japanese bullet train, Laura's editing was stylish, dynamic, and—despite my propensity for derailment—brought us into the station mostly on time and intact. I'm also hugely obliged to Dan Halka and Mike LeGrand, who created the terrific maps throughout the book. They ably spruced up my text like talented guest performers on the lido deck of a budget cruise ship.

Offering invaluable guidance, comfort, and companionship as we make this nonstop circumnavigation of the sun: the LeGrands; the

Bluestone-Cohens; Gwen Edwards, Laura Mattison, and Meredith Mattison Pace; Hillel Gedrich; the gentlemen of the Arnold Club; and all my beloved Brookline brothers and sisters.

I think I can pinpoint when I caught the travel bug. I was in fifth grade, and my parents pulled me out of school a few weeks before summer vacation started. They'd decided to take the whole family on an epic road trip across America. To an eleven-year-old, it was a true adventure. Ever since, as I've charted my own course and pursued my own adventures, my mom, my dad, and my sister, Liz, have been beacons of love, support, and encouragement. They've helped me find my bearings in good weather and in bad, and without them I'd have been lost and drifting more times than I care to imagine.

Seth Stevenson is a contributing writer for *Slate*. His work has also appeared in the *New York Times*, *New York* magazine, *Newsweek*, *Rolling Stone*, and other publications. He's been excerpted three times in the Best American Travel Writing series and won the 2005 Online Journalism Award for commentary. He currently lives in Washington, D.C.